INTERNET
―――――――――― AND ――――――――――
ONLINE PRIVACY:
A LEGAL AND BUSINESS GUIDE

by
Andrew Frackman, Esq.
Rebecca C. Martin, Esq.
Claudia Ray, Esq.

ALM Publishing
New York

Front Cover Design: *Michael Ng*
Interior Page Design & Production: *Mary Beth Quinn*

Library of Congress Cataloging-in-Publication Data

Frackman, Andrew, 1956-
   Internet & online privacy : a legal and business guide / Andrew
Frackman, Claudia Ray, Rebecca C. Martin.
   p. cm.
Includes bibliographical references.
   ISBN 0-9705970-7-X
   1. Internet–Law and legislation–United States. 2. Data
protection–Law and legislation–United States. 3. Privacy, Right
of–United States. I. Title: Internet and online privacy. II. Ray,
Claudia, 1967- III. Martin, Rebecca C., 1962- IV. Title.
   KF390.5.C6 F69 2002
   343.7309'944–dc21

                                                    2002018472

ACKNOWLEDGMENTS

We are grateful for the encouragement and support of our colleagues at O'Melveny & Myers LLP. In particular, we wish to acknowledge the substantial contributions of Samantha Hetherington. We are also greatly appreciative of the efforts of Erica Adelstein, Susan Alter, Nathaniel Bryans, Allen Burton, Charlotte Forssander and Najma Rana. All of their hard work made this book possible.

INTRODUCTION

This book is about the online collection and use of personal data by non-governmental parties. It attempts to explain for both the legal practitioner (including in-house and outside counsel) and the lay reader the primary rules, regulations and statutes that govern the collection and use of personal data online. In exploring these laws, some of their background, and the manner in which they are, or could be, applied to online information gathering, the book strives to give companies and interested individuals a more complete sense of the legal landscape surrounding online privacy issues. It also strives to provide some guidance on good privacy practices that may help companies avoid liability.

This book does not purport to be a full-fledged study of privacy law, but rather focuses on the *collection and use of personal data* and, more particularly, the collection and use of those personal data *on or through the Internet.* We specifically have chosen not to address in detail constitutional issues, or issues relating to *governmental* collection and use of personal data. These are vitally important issues, but outside the scope of this particular book.

The relevance and importance of the topic even as we have limited it, however, can hardly be disputed. Probably the most notorious illustration of its importance is the experience of the company DoubleClick, an online advertising and profiling company. In the early part of 2000, DoubleClick's proposal to merge its clickstream data with the personally identifiable information contained in its recently acquired subsidiary's database of offline consumer preferences collected from direct marketing sources created a cause célèbre in the Internet world. Eventually, DoubleClick was forced to give up its plan to merge these databases. By then, its stock price had fallen 40 percent.

We believe that we are moving relatively rapidly towards regulation of the collection and use of personally identifiable information (PII) on the Internet. The basic ground rules governing the collection and use of PII have already been laid out—and, indeed, have been in existence since 1973, when HEW published its seminal study, *Records, Computers, and the Rights of Citizens*. These fundamental principles are: (1) notice/awareness, (2) choice/consent, (3) access/participation, (4) integrity/security, and (5) enforcement/ redress. Although in 1973 the issue was *governmental* collection and use of PII, in our view, it is only a matter of time until adherence to these principles becomes mandatory for non-governmental actors as well.

We believe there are several imperatives creating momentum toward some kind of increased regulation of data collection and distribution practices in the United States.

First and foremost, most parties to the ongoing debate have now recognized that the basic privacy principles set out above apply, and must apply, to the Internet. Although there are some fringe participants in the debate who still contend that such principles should not apply and that PII is, and should be, freely collectible and transferable, those views are rapidly becoming more and more marginal. The vast majority of U.S. citizens expresses deep concern about privacy and, in particular, privacy on the Internet. The manifest political popularity of regulations or legislation addressing this concern will provide momentum for a legislative solution—whether on a federal or state level. The enormous number of bills introduced by members of Congress on Internet privacy confirms that politicians have recognized the popularity of this issue. State legislators are no less aware of this politically charged issue, and industry will ultimately recognize, as former FTC Chairman Robert Pitofsky counseled in early 2000, that it will likely be better off with a single federal standard than with a patchwork quilt of inconsistent state regulations.

Second, Internet privacy has already emerged from the shadows into the limelight of the press and the courts. Building on common law legal principles and statutes and regulations that long predate the Web, plaintiffs and their industrious counsel have commenced many individual and class action lawsuits alleging violation of privacy or related rights. Whether the threat of intrusion comes from private industry in the form of sales of private customer information, or from the government in the form of new, sophisticated surveillance techniques that monitor criminals' Internet usage, the public's concern for privacy has become a high-profile topic.

Third, the debate on the sufficiency of industry self-regulation in the delicate area of personal data has shifted in favor of regulation. For instance, the FTC previously took the view that governmental intervention was unnecessary. By the middle of 2000, the FTC finally endorsed legislation in at least some areas, such as protection of privacy of children on the Internet. More recently, however, FTC Chairman Timothy J. Muris announced plans for the agency to promote "an aggressive, pro-consumer privacy agenda" through increased enforcement of existing legislation, not the passage of new laws.[1] Since the FTC has emerged as the leading federal regulator in the area of Internet privacy, the views of the FTC carry great weight in this debate.

Fourth, international pressures will mandate legislation or regulation on some level. The Internet is a global marketplace. Even if the U.S. wanted to continue with the regime of industry self-regulation that has governed to date, the pressures of the outside world will make this difficult, if not impossible. The paradigmatic example of this pressure is the Safe Harbor Accord that was negotiated between the U.S. and the European Commission in order to permit the transfer of PII to the U.S. The U.S. had to come up with a solution acceptable to the European Commission in order to permit U.S. companies to collect or receive PII of European citizens. We do not think that the Safe Harbor Accord represents the end of the international debate on the privacy issue. Indeed, comparatively recent legislation in Canada and Australia shows that the U.S. is falling out of step with many other industrialized nations on this issue, and clearly behind our fellow Anglophone nations.

The final consideration in this debate is that the entire issue of regulation may ultimately be made moot by technology itself. The technology to block cookies, surf the Web anonymously, and

---

[1] "Protecting Consumers' Privacy: 2002 and Beyond," remarks of Timothy J. Muris, Chairman, Federal Trade Commission, The Privacy 2001 Conference (Cleveland, Ohio, Oct. 24, 2001), available at http://www.ftc.gov/speeches/muris/privisp1002.htm.

encrypt and eliminate e-mail messages already exists. It may only be a matter of time until the public is sufficiently educated to take advantage of these ways to protect one's privacy. The day when such technologies are available to all—either bundled with a browser or otherwise readily available—is not far off. We do not believe, however, that the theoretical availability of such technology will be sufficient to stave off regulation or legislation mandating compliance with at least the basic privacy principles.

TABLE OF CONTENTS

CHAPTER 1

PRIVACY: DEFINITIONS AND TECHNOLOGY 17

What Is Personally Identifiable Information? 17
How Is Information Collected on the Web? 19

CHAPTER 2

WHY BUSINESS CANNOT AFFORD TO DISREGARD CONSUMER PRIVACY CONCERNS 23

CHAPTER 3

DEVELOPMENT OF REGULATORY PRINCIPLES 29

Common Law Privacy Principles 29
    Intrusion 30
    False Light 31
    Publication of Private Facts 32
    Commercial Appropriation/Right of Publicity 34
Defenses 36
The HEW Report on Records, Computers and the
    Rights of Citizens 38
Personal Privacy in an Information Society (1977) 41

CHAPTER 4

RELEVANT FEDERAL LEGISLATION: PRIVACY PROVISIONS OF COPPA 45

Children's Online Privacy Protection Act 46

Overview   46
Scope of the COPPA Rules   48
    Web Sites and Online Services Subject to the Rules . .   48
    Type of Information Protected by COPPA: Personal
        Information   51
Six Requirements for Online Collection of a Child's
    Personal Information   52
    Notices of Information Practices Must Be Posted on
        the Web Site or Online Service and Sent Directly
        to Parents   52
    Verifiable Parental Consent and How to Obtain It . . .   57
    Certain Exceptions to the Need for Prior Parental
        Consent   59
    Parental Right to Review Collected Information and
        No Conditioning Participation in Online Activities
        on Provision of Personal Information   60
    Confidentiality, Security, and Integrity of Personal
        Information Collected from Children   62
Enforcement and Penalties   62
Safe Harbor   63

CHAPTER 5

RELEVANT FEDERAL LEGISLATION: PRIVACY PROVISIONS OF THE GLB AND HIPAA   65

The Gramm-Leach-Bliley Act   66
    Overview   66
    Scope of the GLB Regulations   68
        Financial Institutions   70
        "Other Persons" Subject to the FTC's Rules   72
        Type of Information Protected by the GLB Act:
            Nonpublic Personal Information   72
    Jurisdiction of the Various Agencies   74
    Time for Compliance   76
    When Disclosure of Nonpublic Personal Information
        Is Permitted   76
    Notice Requirements and Restrictions on Disclosure of
        Nonpublic Personal Information and the "Consumer"/
        "Customer" Distinction   77
        Content of the Privacy Notices   78

Initial Notice   79
Annual Notice   80
Revised Notices   80
Opt-Out Notices   80
Delivery of Notices   82
Primary Exceptions to Privacy and/or Opt-Out Notice
        Requirements   82
Reuse and Redisclosure Limitations   83
Other Restrictions   84
A Further Word on Opt-Out vs. Opt-In Restrictions . .   84
Health Insurance Portability and Accountability
    Act of 1996   86
    Overview   86
    Limitations on Use and Disclosure of Protected Health
        Information   89
    Marketing and Fund Raising   91
    De-Identification of Protected Health Information   92
    Notice   93
    Individual Rights Regarding Protected Health
        Information   94
    Administrative Requirements   96
    Employers That Sponsor Group Health Plans   97
Computer Fraud and Abuse Act   98
The Electronic Communications Privacy Act   99

CHAPTER 6

OTHER LEGISLATIVE APPROACHES   101

Federal and State Efforts   101
State-Sponsored Privacy Bills   107

CHAPTER 7

PRIVACY ISSUES IN THE WORKPLACE   109

Relevant Statutes and Legal Principles   111
    Do Employees Have Any Expectation of Privacy in
        the Workplace?   111
    The Electronic Communications Privacy Act of 1986 . . .   113
    The Fourth Amendment to the U.S. Constitution   118

State Solutions   120
Employer E-Mail and Internet Policies   121

CHAPTER 8

PRIVACY LITIGATION   125

An Overview   125
Characteristics of Lawsuits: Target Defendants and Types
    of Claims   126
Obstacles Facing Privacy Plaintiffs: Lack of an Appropriate
    Theory of Liability   129
Lessons from the Lawsuits: Ways to Avoid or Minimize
    Litigation   131
    The Role of Privacy Policies and User Consent   132
        Taking Care with the Forum Selection Clause:
            Amazon.com Privacy Litigation   133
        Use of the Arbitration Clause: Real Networks Privacy
            Litigation   133
        Certain Considerations for Effective Arbitration
            Clauses   134

CHAPTER 9

THE FEDERAL TRADE COMMISSION:
GUARDIAN OF ONLINE PRIVACY   137

The FTC's Legal Authority   138
Basic FTC Approach to Online Privacy   138
The June 1996 Workshop and December 1996 Report,
    Public Workshop on Consumer Privacy and the
    Global Information Infrastructure   139
The June 1997 Workshop   140
Individual Reference Services: A Report to Congress
    (December 1997)   140
Privacy Online: A Report to Congress (June 1998)   142
Self-Regulation and Privacy Online: A Report to Congress
    (July 1999)   144
Final Report of the Federal Trade Commission Advisory
    Committee on Online Access and Security
    (May 15, 2000)   145

Self-Regulation Will Not Suffice   146
Online Profiling: A Federal Trade Commission Report to
    Congress (Part 1, June 2000)   146
The NAI Principles (July 2000)   148
Online Profiling: A Federal Trade Commission Report to
    Congress (Part 2, July 2000)   149
The FTC Returns to Industry Self-Regulation and Increased
    Enforcement of Existing Laws   151
FTC Enforcement Actions   153
    Privacy Enforcement Actions   153
        Toysmart.com   153
        Online Pharmacies   154
        ReverseAuction.com, Inc.   155
        Liberty Financial Companies, Inc.   155
        GeoCities   156
        Trans Union Corporation   156
    Amazon.com Privacy Investigation   158

CHAPTER 10

PRIVACY REGULATION IN THE EUROPEAN UNION AND THE 2000 UNITED STATES-EUROPEAN COMMISSION SAFE HARBOR ACCORD

. . . .   159

The OECD Guidelines (1980)   160
Council of Europe Convention on Privacy (1981)   162
The EC Directive (Directive 95/46/EC)   164
United States-European Commission "Safe Harbor" Data
    Privacy Accord   165
    Key Benefits of the Safe Harbor Accord   167
    Basic Structure of the Safe Harbor Accord   167
    Checklist of Basic Principles of Safe Harbor Accord   170

CHAPTER 11

PRIVACY REGULATION IN OTHER FOREIGN COUNTRIES

. . . .   175

Canada   176

Canadian Personal Information Protection and Electronic
  Documents Act of 2000 (effective January 1, 2001) . .   176
United Kingdom   179
Australia   179
Austria   181
Brazil   181
China and Hong Kong   181
Finland   182
Germany   183
Greece   184
India   184
Italy   185
Japan   185
The Netherlands   185
Portugal   186
Russia   186
South Africa   186
Sweden   187

CHAPTER 12
PRIVACY POLICIES   189

Introduction   189
The Five Basic Elements of a Privacy Policy   191
  Notice/Awareness   192
  Choice/Consent   194
  Access/Participation   198
  Integrity/Security   199
  Enforcement/Redress   201
Creating a Privacy Policy   203
Chief Privacy Officer   205
Seal Programs   206
  BBBOnLine   206
  CPA WebTrust   207
  ESRB   207
  TRUSTe   208
Other Privacy Organizations   208
  Direct Marketing Association   208
  Online Privacy Alliance   209
  Wireless Advertising Association   209

Interactive Advertising Bureau 210
International Considerations 210

CHAPTER 13

TECHNOLOGY SOLUTIONS ....

213

Personal Firewalls 215
Anonymous Browsing Technology 216
P3P 216
E-Mail Protection 217
    Vanishing E-Mail 217
    Encryption 217
Blocking Web Bugs 218
Education and Exercise of Individual Control 218
The Future 218

CHAPTER 14

GOVERNMENT MONITORING OF INTERNET
USAGE ....

221

Internet Surveillance Technology 222
    KLS and the *Scarfo* Opinion 222
    The FBI's Carnivore System 224
The Legislative Response to the Events of
    September 11, 2001: USA PATRIOT Act 226
The Council of Europe's Convention on Cybercrime 228

POSTSCRIPT ....

231

AUTHOR BIOGRAPIES ....

233

CHAPTER 1

PRIVACY: DEFINITIONS AND TECHNOLOGY

WHAT IS PERSONALLY IDENTIFIABLE INFORMATION?

There is no single definition of personally identifiable information (PII). Some define it broadly to include "anything in an electronic network that can be linked in some way to a flesh-and-blood human being . . . ."[1] Such a definition makes no distinction between publicly available and nonpublic information, or between information that is voluntarily provided and that which is obtained without consent. We have adopted the definition which, although not free from dispute, is used by the Federal Trade Commission: "data that can be linked to specific individuals, and includes but is not limited to such information as name, postal address, phone number, e-mail address, social security number and driver's license number."[2]

We recognize that this definition oversimplifies the complexity of the online privacy problem. The complexity was illustrated in the May 15, 2000 Report of the FTC Advisory Committee on Online Access and Security.[3] While that committee could not reach a consensus as to steps to be taken to address the problem of online privacy, its report sets forth some of the issues and the strongly

---

[1] Jennings and Fena, *The Hundredth Window*, xvii (2000).
[2] FTC, "Online Profiling: A Report to Congress," at 4 n.14 (June 2000) available at http://www.ftc.gov/os/2000/06/onlineprofilingreportjune2000.pdf.
[3] http://www.ftc.gov/acoas/papers/finalreport.htm.

oppositional views that different parties bring to the debate over online privacy.

Is PII limited to data that are tightly tied to an individual's name, address and birth date or not? This question is fundamental in that it determines how one views data about a computer, as opposed to an individual. For instance, clickstream data are information about a computer, not an individual. They can show the path taken by a given computer through the Internet landscape. The clickstream will show where the computer came from when it arrives at an Internet site, where it goes on that site, and where it goes when it leaves the site. The data can also identify which banner ads a computer clicked on, and related information. But, they do not necessarily provide any information about the *individual* who is using the computer. If multiple persons use the same computer, the clickstream data do not—and cannot—distinguish among them. Clickstream data derived from activity of a computer browser, therefore, are similar in some respects to information derived from a telephone extension. Unless the individual who uses that telephone number can be identified, the calling information is imperfectly tied to an individual and, arguably, less problematic from a privacy standpoint. The same holds true for clickstream data.

Should all personal information be treated the same, regardless of source? A business can collect personal information itself, or it can purchase such information from third parties. (This, obviously, applies to bricks and mortar as well as Internet companies.) The offline direct marketing business is huge, and has been collecting and selling personal data about consumers for years. Should information collected by a business itself be treated differently (that is, with fewer restrictions) from information offered for sale by a third party? Some believe that it should.

Should any effort to regulate the collection and use of personal information be limited to information that is obtained non-consensually? Information is often collected when an individual willingly fills out a registration form at a Web site. In contrast, clickstream data are collected without any active participation of the individual and without the individual's knowledge. Such passively obtained data arguably should be treated differently from personal information that is volunteered by an individual.

Should any effort to regulate be limited to factual data? Many believe that derived or inferred data—information about an individual that is derived from facts, as opposed to the facts themselves—do not raise the same privacy concerns as factual data. Statistical data are inferred or derived data. Some privacy advocates assert that inferred data should be treated no differently from factual data.

Finally, should all parties in the data collection process be regulated in the same manner? Were the question simply one of regulating the site that collects the personal data, the task might be an easy one. All information is easily transferred in this day and age, however, and personal data are no exception. Should information obtained by a site from a third party be subject to the same controls as information that a site collects itself, for instance? Should a site that originally collected the information be responsible for and have to provide or ensure access to that information when it is in the hands of downstream third parties? Should the third parties have to "step into the shoes" of the site that collected the information in the first instance and treat the information in a manner that is consistent with the collecting site's controls? These issues raise serious obstacles to an effective and efficient regulatory scheme, even if one believes that there should be increased regulation of PII online.

HOW IS INFORMATION COLLECTED ON THE WEB?

Before one can answer any of these questions—and we do not suggest that there are easy answers—one must understand how information is collected on the Internet.

First, information is collected when an individual visits a site and registers or otherwise voluntarily provides information about him- or herself.

Second, information can be obtained from the computer or browser passively from clickstream data.

For the Internet to work, computers must be able to identify one another. The Internet Protocol evolved so that each computer would have a unique address (e.g., 123.45.789.14), its IP address. The IP address is communicated among computers every time they speak to one another over the Internet, and Internet transaction logs record the IP addresses of computers with which a server communicates. In some cases, the IP address is temporary; in other cases, the address is permanent. With most dial-up ISPs, each time a user dials up, he or she is given a temporary or "dynamic" IP address from the set of IP addresses that the ISP possesses. Thus, while it is possible in such instances to know that the user is an AOL or MSN subscriber, it is not possible to connect the IP address to a particular computer. With a dedicated line, such as a DSL connection, however, the computer is given a unique and permanent IP address.

Cookies are small bits of data (not code) placed on a remote browser's computer hard drive by a Web site or server that the browser visits. In other words, when a user visits a Web site, that site places a cookie on his or her hard drive. The cookie resides on the user's hard drive, so that when he visits the site in the future, the site knows that he has been there before.[4] Some cookies do not remain on a browser's hard drive. Often, however, the cookies are "persistent," and they are intended to remain on the browser's hard drive for some period of time. When a browser sends a request to a server for a cookie, it communicates a variety of information about the browser computer, including: IP address, type of browser that the computer is using, domain and URL information, and the operating system.

Cookies are useful in that they assist in customizing a user's computer. The user does not have to re-input information each time he or she visits a site. The site is able to recognize her and recall her preferences. It is the cookie that permits an Internet shopping site to track the user's shopping cart. Cookies can also be used to personalize advertising, so that a given computer is not bombarded with broad advertising that does not interest the user, but rather is sent only those ads that the computer has indicated it is interested in through its surfing profile.

A third way in which information can be gathered over the Internet is through the use of "Web bugs"—a form of GIFs (graphic

---

[4] A useful, non-polemical description of cookie technology can be found in U.S. Dept. of Energy, "Computer Incident Advisory Capability Information Bulletin on Internet cookies," at http://www.llnl.gov/ciac/bulletins/i-034.shtml.

image files). Web bugs are also referred to as 1-by-1 GIFs, "invisible" or "clear" GIFs, or "tracker" GIFs.

Web bugs are tiny graphic image files embedded in a Web page, generally the same color as the background on which they are displayed, which are invisible to the naked eye. The Web bug sends back to its home server (which can belong to the host site, a network advertiser, or some other third party): the IP (Internet Protocol) address of the computer that downloaded the page on which the bug appears; the URL (Uniform Resource Locator) of the page on which the Web bug appears; the URL of the Web bug image; the time the page containing the Web bug was viewed; the type of browser that fetched the Web bug; and the identification number of any cookie on the consumer's computer previously placed by that server.[5]

The information collected through the monitoring of IP addresses and other forms of tracking by cookies and Web bugs is known as "clickstream" data. Clickstream data will tell the company mining the data where the computer has been before it visited the company's site, and where it goes when it leaves the company's site. Clickstream data also describe the information collected from banner ads—what computer has clicked on a banner ad, what Web page that computer was visiting when it clicked on the banner. Clickstream data derived from IP addresses and cookies generally only give information about the computer, but not necessarily about the user of the computer.[6] Thus, in order to drill down to individual data, a company seeking to mine the clickstream data needs to link them with additional information about the particular

---

[5] "Online Profiling: A Report to Congress," N. 2 *supra*, at 3 n.12.

[6] One commentor before the FTC noted that in some cases Web bugs can actually retrieve a user's e-mail address when sending graphic files loaded from a Web server belonging to a banner ad company through an HTML-formatted message. When such a message is sent and read, a cookie for the banner ad company is sent, with the e-mail address, to the banner ad company supplying the graphic image. Thus, the e-mail address can then be combined with the previously anonymous customer ID number associated with the cookie. See Smith, "Online Profiling Project-Comment," P994809/Docket No. 990811219-9219-01 (Dec. 1, 1999) at http://www.ftc.gov/bcp/profiling/comments/rsmith.htm.

individual visiting its site. The clickstream data possessed by a single Web site are unlikely to be a source of great concern because they are, by definition, limited, and typically may just be used by a Web site to market better to its willing customer. But, when clickstream data about a given computer are collected from multiple Web sites, so that a profile is constructed that identifies where that computer goes and its preferences, privacy concerns can grow.

Another increasingly common way for information to be gathered is through tracking software. Many companies, such as RealNetworks, will provide free or low-cost software that can assist users in various ways in their browsing activities on the Internet. For instance, the software can assist users in downloading music. Or it can assist users in increasing the speed of downloading files. Some, though not all, of these types of software will track the movements of the user through the Internet and send some or all of the information back to the company that issued the software. This information can be particularly valuable because it can be linked to the specific individual who downloaded the software and who may have given personal information in the process of doing so.

Though much of the information collected over the Internet is not immediately personally identifiable, over the last few years, an entire category of companies specializing in collection and mining of clickstream data has emerged. This market is not limited to high profile companies such as DoubleClick and its fellow online advertising companies. There are numerous other players in this market segment, apart from the online advertising companies. Mining clickstream data and converting them into usable data is big business. The key for businesses interested in personal data, though, is combining clickstream data—data that are somewhat anonymous—with offline data, so as to put those clickstream data together with an individual. It is the specter of such a database, consisting of the offline marketing data already in existence, plus the clickstream and related data from the Internet, that concerns privacy advocates the most.

CHAPTER 2

WHY BUSINESS CANNOT AFFORD TO DISREGARD CONSUMER PRIVACY CONCERNS

Internet privacy is a front-line issue not only for privacy advocates, who view the gradual intrusion on individual privacy as a moral issue, but for the average consumer and Internet user as well. And privacy is a concern not only for individuals; it is a paramount issue for any business that intends to utilize the Internet. Today, that means almost every business, on some level.

Study after study has demonstrated that one of the principal barriers to consumers using the Internet, in general, and using it to make purchases, in particular, is concern over personal privacy—a concern notably absent in their other commercial dealings.

- An early 2000 survey by Forrester Research concluded that approximately two-thirds of the respondents were concerned about Internet privacy, but only 12 percent would pay for enhanced protection.[1]
- Another survey by Odyssey, a San Francisco-based research firm, reported that 92 percent of respondents do not trust companies to keep personal information confidential.[2]

---

[1] "Online Consumers Fearful of Privacy Violations" (Oct. 1999), http://www.forrester.com/ER/Press/Release/0,1769,177,FF.html.

[2] "Privacy Online: Fair Information Practices in the Electronic Marketplace" (May 25, 2000), at 2 n.8, at http://www.ftc.gov/os/2000/05/testimonyprivacy.htm.

- In what is known as the "1999 AT&T Study," 87 percent of the respondents, experienced Internet users, stated that they were concerned about threats to their privacy online.[3]
- A 1999 survey, by the well-known pollsters Louis Harris & Associates, this time for the National Consumers League, reported 70 percent of respondents were uncomfortable providing personal information online.[4]
- A 1998 Business Week/Harris Poll indicated that privacy was the *number one* reason why individuals stay off the Internet.[5]
- A 1998 Harris survey disclosed that over 90 percent of Internet users and those who purchase online felt that it was important for Internet sites to post privacy policies, and that of those who said it was likely that they would use the Internet in the next year, 44 percent stated that assured privacy of personal information would have a positive effect on whether they would use the Internet.[6]
- A 1996 Harris survey revealed that four out of five Americans felt that consumers had lost control over how personal information about them is collected and used by companies.[7]

One could go on and on. The surveys are remarkably consistent in their conclusions: online privacy is an enormously sensitive issue for individuals. And because it is such a major issue for consumers, it is a major source of concern for businesses trying to attract individuals to the Internet and to induce them to engage in commercial transactions online.

---

[3] Crano et al., "Beyond Concern: Understanding Net Users' Attitudes About Online Privacy," 5 (1999), available at http://www.research.att.com/projects/privacystudy.

[4] Louis Harris & Associates, Inc., "National Consumers League: Consumers and the 21st Century," 4 (1999).

[5] Louis Harris & Associates, Inc., "Business Week/Harris Poll on Online Security" (March 1998).

[6] Louis Harris & Associates, Inc., "E-Commerce & Privacy: What Net Users Want" (June 1998), sponsored by Privacy & American Business and PricewaterhouseCoopers LLP.

[7] Louis Harris & Associates, Inc., "Equifax/Harris Consumer Privacy Survey" (Feb. 1996).

Online privacy, however, does not merely affect the number of visitors to a given Web site or the number of transactions that they may engage in. Because online privacy is one of the most exposed areas of debate in the Internet world, and because it elicits such emotional, as well as practical, responses, online privacy can affect a business on other levels, too.

The story, or debacle, of DoubleClick is illustrative of the risks associated with privacy issues in the current marketplace.

DoubleClick is an Internet advertising company that was one of the leaders in developing online banner advertising. When an individual clicks on a banner, a cookie is deposited on the browser's hard drive. When the individual then visits a Web site on which DoubleClick serves ads, DoubleClick's technology is able to read the cookie that has been previously deposited on the individual's hard drive. Usually, the cookies are placed on a hard drive without the knowledge or consent of the individual (although it is possible, of course, to prevent a computer from accepting cookies). DoubleClick's DART technology is then able to use the cookies from a given computer to deliver targeted ads. For instance, if a user previously clicked on a banner ad for books, and then went to a Web site where DoubleClick served ads, DoubleClick would know to deliver banner ads for books to the user's computer. DoubleClick described its own capability as follows:

> DART's dynamic matching, targeting and delivery functions enable Web advertisers to target their advertising based on a variety of factors, including user interests, time of day, time of week, organization name and size, domain type (i.e., commercial, government, education, network), operating system, server type and version, and keywords.

Notably, while DoubleClick's technology tracks information about sites visited by a computer and about the particular computer, it cannot link that information with individual personal data unless it also knows who uses a given computer. Thus, at least until it acquired Abacus, DoubleClick's data was not personally identifiable.

On November 23, 1999, DoubleClick consummated its acquisition of Abacus Direct Corporation. Abacus is in the business of providing specialized consumer information to direct marketers. Over 1,000 direct marketers belonged to the Abacus Alliance. These direct marketers contributed information about their customers' purchasing histories to Abacus, which then incorporated that data into the Abacus database. Prior to the DoubleClick acquisition, the Abacus database contained over 88 *million* detailed buyer profiles. These profiles clearly consisted of personally identifiable information about consumers, containing such information as a user's name, address, purchasing history and other demographics.

Following the acquisition of Abacus, DoubleClick for the first time announced its intention to combine its online databases with Abacus's offline databases. If the databases were combined, DoubleClick would be able to put its anonymous clickstream data together with the individualized data of the Abacus database. Although DoubleClick asserted that this would permit Internet users "to receive advertising messages tailored to their individual interests," and asserted that this was no different from what had been going on in the direct marketing business for years, the public vehemently objected.

DoubleClick's announcement of its intention to merge the databases elicited a firestorm of criticism. On February 10, 2000, EPIC, one of the leading privacy watchdog organizations, filed a complaint with the FTC, alleging that DoubleClick was engaging in unfair and deceptive trade practices by tracking online activities of Internet users and combining that tracking data with detailed personally identifiable information contained in a massive, national marketing database. EPIC asked the FTC to investigate and to enjoin DoubleClick's practices.[8] Individuals filed numerous civil lawsuits against DoubleClick. Eventually, sixteen different civil actions, some of them class actions, were brought against DoubleClick.[9]

DoubleClick's initial response was that it was doing nothing improper. On February 14, after the public outcry had made it apparent that the public relations problem was not simply going to

---

[8] The EPIC complaint can be found at http://www.epic.org/privacy/internet/FTC/DCLK_complaint.pdf.

[9] These lawsuits are discussed in greater detail in Chapter 8.

disappear for DoubleClick, the company announced that it would: (1) hire a chief privacy officer; (2) commence a substantial public information campaign (the "Internet Privacy Education Campaign") to inform and to permit consumers to opt out of having their personal data collected, including distribution of 50 million banner ads for privacychoices.org, a privacy watchdog organization; (3) appoint an independent privacy advisory board; (4) retain PricewaterhouseCoopers LLP to conduct privacy audits to ensure compliance; and (5) do business only with Web sites that adopt and post "effective" privacy policies. However, at this stage of the debate, DoubleClick believed it would be able to proceed with its plans to merge the databases and create the personal profiles. Furthermore, DoubleClick adhered to the policy of requiring consumers to opt out of the data collection, as opposed to opting in, as privacy advocates urged.[10]

By late February, the heat of adverse publicity had already contributed to several of DoubleClick's clients deciding to withdraw from its program. Immediately thereafter, on March 2, DoubleClick announced that it would delay its plan to merge its databases with those of Abacus. By this time, however, DoubleClick's share price had dropped precipitously (and this was before the industry-wide decline in stock values commencing in late March). The stock closed as high as $134 per share on January 3, 2000. By March 1, it closed at $80.56 per share, a 40 percent decline. Although other factors doubtless also affected the DoubleClick stock price during this two-month period, the storm of adverse publicity and legal actions contributed substantially to the significant drop in stock value.

By this time, DoubleClick had lost the battle of public opinion. DoubleClick's claim that offline marketing companies had combined catalog and retail data for years missed the point. The issue of online privacy was an exposed nerve. The private lawsuits had been commenced, and the public relations disaster had occurred.

There is little question that the DoubleClick fiasco contributed to the willingness of the Network Advertising Initiative, an industry

---

[10] http://interactive.wsj.com/archive/retrieve.cgi?id=SB950550727796148720.djm; http://www6.nytimes.com/library/tech/00/02/cyber/articles/15privacy.html.

group of which DoubleClick is a member, to reach a compromise with the FTC in July 2000.[11] Ultimately, in January 2001, the FTC closed its investigation of DoubleClick without taking action, concluding that DoubleClick had not violated its privacy policy.[12] DoubleClick's stock price immediately rose.

In sum, the DoubleClick incident provides ample evidence that the public concern over Internet privacy has real-world implications for any business.

---

[11] See Chapter 9.
[12] http://www.ftc.gov/os/closings/staff/doubleclick.pdf.

CHAPTER 3

DEVELOPMENT OF REGULATORY PRINCIPLES

Internet privacy is a front-page topic. However, to understand what is transpiring in the Internet privacy debate today, one must look at the historical perspective—at least a bit. The Internet may be a relatively new technology, but concern about personal data collection practices dates back about thirty years. The principles on which the FTC and governmental regulatory bodies have based their recent enforcement efforts regarding the Internet began with the 1973 HEW report on personal data collection practices, *Records, Computers, and the Rights of Citizens.* That HEW report sets out what has become known as the "Fair Information Collection Practices" that have formed the intellectual basis for all regulation of personal data collection since that time. Indeed, in what has turned out to be a prescient statement, in 1973, HEW Secretary Casper Weinberger wrote in the foreword to the report: "Computers linked together through high-speed telecommunications networks are destined to become the principal medium for making, sorting, and using records about people."

COMMON LAW PRIVACY PRINCIPLES

The legal notion of privacy has a fairly recent history. Most U.S. scholars trace the development of the common law civil legal right to the seminal 1890 *Harvard Law Review* article by Louis Brandeis and Samuel Warren.[1] The focus of that article was on whether an

---

[1] Warren and Brandeis, "The Right to Privacy," 4 Harv. L. Rev. 193 (Dec. 15, 1890).

individual possessed a "right to be let alone" that protected against unwarranted invasion by gossip columnists in the newspapers of the day. Since that time, we have seen a steady development of privacy concepts, both common law and statutory. Claims for invasion of privacy typically are governed by state common law.

In general, the common law of privacy can be divided into four areas: intrusion; false light; publication of private facts; and commercial misappropriation.

In deciding disputes, courts generally apply the common law of the state where the *plaintiff* resides. This is important because privacy law can vary significantly from state to state. For example, New York does not recognize *any* common law right of privacy, restricting plaintiffs instead to a narrow statutory cause of action when a living person's name or likeness is used in connection with trade or advertising without permission.[2] However, states such as California recognize a broad common law right of privacy, including all four of the traditional common law privacy torts.[3] Thus, it is important to consider which state's law is likely to apply to any privacy claim before considering whether a claim may exist.

INTRUSION

The privacy tort that most people are familiar with is the tort of intrusion. One common definition of the "intrusion" tort states that it is an intentional intrusion, physical or otherwise, upon a person's solitude, private affairs or concerns, where such intrusion would be *highly offensive* to a reasonable person.[4] Thus, in order to state a claim a plaintiff must show that there was something more than merely annoying or obnoxious behavior on the part of the defendant. Whether an invasion meets this standard generally depends

---

[2] See: Messenger v. Gruner & Jahr Printing and Publishing, 2000 WL 190553 (N.Y. 2000) (the legislature has rejected bills that would have created a cause of action for privacy torts); Howell v. New York Post, 81 N.Y.2d 115, 596 N.Y.S.2d 350 (1993) ("we have no common law of privacy"); N.Y. Civil Rights L. §§ 50-51 (providing a cause of action for a living person whose name or likeness is used in connection with trade or advertising without permission and making such use a misdemeanor).

[3] See Shulman v. Group W Productions, Inc., 18 Cal.4th 200, 74 Cal. Rptr.2d 843, 26 Media L. Rep. 1737 (1998).

[4] See *Restatement (Second) of Torts*, § 652B (1977).

on where the person was when the approach occurred, whether the defendant was invited to approach the person, whether the defendant used any electronic devices, and the intensity of the approach.[5]

One state court found an invasion of privacy when a person at a checkout counter was accused in front of witnesses of writing a bad check.[6] Another state court found intrusion when a person's blood was tested for the HIV virus without his consent and the results disclosed to the state and to third parties.[7]

FALSE LIGHT

A person may be liable for invasion of privacy if he or she places another person before the public in a false light, if doing so would be highly offensive to a reasonable person, and if the defendant knew or acted in reckless disregard of the falsity of the publicized matter and the false light in which the person would be placed.[8]

The tort of false light is similar to, and in most jurisdictions has been subsumed within, that of defamation.[9] Some jurisdictions, however, require that a plaintiff demonstrate *either* that the publication was libelous on its face, *or* that the plaintiff incurred special damages.[10] Other jurisdictions have held that the tort simply

---

[5] See Sanford, *Libel and Privacy*, § 11.2.1 (2d ed. 1994 and 2000 Supp.). See also, Aisenson v. American Broadcasting Cos., Inc., 269 Cal. Rptr. 379 (1990) (television crew that taped judge walking from his home to his car in public view did not commit actionable intrusion).

[6] See K-Mart Corp. v. Weston, 530 So.2d 736 (Ala. 1988).

[7] See Doe v. High-Tech Institute, Inc., 972 P.2d 1060 (Colo. App. 1998).

[8] See *Restatement (Second) of Torts*, § 652E. See also:

Colorado: Bueno v. Denver Pub. Co., 2000 WL 231993 (Colo. App. March 2, 2000) (oldest son of alleged crime family who had never been charged or arrested recovered when article stated that the family's oldest sons had engaged in criminal activities).

Illinois: Lovgren v. Citizens First National Bank, 126 Ill. 411, 534 N.E.2d 987 (1989) (plaintiff stated cause of action when defendant placed ad in newspapers and circulated handbill stating that plaintiff was selling his farm at auction).

Michigan: Morganroth v. Whitall, 161 Mich. App. 785 (1987) (newspaper article describing hairdresser as "blowtorch lady" and describing her technique as the "blowtorch technique" did not support a false light claim when statements were true).

[9] See Time, Inc. v. Hill, 385 U.S. 374 (1967).

[10] See Newcombe v. Adolph Coors Co., 157 F.3d 686, 26 Media L. Rep. 2364 (9th Cir. 1998) (applying California law; summary judgment was proper because alcohol ad depicting plaintiff was not defamatory without the aid of "explanatory matter" outlining his battle with alcoholism, and plaintiff failed to show special damages).

requires a false statement about the plaintiff, not necessarily a defamatory one.[11]

In states that follow the *Restatement (Second) of Torts*, the publication of the information must be made to the public at large, whereas "publication" for purposes of a defamation claim need only be made to one person.[12] For instance, a Connecticut Superior Court held that there was no false light invasion of privacy when a memorandum regarding plaintiff's job performance was not circulated to the general public.[13]

In general, the statement must also be recognizably "of and concerning" the plaintiff, meaning that a person hearing it would know that it was a statement about the plaintiff.[14]

PUBLICATION OF PRIVATE FACTS

A person may be subject to liability for publicizing true facts about a nonpublic figure's private life, when such publicity would be highly offensive to a reasonable person and is not a matter of public interest.[15] For example, a cosmetic surgery patient successfully stated a private facts claim when a department store displayed before and after photos.[16] In another case, a plaintiff's sex change

---

[11] See:
Alabama: Phillips v. Smalley Maintenance Services, 435 So.2d 705 (Ala. 1983).
Arizona: Godbehere v. Phoenix Newspapers, Inc., 783 P.2d 781 (Ariz. 1989).
[12] See Pace v. Bristol Hospital, 964 F. Supp. 628 (D. Conn. 1997).
[13] See Hankard v. Town of Avon, 1999 WL 482635 (Conn. Super. 1999). See also, Dzierwa v. Mich. Oil Co., 152 Mich. App. 281 (1986) (incident that occurred only within presence of a few co-employees or visitors to office was not published to sufficiently large group so as to constitute substantial publicity). Another Connecticut Superior Court more recently noted, however, that there is no "magic number" of persons to constitute publication for purposes of invasion of privacy, and communication to persons outside of an organization may be sufficient. See Beveridge v. Briston Spring Manufacturing Co., 2000 WL 254654 (Conn. Super. 2000). See also, Kinsey v. Macur, 165 Cal. Rptr. 608 (1980) (mailing thirty letters to approximately twenty people was sufficient publication).
[14] Blatty v. New York Times Co., 232 Cal. Rptr. 542 (1986) (failure to place plaintiff's book on bestseller list was not a statement "of and concerning" the plaintiff), *cert. denied* 485 U.S. 934 (1988).
[15] See *Restatement (Second) of Torts*, § 652D. See also, Melvin v. Reid, 112 Cal. App. 285 (1931) (story about married woman's former life as a prostitute stated claim for invasion of privacy based on publication of private facts).
[16] See Vassiliades v. Garfinckel's, 492 A.2d 580 (D.C. 1985).

operation was held to be a private fact and not sufficiently news-worthy to be considered a matter of public interest.[17]

Some jurisdictions require that the statement identify the plaintiff, although the plaintiff does not necessarily have to be identifiable to all members of the public.[18]

Because the essence of the offense is the publicizing of private matters, the key question is whether the information revealed was public or private.[19] Merely giving wider publicity to facts that the plaintiff has left open to the public eye is not actionable.[20]

In practice, such claims very rarely succeed. For example, there is no liability when the private information comes from a public record.[21] Similarly, although cases involving disclosure of a plaintiff's AIDS status are fairly common, they do not appear to have a high success rate.[22]

---

[17] See Diaz v. Oakland Tribune, 139 Cal. App.3d 118, 188 Cal. Rptr. 762 (Cal. App. 1983).

[18] See Shulman v. Group W Productions, Inc., 18 Cal.4th 200, 74 Cal. Rptr.2d 843, 26 Media L. Rep. 1737 (1998) (broadcast of rescue and medivac flight of plaintiff, an automobile accident victim, by defendants was held to be an invasion of privacy even though the broadcast did not use plaintiff's full name or directly display her face because the plaintiff was still generally identifiable by her first name, voice, general appearance, and the circumstances of the accident, which had previously been published in a newspaper).

[19] See Virgil v. Time, Inc., 527 F.2d 1122 (9th Cir 1975), *cert. denied* 425 U.S. 998 (1976).

[20] See Sipple v. Chronicle Publishing Co., 201 Cal. Rptr. 665 (1984) (where plaintiff openly participated in events in the gay community, fact that he was gay was not a "private fact").

[21] See, e.g.: Florida Star v. B.J.F., 491 U.S. 524 (1989) (no liability for publishing rape victim's name when information came from accident report inadvertently left in sheriff's press room); Cox Broadcasting Co. v. Cohn, 420 U.S. 469 (1975) (no liability for publication of rape victim's name when information was obtained from official court records open to the public).

[22] See, e.g.:
Seventh Circuit: Woody v. West Pub. Co., 1995 WL 686028 (N.D. Ill. 1995) (legal publisher was immune from privacy claim when it published court decision in criminal sentencing matter that disclosed plaintiff's HIV status).
State Court:
New York: Cruz v. Latin News Impacto Newspaper, 216 A.D.2d 50, 627 N.Y.S.2d 388 (N.Y. App. 1995) (finding that statutes providing for confidentiality of AIDS diagnosis apply only to health care workers, not to news media).

Commercial Appropriation/Right of Publicity

A person may have a claim when his or her name, voice or likeness has been appropriated for commercial or advertising purposes, or for the defendant's own use or benefit.[23] The right of publicity is not violated, however, when a person's identity is used in a news, sports or public affairs context.[24]

But see, Multimedia WMAZ v. Kubach, 212 Ga. App. 707, 443 S.E.2d 491 (Ga. App. 1994) (split opinion affirming jury verdict for AIDS victim in private facts case when his identity was revealed during call-in show, despite fact that his identity was known to family, friends, and AIDS support group).

[23] See:

Sanford, *Libel and Privacy*, § 11.5.1 (2d ed. 1994 and 2000 Supp.).

Second Circuit: Haelan Laboratories, Inc. v. Topps Chewing Gum, Inc., 202 F.2d 866 (2d Cir. 1953) (finding that chewing gum company that had obtained exclusive right to use baseball player's image in its ads had valid cause of action against rival gum company that used image in its own ads), cert. denied 346 U.S. 816 (1953).

Ninth Circuit: Newcombe v. Adolf Coors Co., 157 F.3d 686, 26 Media L. Rep. 2364 (9th Cir. 1998) (reversal of grant of summary judgment for defendants Coors and its advertising agency, finding that whether the plaintiff was immediately identifiable from his pitching stance and player number in an artist's rendering of a 1949 newspaper photograph was a triable issue); Abdul-Jabbar v. General Motors Corp., 85 F.3d 407 (9th Cir. 1996) (car ad using name of former athlete violated his right of publicity); Cher v. Forum Int'l., Ltd., 692 F.2d 634, 639 (9th Cir. 1982) (magazine appropriated celebrity's right of publicity where it falsely stated that celebrity told magazine information she would not give to magazine's competitor, and that she had endorsed magazine), cert. denied 462 U.S. 1120 (1983).

State Court:

Arkansas: Olan Mills, Inc. v. Dodd, 353 S.W.2d 22 (Ark. 1962) (housewife whose photo was used in ad campaign for photo studio, including appearing on tens of thousands of postcards, could recover).

[24] See:

Second Circuit: Ann-Margret v. High Society Magazine, Inc., 498 F. Supp. 401 (S.D.N.Y. 1980) (actress's right of publicity was not violated by use of nude photo in magazine article).

Ninth Circuit: Baugh v. CBS, Inc., 828 F. Supp. 745 (N.D. Cal. 1993) (crime victim's right of publicity was not infringed where likeness was used in television news magazine program).

State Courts:

California: Montana v. San Jose Mercury News, Inc., 34 Cal. App.4th 790, 40 Cal. Rptr.2d 639 (Cal. App. 1995) (distribution of posters featuring Joe Montana did not violate his right of publicity because they depicted newsworthy matters in the public interest).

New York: Finger v. Omni Publications Int'l., 77 N.Y.2d 138, 564 N.Y.S.2d 1014 (1990) (publication of family's photo in magazine article did not infringe right of publicity).

Furthermore, even a commercial use may be privileged if its purpose is to advertise a book that contains news or is newsworthy.[25] For example, one New York court found that when a filmmaker had the right to use the likenesses of Ginger Rogers and Fred Astaire in a film, the use of the likenesses in advertising for the film was also permissible.[26]

It is important to note that some states, such as California, allow individuals to grant their heirs the right to exploit their name and likeness.[27] The California statute was amended in 1999 to provide a transferable property right in the "name, voice, signature, photograph, or likeness of any natural person who has commercial value at the time of his or her death."[28] While certain uses such as news reporting are exempted, the statute does not exempt uses that the claimant proves are "so directly connected with a product, article of merchandise, good or service as to constitute an act of advertising, selling, or soliciting purchases of that product, article of merchandise, good or service by the deceased personality without prior consent" from the claimant.[29] Registration of rights under the statute before the infringement occurs is a precondition for the recovery of damages.[30] The statute applies to any act in California regardless of the domicile of the celebrity at his or her death.[31]

---

[25] See:

Second Circuit: Friedan v. Friedan, 414 F. Supp. 77 (S.D.N.Y. 1976) (husband of feminist leader did not state cause of action for appropriation under civil rights statute where his photograph was used in advertising for magazine article written by wife; advertisements shared the privilege accorded news or newsworthy articles).

Ninth Circuit: Cher v. Forum Int'l., Ltd., 692 F.2d 634, 639 (9th Cir. 1982); New Kids on the Block v. News America, 745 F. Supp. 1540 (C.D. Cal. 1990) (900 number to vote for your favorite "New Kid" protected by First Amendment against misappropriation claim), *aff'd* 971 F.2d 302 (9th Cir. 1992).

[26] See Rogers v. Grimaldi, 695 F. Supp. 112 (S.D.N.Y. 1988) (because film maker had right to use likenesses of Ginger Rogers and Fred Astaire in film, use in advertising for film also was not actionable), *aff'd* 875 F.2d 994 (2d Cir. 1989).

[27] See Cal. Civ. Code § 3344.1 (formerly § 990) (rights last for 70 years after death).

[28] Cal. Civ. Code § 3341.1(h).

[29] Cal. Civ. Code § 3341.1(g).

[30] Cal. Civ. Code § 3341.1(f)(1).

[31] *Id.*

In states such as New York, with a very limited right of publicity for living persons, the right of publicity is not descendible.[32] Domicile at death may therefore be an important fact.

DEFENSES

Civil defendants in actions alleging invasion of privacy have a number of defenses available to them, but the most common are consent[33] and newsworthiness.

A written release of liability, expressly consenting to the publication or other activity, is perhaps the best defense to a privacy claim. If one knows in advance that one is going to be publicizing information about someone, or using a person's name or likeness, it is a good idea to get a written release beforehand. The release should be very short and simple, basically stating that the person is allowing his or her name, voice, likeness and possibly biographical information to be used in the program. It might be appropriate to include permission to use the material in advertising or promotions, and to grant the producer sole editorial discretion.

Publication of private information that is of public interest, or "newsworthy," is not an invasion of privacy.[34] For example, in California, the sexual orientation of a gay man who saved President Ford from assassination was deemed newsworthy and thus was not an invasion of his privacy.[35] The identity of young mother who abandoned her child was also deemed newsworthy by a California court of appeal.[36] In Alabama, the mismanagement of an electrical co-op was found to be a matter of public interest.[37] There are

---

[32] See Pirone v. MacMillan Inc., 894 F.2d 579 (2d Cir. 1990) (no post-mortem rights under N.Y. Civil Rights L. §§ 50-51).

[33] See Ault v. Hustler Magazine, 860 F.2d 877 (9th Cir. 1988) (plaintiff's consent to be photographed barred claim for publication of photos), *cert. denied* 489 U.S. 1080 (1989).

[34] See: Metcalf, 1 *Rights and Liabilities of Publishers, Broadcasters, and Reporters (Individual Rights)*, § 2.28 (1982); Sanford, *Libel and Privacy*, § 11.3.3.1 (2d ed. 1994 and 2000 Supp.).

[35] See Sipple v. Chronicle Publishing Co., 154 Cal. App.3d 1455, 201 Cal. Rptr. 665 (1987).

[36] See Pasadena Star News v. Superior Court, 203 Cal. App.3d 131, 249 Cal. Rptr. 729 (1988).

[37] See McCaig v. Talladega Pub. Co., 544 So.2d 875 (Ala. 1989).

limits, however, to the "newsworthiness" defense, depending in part on "public notions of decency." For instance, the disclosure of the HIV status of a person may be actionable.[38]

Courts generally examine three factors in evaluating newsworthiness: (1) the social value of the facts published; (2) the depth of intrusion into the person's private affairs; and (3) the degree to which the person involved is a voluntary public figure. With respect to the third factor, courts have recognized that when a private person has been caught up involuntarily in events of public interest, the publication of private facts about that person may be newsworthy if they "bear a logical relationship to the newsworthy subject of the broadcast" and are not intrusive beyond the scope of their relevance.[39]

Although the newsworthiness privilege most often arises in the context of breaking news, such as contemporary news accounts of criminal activity, sports events or highway accidents, it applies equally to reports of newsworthy events after a lapse of time. The Second Circuit has held that the decline of a child prodigy remained a matter of general interest twenty-seven years after wide publicity for his academic accomplishments as a ten-year-old boy.[40] In California, the photo of a former actress as shown on a television program concerning the murder of her fiancé/director forty-eight years earlier was still newsworthy.[41] Even the identity of those involved in historical events may be disclosed if disclosure is based on accurate information obtained from judicial records.[42]

The Second Circuit reaffirmed that New York's Civil Rights Law Section 51 does not provide a cause of action for invasion of privacy for photographs that are used to illustrate a magazine article when the article is "newsworthy," there is a real relationship

[38] See Urbaniak v. Newton, 226 Cal. App.3d 1128, 277 Cal. Rptr. 354 (1991).

[39] Shulman v. Group W Productions, Inc., 18 Cal.4th 200, 215, 74 Cal. Rptr.2d 843, 26 Media L. Rep. 1737 (1998).

[40] See, e.g., Sidis v. F-R Pub. Corp., 113 F.2d 806 (2d Cir.), cert. denied 311 U.S. 711 (1940).

[41] See O'Hilderbrandt v. Columbia Broadcasting Systems, Inc., 40 Cal. App.3d 323, 114 Cal. Rptr. 826 (1974).

[42] See Cox Broadcasting Co. v. Cohn, 420 U.S. 469 (1975).

between the photograph and the article, and the article is not an advertisement in disguise.[43] In cases involving media "ride-alongs," in which members of the media accompany law enforcement or rescue workers on their rounds, the California Supreme Court has ruled that a plaintiff must show lack of newsworthiness as an element of a claim for public disclosure of private facts.[44] The California Supreme Court assumed that the newsworthiness defense and the "absence of legitimate public concern" in a publication of private facts claim have "congruent" boundaries.[45]

The person asserting the privacy violation need not have been accused of a crime in order for information about the person to be considered newsworthy; even innocent bystanders may lose their privacy rights regarding reports of newsworthy events.[46] For example, in one California case, when the plaintiff was one of the last known people to see a missing person alive, the plaintiff was found to have no valid privacy claim.[47]

It is with this backdrop of common law privacy principles that we turn to the evolution of the principles relating to the rights of individuals to prevent unwanted collection of their personal data.

THE HEW REPORT ON RECORDS, COMPUTERS AND THE RIGHTS OF CITIZENS

In 1972, then-HEW Secretary Elliot L. Richardson formed the Secretary's Advisory Committee on Automated Personal Data Systems to study the effect of new computer and telecommunications technology on the collection, storage and use of data about individual citizens. The result was the HEW Report, issued in July 1973. The Report set out the following principles, entitled "Rights of Individual Data Subjects":

---

[43] See Messenger v. Gruner & Jahr Printing and Publishing, 2000 WL 190553 (N.Y. 2000), 2000 WL 267749 (2d Cir. 2000).

[44] See *Shulman v. Group W Productions, Inc.*, N. 39 *supra.*

[45] *Id.*, 18 Cal.4th at 216.

[46] See, e.g., Forsher v. Buglioso, 26 Cal.3d 792, 163 Cal. Rptr. 628 (1980). See also, Sipple v. Chronicle Publishing Co., 154 Cal. App.3d 1040, 201 Cal. Rptr. 665 (1984).

[47] See *Forsher,* N. 46 *supra.*

(1) The Choice Principle. Inform an individual asked to supply personal data for the system whether he is legally required, or may refuse, to supply the data requested, and also of any specific consequences for him, which are known to the organization, of providing or not providing such data;

(2) The Notice Principle (I). Inform an individual, upon his request, whether he is the subject of data in the system, and, if so, make such data fully available to the individual, upon his request, in a form comprehensible to him;

(3) The Consent Principle. Assure that no use of individually identifiable data is made that is not within the stated purposes of the system as reasonably understood by the individual, unless the informed consent of the individual has been explicitly obtained;

(4) The Notice Principle (II). Inform an individual, upon her request, about the uses made of data about her, including the identity of all persons and organizations involved and their relationships within the system;

(5) The Security Principle. Assure that no data about an individual are made available from the system in response to a demand for data made by means of compulsory legal process, unless the individual to whom the data pertain has been notified of the demand;

(6) The Integrity and Access Principles. Maintain procedures that (i) allow an individual who is the subject of data in the system to contest their accuracy, completeness, pertinence, and the necessity for retaining them; (ii) permit data to be corrected or amended when the individual to whom they pertain so requests; and (iii) assure, when there is disagreement with the individual about whether a correction or amendment should be made, that the individual's claim is noted and included in any subsequent disclosure or dissemination of the disputed data.[48]

Elsewhere in the Report, the authors drafted what has become known as the "Code of Fair Information Practices":

---

[48] *HEW Report*, 59-63 (July 1973).

- There must be no personal-data record-keeping systems whose very existence is secret.
- There must be a way for an individual to find out what information about him is in a record and how it is used.
- There must be a way for an individual to prevent information about her obtained for one purpose from being used or made available for other purposes without her consent.
- There must be a way for an individual to correct or amend a record of identifiable information about him.
- Any organization that creates, maintains, uses, or disseminates records of identifiable personal data must assure the reliability of the data for their intended use and must take reasonable precautions to prevent misuse of the data.[49]

This "Code of Fair Information Practices" supplied the framework for the Privacy Act of 1974 (see below). And, as we will see later, it forms the basis for most of the U.S. legislative and regulatory enforcement efforts, including that of the Federal Trade Commission, that have followed.

While many of the concerns that citizens, legislators and businesses are struggling with today existed back in 1973, much has changed. Back in the 1970s, the focus of privacy initiatives was on protecting the individual from abuses by government. In part, this was a reflection of the times, and of the paramount concerns about the rights of individuals to be free from *governmental* intrusion into their privacy.[50] That is, the preoccupation with governmental intrusion into individual privacy was a function of the fact that only the government had the technology to permit the consolidation of personal information from various databases. Private organizations simply lacked any serious capability to transfer personal data across private networks. In the words of the HEW Report:

> [W]e recognize that combining bits and pieces of personal data from various records is one way of creating an intelligence record, or dossier. The possibility of using a large computer to

---

[49] *Id.* at 41.

[50] This concern with governmental intrusion into the privacy of citizens resurfaced in Congress and in public debate following the terrorist attack on New York City and Washington, D.C. on September 11, 2001.

assemble a number of data banks into a "master file" so that a dossier on nearly everybody could then be extracted is currently remote, since the ability to merge unrelated files efficiently depends heavily upon their having many features of technical structure in common, and also on having adequate information to match individual records with certainty. These technical obstacles are avoided if the capability to merge whole files is designed into a group of systems at the outset, a practice now characteristic of only a few multi-jurisdictional systems but perhaps becoming more prevalent. *At the present time, however, compiling dossiers from a number of unrelated systems presents problems that few organizations, and probably no organizations outside of governmental, have the resources to solve.*[51]

The big change over the past thirty years, then, has been the change in technology, rather than a change in legal principles or public concern with privacy. The "technical obstacles" that led the authors of the HEW Report to focus on governmental data protection practices rather than private data protection practices no longer exist. Private companies now have the technology to create dossiers and share the information across companies and systems in a manner that was inconceivable thirty years ago.

PERSONAL PRIVACY IN AN INFORMATION SOCIETY (1977)

In 1974, Congress passed the Privacy Act of 1974.[52] This Act was directed to agencies of the Executive Branch of the U.S. government and had no direct impact on data collection by private entities. However, in the Act, Congress adopted the principles of the HEW Report. Those tenets are contained in the "Congressional findings and statement of purpose" of the Act, which are to:

(1) permit an individual to determine what records pertaining to him are collected, maintained, used, or disseminated by such [federal] agencies;

(2) permit an individual to prevent records pertaining to him obtained by such agencies for a particular purpose from

---

[51] *HEW Report,* N. 48 *supra* at 20-21. (Emphasis added.)
[52] Privacy Act, Pub. L. No. 93-579, 88 Stat. 1896.

being used or made available for another purpose without his consent;

(3) permit an individual to gain access to information pertaining to him in federal agency records, to have a copy made of all or any portion thereof, and to correct or amend such records;

(4) collect, maintain, use, or disseminate any record of identifiable personal information in a manner that assures that such action is for a necessary and lawful purpose, that the information is current and accurate for its intended use, and that adequate safeguards are provided to prevent misuse of such information;

(5) permit exemptions from requirements with respect to records provided in this Act only in those cases where there is an important public policy need for such exemption as has been determined by specific statutory authority; and

(6) allow Executive Branch agencies to be subject to civil suit for any damages which occur as a result of willful or intentional action which violates any individual's rights under this Act.[53]

Following enactment of the Privacy Act, Congress revisited the question of whether privacy protections should apply to non-governmental organizations and asked for a recommendation as to whether the standards of the Privacy Act should be extended beyond federal Executive Branch agencies. In response, the Privacy Protection Study Commission was formed to conduct a "study of the data banks, automatic data processing programs, and information systems of governmental, regional, and private organizations, in order to determine the standards and procedures in force for the protection of personal information." After two years' work, in 1977, it issued its report, entitled *Personal Privacy in an Information Society*, which was by its own terms focused on the very issues that drive the Internet privacy debate today: "This report is about records and people. It looks toward a national policy to guide the way public and private organizations treat the records they keep about individuals."[54]

---

[53] *Id.* at § 2.
[54] Privacy Protection Study Commission, *Personal Privacy in an Information Society*, 4 (1977).

Although the report acknowledged that individuals should "be concerned about the long-term effect record-keeping practices can have . . . on relationships between individuals and organizations,"[55] it ultimately recommended that the Privacy Act not be extended beyond the Executive Branch agencies.[56]

Nonetheless, the report concluded that the personal data record-keeping practices of the day poorly protected the individual's interest, and identified five "systemic features of personal-data record-keeping in America today":

First, while an organization makes and keeps records about individuals to facilitate relationships with them, it also makes and keeps records about individuals for other purposes, such as documenting the record-keeping organization's own actions and making it possible for other organizations—government agencies, for example—to monitor the actions of individuals;

Second, there is an accelerating trend most obvious in the credit and financial areas, toward the accumulation in records of more and more personal details about an individual;

Third, more and more records about an individual are collected, maintained, and disclosed by organizations with which the individual has no direct relationship but whose records help to shape his life;

Fourth, most record-keeping organizations consult the records of other organizations to verify the information they obtain from an individual and thus pay as much or more attention to what other organizations report about him than they pay to what he reports about himself; and

Fifth, neither law nor technology now gives an individual the tools he needs to protect his legitimate interests in the records [that] organizations keep about him.[57]

The Commission concluded that an effective privacy policy must have the following three objectives:

---

[55] Id. at 5.
[56] Id. at 497.
[57] Id. at 8.

- to create a proper balance between what an individual is expected to divulge to a record-keeping organization and what he seeks in return *(to minimize intrusiveness)*;
- to open up record-keeping operations in ways that will minimize the extent to which recorded information about an individual is itself a source of unfairness in any decision about him made on the basis of it *(to maximize fairness)*; and
- to create and define obligations with respect to the uses and disclosures that will be made of recorded information about an individual *(to create legitimate, enforceable expectations of confidentiality)*.[58]

The Commission then analyzed three alternative approaches to address the observed deficiencies in privacy policy. These alternatives are precisely those being discussed today as a way to address the concerns about Internet privacy:

(1) voluntary compliance;
(2) statutory creation of rights and interests enforceable through individual or governmental action; and
(3) establishment of ongoing governmental mechanisms to investigate, study, and report on privacy protection issues.[59]

Notably, the Commission concluded that in most cases voluntary compliance will not be sufficient.[60]

Following the Privacy Commission report, and the recommendation that the Privacy Act not be extended beyond the Executive Branch, privacy issues receded from the forefront of public debate in the United States, although Europe focused on them in 1980 and 1981 in the *OECD Guidelines on the Protection of Privacy and Transborder Flows of Personal Data* (1980) and the Council of Europe's *Convention on Privacy* (1981). Privacy issues resurrected themselves in the U.S. in more limited ways in a series of statutes that were primarily focused on other matters, but which had privacy concerns embedded in them.[61]

---

[58] *Id.*
[59] *Id.* at 33.
[60] *Id.* at 34.
[61] A number of these initiatives are discussed in Chapters 4 and 5.

CHAPTER 4

RELEVANT FEDERAL LEGISLATION: PRIVACY PROVISIONS OF COPPA

Congress has embarked on many privacy initiatives since the early 1970s, from the Privacy Act of 1974 to the Cable Communications Policy Act of 1984 to the Telecommunications Act of 1996. As we have seen in the preceding chapter, the initial legislative efforts focused on and regulated governmental entities and their ability to collect and use personal information. Other statutes created protections for certain types of personal information (for instance, cable television subscriber information and credit reports) and regulate the ability of private—not just governmental—entities to collect and use the information.[1] These statutes existed for years, if not decades, prior to the widespread use of the Internet.

More recently, Congress has enacted another spate of privacy legislation, namely, the Children's Online Privacy Protection Act (COPPA), the Gramm-Leach-Bliley Act (the GLB Act), and the Health

---

[1] See, e.g.: Fair Credit Reporting Act, 15 U.S.C. §§ 1681 *et seq.* (governing consumer credit reports); Cable Communications Policy Act of 1984, 47 U.S.C. §§ 551 *et seq.* (governing cable television subscriber information); Right to Financial Privacy Act of 1978, 12 U.S.C. §§ 3401 *et seq.* (governing individual bank records); Video Privacy Protection Act of 1988, 12 U.S.C. §§ 2719 *et seq.* (governing video rental records); Family Educational Rights and Privacy Act of 1974, 20 U.S.C. §§ 1232g (governing student records); Telephone Consumer Protection Act of 1991, 47 U.S.C. § 227 (governing unsolicited telephone calls); Telecommunications Act of 1996, 47 U.S.C. § 222 (governing information concerning use of telecommunication services).

Insurance Portability and Accountability Act (HIPAA), with a vivid awareness of online privacy issues.[2] The privacy provisions of each of these statutes were, at least in part, intended to address privacy threats posed by digital commerce, where information is collected and widely disseminated with unprecedented speed, including information that was generally understood to be confidential. One of these laws, COPPA, is drafted to apply solely to entities that collect personal information online. This chapter describes the contours and basic requirements of COPPA, pursuant to which the Federal Trade Commission and other federal agencies have promulgated detailed regulations. These regulations impose substantial affirmative duties on certain entities, such as Web site operators, financial institutions and/or healthcare entities.

CHILDREN'S ONLINE PRIVACY PROTECTION ACT

OVERVIEW

Enacted on October 21, 1998, the Children's Online Privacy Protection Act is the first major piece of federal legislation directly targeting online data-collection practices. COPPA was enacted in response to the 1998 survey conducted by the FTC that found that among the 212 children's Web sites surveyed, very few were disclosing their information practices and even fewer were providing mechanisms for parental notice of and consent to the collection and disclosure of children's personal information. With COPPA, Congress responded to these practices by establishing a regulatory framework for the collection and use of personal information from and about children on the Internet, with the following four goals: (1) enhancing parental involvement in a child's online activities in order to protect the privacy of children in the online environment; (2) helping to protect the safety of children in online situations (such as chat rooms, home pages and pen-pal services in which children may make public postings of identifying information); (3) maintaining the security of children's personal information collected online; and (4) limiting the collection of personal information from children without parental consent.

---

[2] The GLB Act and HIPAA are discussed in detail in Chapter 5.

The name "Children's Online Privacy Protection Act" correctly suggests that COPPA applies only to a limited range of data—specifically, personal information that is collected online and that can serve to identify an individual child. Significantly, COPPA does *not* apply to any personal information collected prior to the effective date, April 21, 2000. Although limited in its reach with respect to the type of information it affects, COPPA does apply to an extremely broad range of Internet actors—from operators of Web sites and online services that directly target children to certain operators of general audience Web sites or online services (which, while not targeting children, nonetheless receive visits from children) to persons who have an interest in the online collection of children's personal information. Thus, every such operator or person should be familiar with the requirements of COPPA.

Congress delegated to the FTC the responsibility of promulgating regulations to implement COPPA's various requirements. In October 1999, the FTC promulgated final rules, which became effective April 21, 2000.[3] Generally speaking, the rules require an "operator" of a commercial site or online service that collects personal information from children under thirteen years of age to follow six basic guidelines:

- Provide clear and prominent notice on the site of what information it collects about children, how the information is used, and the site's disclosure practices;
- Obtain "verifiable consent" from parents prior to collecting, using or disclosing any of this information;
- Provide a reasonable means for parents to review the information that is collected from their child;
- Allow parents to refuse to permit the use or continued maintenance of information that is collected about their child;
- Not condition a child's participation in a game, the offering of a prize, or other activity, on the child's disclosure of more personal information than is reasonably necessary to participate in the activity;
- Set up and maintain procedures to protect confidentiality, security and integrity of personal information collected from children.

---

[3] 16 C.F.R. Part 312. The rule is available online at http.www.ftc.gov/privacy/index.html.

As detailed below, the rules also delineate with a fair amount of precision exactly how operators are to go about implementing these six requirements.

A commercial Web site or online service must comply with *each* of the six COPPA requirements (each of which implicates many other subsidiary requirements). Failure to comply can result in penalties of up to $11,000 per violation. If a commercial site or service collects information from children under thirteen years of age and is not in full compliance, it should stop collecting personal information from children until full compliance is achieved. Because compliance requires such actions as implementing notice and consent mechanisms for every child from whom a site or service collects information and instituting appropriate methods for protecting children's information and for verifying the identity of persons requesting children's information, the costs of compliance are substantial. Thus, numerous sites and services will no doubt conclude that the cost of achieving compliance is simply too high to warrant the continued collection of children's personal information. In addition, there may be a fair amount of uncertainty as to whether compliance has been achieved even if substantial efforts to comply are made, thus making collection of children's information somewhat risky, particularly in light of the possible penalties.

In an effort to lessen the risks of inadvertent noncompliance, COPPA requires the FTC to approve "self-regulatory guidelines," issued by representatives of the marketing or online industries, in order to provide operators with a "safe harbor." In other words, if an operator fully complies with self-regulatory guidelines that have been approved by the FTC, such compliance will be deemed a defense (or "safe harbor") in any enforcement action under the rules. For example, the FTC has approved a set of safe harbor rules issued by the Children's Advertising Review Unit of the Council of Better Business Bureaus, Inc. (the CARU safe harbor rules).

SCOPE OF THE COPPA RULES

WEB SITES AND ONLINE SERVICES SUBJECT TO THE RULES

The COPPA rules apply to operators of commercial Web sites or online services that collect personal information from users and (1) are directed to children or (2) have actual knowledge that they are collecting personal information from children under thirteen years of age.[4] An "operator" includes not only the entity that actually runs the day-to-day operations of the Web site, but also any person or entity on whose behalf the personal information is collected.[5] To determine whether a party is an "operator" and thus comes within the COPPA rules, certain factors, such as whether a party (1) owns, controls or has access to the information, (2) pays for or plays a role in its collection or maintenance, or (3) has some other interest in the information, are considered in making this determination. The FTC has clarified that those entities that merely provide access to the Internet, without providing content or collecting information from children, would not be considered operators and thus are not subject to the rules.[6]

Directed to Children. There is no bright line to determine whether a Web site or online service is "directed to children"—and thus subject to the rules. Instead, whether a site or service is directed to children depends on the overall character of the site. Some relevant factors in determining the character of a site or service are, for instance, subject matter, visual or audio content, age of any models, language, as well as whether advertising promoting or appearing on the Web site or online service is directed to children and whether the site uses animated characters and/or child-oriented activities and incentives.[7] In addition, in any investigation the FTC would take into account empirical evidence of the age of actual visitors and evidence of the intended audience. While most Web sites or services will know whether they are directed to children, sites or services that use animation or younger models should look closely at the character of the sites or services (as well as at their actual audience) to determine whether they could be viewed (by the FTC) as being directed at children.

Actual Knowledge. The rules do not impose a duty on an operator to inquire as to the age of the site's visitors. However, once the operator obtains actual knowledge that a visitor is a child, the rules apply. Actual knowledge can be obtained in many ways, and the

---

[4] 16 C.F.R. § 312.3.
[5] 16 C.F.R. § 312.2 (definition of "operator").
[6] 64 Fed. Reg. 59,891 (Nov. 3, 1999).
[7] 16 C.F.R. § 312.2 (definition of "Website or online service directed to children").

FTC has provided certain examples of how such knowledge can be obtained. For instance, actual knowledge that a visitor is a child is obtained when an operator learns of a child's age or grade from the child's registration at the site or from a concerned parent who has learned that his or her child is participating at the site. The FTC has raised a red flag that it will closely examine operators of general audience sites who "*do not directly ask age or grade, but instead ask 'age identifying' questions, such as 'what type of school do you go to: (a) elementary; (b) middle; (c) high school; (d) college.'*" The FTC has stated that it will look closely at such sites because "*through such questions, operators may acquire actual knowledge that they are dealing with children under 13.*"[8] In addition, the FTC is on the lookout for efforts to avoid COPPA. Disclaimers or warnings posted on a site, such as "Children under 13 not permitted," will not avoid the need to comply with COPPA. The FTC will also examine practices that encourage children to falsify their ages, and even making the provision of personal information optional will not avoid the need to comply with COPPA.[9]

Advertisers. The FTC has specifically stated that online advertising companies *are* subject to the rules if such companies collect personal information directly from children who click on ads placed on Web sites or online services directed to children. The FTC has also explicitly stated that advertising companies that collect personal information from visitors who click on the companies' ads at general audience sites are subject to the rules if any information reveals that the visitor is a child. Finally, the FTC has noted that advertising companies are subject to COPPA even if they do not collect information from children directly, if they own or control information collected at a host children's site.[10] In these instances, the FTC has recommended that the advertising company provide a joint notice with the operator of the host site.[11] To ensure compliance with the rules, advertisers can now take advantage of the safe harbor rules that were submitted by CARU and approved by the FTC.

---

[8] 64 Fed. Reg. 59,891 (Nov. 3, 1999).
[9] See http://www.ftc.gov/bcp/conline/edcams/kidzprivacy.
[10] 64 Fed. Reg. 59,892 (Nov. 3, 1999).
[11] *Id.*, n.57.

TYPE OF INFORMATION PROTECTED BY COPPA: PERSONAL INFORMATION

The COPPA rules restrict the collection and maintenance of "personal information," which is, generally speaking, information that on its own or in combination with other information could be used to identify or locate an individual either online or offline. This includes, for instance, the following fairly obvious types of identifiers:

- A first and last name;
- A home or other physical address, including street name and name of a city or town;
- An e-mail address or other online contact information, including, for example, an instant messaging user identifier or screen name that reveals an individual's e-mail address;
- A telephone number;
- A Social Security number.

While names, addresses, telephone and Social Security numbers are straightforward identifiers, other types of information that do not obviously identify an individual are also considered "personal information" if they permit such identification in combination with other information. For instance, a "persistent identifier," such as a last name or even a photograph of an individual, is "personal information" when it is combined with other information that would permit online or physical contacting. Similarly, a customer number that is held in a cookie or a processor serial number is considered "personal information" when it is associated with information that identifies the individual. Moreover, information that exists *only in storage in an operator's cookie that the operator implanted on a user's hard drive* is considered "personal information" if that information is an identifier on its own or is combined with an identifier. The FTC has also indicated that if children are invited to download software that tracks their online activities and the information sent back to the Web site contains personal information, then this collection of information would be subject to the COPPA rules.

The last component of the FTC's definition of "personal information" goes beyond information that serves as an identifier and includes any information (e.g., age, gender, a hobby or favorite toy) about a child or the parents of a child that is collected online and combined with an identifier, such as those described above.

This information must be *collected over the Internet* to be subject to the rules. So even if a company collects "personal information," it would not be subject to the strictures of the rules unless it does so over the Internet. Thus, personal information collected only at a physical retail outlet would not be regulated by COPPA. But when children are requested to give information online or are enabled to make information public online (i.e., in a chat room or message board), or when children are tracked and the "track" is linked to personal information, any personal information derived must be collected in conformity with the COPPA rules.

SIX REQUIREMENTS FOR ONLINE COLLECTION OF A CHILD'S PERSONAL INFORMATION

The rules make it unlawful for an operator of a Web site or online service directed to children, or an operator who actually knows that it is collecting or maintaining personal information from a child, to collect personal information from a child unless the Web site or service operator complies with the six requirements of COPPA: (1) provide the required notice, (2) obtain verifiable parental consent, (3) provide a reasonable means for parents to review the information, (4) allow parents to refuse to permit further use or maintenance of the information, (5) do not condition a child's participation in a game or offering on giving personal information, and (6) protect the confidentiality and security of the personal information. It is worth emphasizing that these requirements must still be complied with *even if a company only uses the information internally and does not disclose it to third parties.*

NOTICES OF INFORMATION PRACTICES MUST BE POSTED ON THE WEB SITE OR ONLINE SERVICE AND SENT DIRECTLY TO PARENTS

The rules require two types of notice: (1) a notice that appears on the Web site or online service and that, among other things, describes the information practices that relate to the personal information that is collected and used by or through the site/service, and (2) a notice similar in content to that appearing on the Web site or online service and that is sent directly to parents of children whose personal information is to be collected.

Operators of Web sites and online services directed to children *and* general audience Web sites *that have a separate children's area* must post on the homepages of their Web sites or online services *and* at each area on the Web sites or online services where personal information is collected from children prominent and clearly labeled links to notices of their information practices with regard to children. An operator of a general audience site that has a separate children's area must post these links on the home page of the children's area *and* where personal information is collected from children.[12] Operators must ensure that the links are:[13]

- Clearly labeled as links to the sites' information practices regarding children; for instance, such a link could be labeled as a "Privacy Policy," "Notice of Information Practices," "Privacy Notice," or with a similar description;
- Prominently placed on the home page and in close proximity to all areas where personal information is collected from children—not in small print at the bottom of the page; instead, the link to the notice should stand out and be noticeable to the site's visitors through, for example, a larger font size in a different color on a contrasting background;
- Clearly distinguishable from other links.

The actual notice that sets out a site's child-related information practices must also conform to the particular requirements of the rules.[14] Specifically, the contents of the actual notice:

- Must be clear and understandable—no legalese;
- Must be a complete statement of the information practices that govern the collection, maintenance, use and/or disclosure of children's personal information collected by the Web site or online service;
- Cannot contain any unrelated, confusing or contradictory materials—including, for example, materials promoting products, services or other Web sites;
- Must include the following detailed information:

---

[12] 16 C.F.R. § 312.4(b).
[13] *Id.* and 64 Fed. Reg. 59,894-59,897 (Nov. 3, 1999).
[14] 64 Fed. Reg. 59,894-59,897 (Nov. 3, 1999).

- Operators' contact information (i.e., name, address, telephone number and e-mail address of all operators collecting or maintaining personal information from children through the Web site or online service (contact information for one operator who will respond to all inquiries is permitted, so long as the *names* of all other operators are listed in the notice));
- Kinds of personal information (e.g., names, addresses, telephone numbers, Social Security numbers, hobbies, investment information) that are collected—and whether such information is collected actively (with the child's participation) or passively (through cookies, GIFs, IP addresses or other tracking devices);
- How the information is to be or may be used (e.g., to fulfill requests, for record-keeping, for marketing purposes, or making information publicly available through a chat room, bulletin board, personal home pages or personal profiles, or other means);
- Whether the information is disclosed to third parties and, if so, what business the third parties are engaged in (e.g., advertising, list brokering, magazine publishing, retailing), how they use the information, and whether they have agreed to maintain the confidentiality of the information;
- That parents can permit the collection of their child's personal information, but prohibit the disclosure of such information to third parties;
- That a child's participation in the Web site or online service cannot be conditioned upon providing more personal information than is reasonably necessary to participate in the offerings of the site or service;
- That parents can at any time review and delete any personal information that has been collected *and* refuse to permit future collection of personal information;
- How parents can review and delete the information and how they can prevent future collection.

When multiple operators collect and use the information and when those operators do not have identical information practices, a summary of *all* the information practices that govern the collection, maintenance, use and disclosure of children's personal information—not just the host information practices—must be included in the notice.[15] In addition, the FTC has made clear that it expects operators to keep the notice on the site current. Thus, the quick-changing world of online data-sharing relationships requires an equally quick method of updating the site to reflect these shifting relationships.[16]

Operators must make reasonable efforts to ensure that a parent of a child receives notice of the operator's information practices regarding the collection, maintenance, use, and/or disclosure of the child's information. "Reasonable efforts" to provide a parent with notice can include sending the notice by postal mail or e-mail or even having the child print out a form to give to the parent.[17] Other reasonable means can be used as well.

The parental notice must contain the following:

- That the operator wishes to collect personal information from the child;
- That the parent's consent is required for the collection, use and/or disclosure of such information;
- An explanation of the means by which the parent can provide verifiable consent to the collection of information;
- All the information required by the rules to appear in the Web site notice.

If an operator collects online contact information from a child solely to respond more than once to a specific request (for instance, an online newsletter), the operator must also state in its parental notice that: (1) the operator has collected the child's e-mail address or other online contact information to respond to the child's request and that the request will require more than one con-tact with the child; (2) the parent may refuse to permit further con-tact with the child and require the operator to delete the informa-tion and explain how the parent can do so; and (3) if the parent fails to respond to the notice, the operator may use the contact information for the purpose stated in the notice (i.e., to fulfill the child's request).

---

[15] 64 Fed. Reg. 59,896 (Nov. 3, 1999).
[16] 64 Fed. Reg. 59,895 (Nov. 3, 1999).
[17] 64 Fed. Reg. 59,897 (Nov. 3, 1999).

If an operator collects a child's name and online contact information to protect the safety of a child participant on the Web site or online service, the operator must also state in its parental notice that (1) it did so, (2) the parent may refuse to permit use of and require deletion of the information and explain how the parent can do so, and (3) if the parent fails to respond to the notice, the operator may use the contact information for the purpose stated in the notice (i.e., to protect the child's safety).

Finally, a *new* notice must be sent to parents whenever *material* changes in the relevant information practices occur. For instance, if an operator plans to disclose children's personal information to an operator whose contact information is not listed in the notice sent to parents, but that operator's information practices are consistent with the practices already described in the prior parental notice, an operator would have to update its site/service notice, but would *not* be required to send a new, revised notice directly to parents.

If, however, the information practices of the new operator are *not* consistent with the practices described in the prior notice, a new, updated parental notice would have to be distributed. For example, if an operator previously obtained consent for purposes of allowing the child to participate in games on the Web site, but now wishes to offer chat rooms to the child, a new notice and consent will be required. Or if an operator that previously had permission to market toys to the child now wishes to market materially different items, such as diet pills, a new notice and consent would be required.[18] In order to ease the burden of re-notification, the FTC has permitted the new notice to consist of an e-mail with an embedded hyperlink to the updated notice on the Web site or online service *so long as* all the additional information (i.e., the information required in the parental notice, but not contained in the Web site/service notice, such as the fact that parental consent is needed for collection and how to provide parental consent) is clearly communicated to the parents in the e-mail and the hyperlink to the notice is clear and prominent.[19]

---

[18] *Id.*
[19] *Id.*

VERIFIABLE PARENTAL CONSENT AND HOW TO OBTAIN IT

Once an operator has sent the required parental notice and has made a request for parental consent, the operator must then receive *verifiable* parental consent prior to collecting any information. The rules specifically require that the operator use a method to obtain consent that is reasonably calculated to ensure that the person providing consent *is the child's parent* and not another person—such as the child. The FTC has specifically approved certain methods as sufficiently secure for all purposes (i.e., collection, maintenance, use and disclosure to third parties), including when higher risk activities such as chat rooms or message boards are involved. These methods (which are listed below) are either cumbersome or not widely available and thus inevitably will lower the parental consent rate:

- Providing a consent form to be signed by the parent and returned to the operator by postal mail or facsimile;
- Requiring a parent to use a credit card in connection with a transaction (most credit card companies require an actual payment to be made; thus, this method may not prove feasible if the operator does not wish to charge the parent a fee);
- Having a parent call a toll-free telephone number staffed with appropriately trained personnel (trained, for instance, to differentiate between children and adult callers);
- Using a digital certificate (which uses public key technology) to establish that the person responding is the parent of the child;
- Using e-mail accompanied by a digital parental signature or a PIN or password, which has been obtained through one of the approved methods set out above.

These methods are not only cumbersome and expensive, but in many cases not viable. For example, digital signatures and certificates are simply not widely enough available at this time to present viable options. Staffing a telephone line with a live operator has been estimated to cost $55 per hour, plus training costs.[20] With respect to the "print and send" method, the cost may be as high as

---

[20] 64 Fed. Reg. 59,901 n.194 (Nov. 3, 1999).

$2.81 per child to process mailed or faxed parental consent forms. In addition, the response rate will no doubt decline substantially if online response is not permitted.[21]

Obviously, the least costly and most effective method of obtaining consent would be via e-mail. The FTC and numerous commentators, however, have no doubt correctly observed that a child using e-mail could pretend to be a parent and effectively bypass the consent process. They have also correctly observed that while cost-efficient secure technologies are anticipated to be widely available in the near future, these technologies have not yet reached that level of wide distribution. Therefore, the FTC has *temporarily* approved the use of e-mail for purposes of obtaining verifiable parental consent for uses that do not pose significant risks to children, such as marketing to a child based on his or her hobby or toy preferences or sending promotional updates about site content or offerings. Even in these low-risk situations, the operator must take additional steps to increase the likelihood that the parent has, in fact, provided the consent, such as seeking confirmation from a parent in a delayed, subsequent e-mail asking whether the parent had actually provided the previously received consent or by seeking confirmation of the parent's consent by letter or phone call. When, however, the operator wishes to disclose the information to third parties or when the information is made public via chat rooms or message boards, confirmatory e-mail is not sufficient and the more secure approved methods listed above must be used. This "sliding scale" approach to verifiable consent is expected to be used until the FTC is presented with evidence showing that the anticipated progress in available technology has not occurred.[22]

Regardless of the approach initially used to obtain consent, operators should almost certainly include in their communications with parents a PIN number or password that can be used to verify future communications with parents. Using such an identifier can ease the

---

[21] The FTC noted that one commentator noted an 80 percent decline in online subscriptions to its magazine when it switched from an online subscription model to a form that had to be downloaded and mailed. 64 Fed. Reg. 59,900 (Nov. 3, 1999).
[22] 64 Fed. Reg. 59,902 (Nov. 3, 1999).

burden of obtaining verifiable parental consent if (or, more likely, *when*) a new consent must be obtained because of material changes in information practices. In addition, the use of PIN numbers or passwords can ease the burden of verifying that a person requesting access to a child's information is actually the parent of the child.

CERTAIN EXCEPTIONS TO THE NEED FOR PRIOR PARENTAL CONSENT

In general, the rules do not permit companies to collect first, and then get consent later. Operators, however, may collect information *without* prior parental consent in certain limited circumstances. These exceptions to the prior-consent rule were developed to facilitate compliance with the rules and were designed to allow for "seamless interactivity" in certain circumstances (such as responding to specific requests from a child) and to enable operators to respond to safety and liability concerns.[23] These limited exceptions are as follows:[24]

- Operators may collect a child's or parent's name and/or e-mail address or other online contact information for the purposes of providing the required notice and obtaining consent;
- Operators may collect a child's e-mail address (or other online contact information) to respond *once* to a specific request from a child *so long as* the operator deletes the e-mail address immediately after responding to this request;
- Operators may collect a child's e-mail address (or other online contact information) to respond on more than one occasion to a specific request of a child and only to that request (for instance, a request for a subscription to an online newsletter or for site updates or to provide a contest entry and subsequent award) *so long as* the operator sends a notice to the parent (after the first communication with the child) to provide an opportunity for the parent to opt out of the information collection and to order the operator to delete the e-mail address and stop contacting the child;

---

[23] *Id.*
[24] 16 C.F.R. § 312.5(c).

- Operators may collect a child's name and e-mail address (or other online contact information) to protect the safety of a child participating on the Web site or online service (for instance, operators may collect online contact information from children participating in their chat rooms in order to report to authorities a child's claim that he or she is being abused); in this circumstance the operator must give notice to the parent and use the information only for safety purposes;
- Operators may collect a child's name and e-mail address (or other online contact information) for the purposes of protecting the security and integrity of the site, taking precautions against liability, responding to judicial process, or for law enforcement on a matter related to public safety.

PARENTAL RIGHT TO REVIEW COLLECTED INFORMATION AND NO CONDITIONING PARTICIPATION IN ONLINE ACTIVITIES ON PROVISION OF PERSONAL INFORMATION

Upon a parent's request, an operator must provide the parent with reasonable access to any personal information collected about his or her child and an opportunity to prevent any further use or online collection of personal information from that child *and* to direct the operator to delete any of the information.[25]

In return for the parent's right to delete information, the operator has the ability to terminate any service provided to the child, *but only if the information to be deleted is reasonably necessary for the child's participation in that activity.*[26] For example, an operator may reasonably require children to provide their e-mail addresses to participate in a monitored chat room so the operator can contact a particular child if he or she is disrupting the chat room. If a parent directs the operator to delete the e-mail address, the operator may reasonably refuse to allow the child to participate in the chat room. If, however, other activities on the Web site do not require an e-mail address, the child must be permitted to have access to those activities.

---

[25] 16 C.F.R. § 312.6.
[26] *Id.* §§ 312.6(c) and 312.7.

While the notion of giving parents control over their children's information is in the interest of safety, implementing such a policy creates the danger that the information will be released to a person other than the child's parent. The rules, therefore, place upon the operator the uncomfortable burden of having to ensure that the person seeking to review the information is the child's parent, but to do so without "unduly burdening" the parent.[27] Fortunately, however, the rules also provide that any disclosure made to a person requesting the information would not result in liability so long as the disclosure was made in good faith and by following reasonable procedures designed to ensure that the requestor is the parent of the child whose information was requested.[28]

Although the rules themselves do not specifically define what a "reasonable procedure" might be, the FTC has indicated that "acceptable methods" for ensuring that a requestor is the parent would include the types of secure methods approved for obtaining verifiable parental consent: (1) printing and sending of forms (which should be signed by the parent and sent via postal mail or facsimile), (2) use of a credit card in connection with a transaction, (3) use of a toll-free number staffed by trained personnel, (4) use of digital signatures, and (5) use of an e-mail accompanied by a PIN number or password obtained through one of the verification methods listed above.[29] Given that a parent requesting access to information, in most circumstances, will have already received a request for parental consent from the operator of the Web site or service, operators should consider giving out PIN numbers or passwords to parents in the initial consent requests as these identifiers will ease the task of having to verify the fact that the requestor is actually the parent.

The FTC also recognized that other methods of parental verification might be appropriate, such as requiring requests to be made in writing, with confirmation sent to the home address, or using photocopies of drivers' licenses. The FTC has not precluded use of

---

[27] Id.
[28] Id. § 312.6(b).
[29] 64 Fed. Reg. 59,905 (Nov. 3, 1999).

these or other means that are "reasonable" and has made clear that it will continue to monitor technological advances that might ease parental verification.[30] Given the potential for liability, however, the most prudent course is to use one of the secure methods specifically blessed as "acceptable" by the FTC.

CONFIDENTIALITY, SECURITY, AND INTEGRITY OF PERSONAL INFORMATION COLLECTED FROM CHILDREN

Operators must establish procedures to protect the confidentiality, security and integrity of the personal information collected from children. Specifically, operators must protect children's information from loss, misuse, unauthorized access or disclosure. Appropriate measures to be taken to accomplish this goal are: (1) using secure Web servers and firewalls, (2) deleting personal information once it is no longer being used, (3) limiting employee access to data and providing those employees who have access with data-handling training, and (4) carefully screening the third parties to whom the information is disclosed.[31]

ENFORCEMENT AND PENALTIES

The FTC has primary responsibility for enforcing COPPA, but state attorneys general and certain federal agencies, such as the Office of the Comptroller of the Currency and Department of Transportation, have jurisdiction to enforce COPPA as well.[32] Violations of the rules can result in civil penalties of up to $11,000 per violation. The level of penalties can fluctuate and will likely depend on various factors such as the number of children involved, the amount and type of personal information collected, how the information was used, and whether it was shared with third parties.

The FTC demonstrated the seriousness with which it takes COPPA enforcement by marking the first anniversary of the

---

[30] Id.

[31] 16 C.F.R. § 312.8 and 64 Fed. Reg. 59,906 (Nov. 3, 1999).

[32] Other agencies with jurisdiction to enforce COPPA are the Federal Reserve Board, the Board of Directors of the Federal Deposit Insurance Corporation, the Director of the Office of Thrift Supervision, the National Credit Union Administration Board, the Secretary of Transportation, the Secretary of Agriculture, and the Farm Credit Administration.

statute's enforcement date with the announcement that it had reached settlements with three Web site operators for violation of the COPPA rules.[33] The operators—Monarch Services, Inc., Looksmart Ltd. and BigMailbox.com, Inc.—had been charged with collecting personally identifiable information (PII) from children under age thirteen without parental consent. The three sites had partnered to provide girls aged nine to fourteen with online articles, advice columns, contests, pen-pal opportunities, free e-mail accounts and message boards. In doing so, the sites collected children's personal information for the sites' own internal uses, enabled children to reveal their personal information publicly online without parental consent, and, in the case of BigMailbox.com, provided children's personal information to third parties without parental consent. To settle the enforcement action, the sites were required to pay a total of $100,000 in civil penalties, as well as bring their sites into compliance with COPPA and delete any PII collected from children since the rules' effective date. Furthermore, the BigMailbox settlement barred the company from making deceptive claims in its privacy policy regarding how it shared the information it collected.[34]

In a similar action, the FTC imposed a $30,000 fine on Lisa Frank, Inc., a company specializing in school supplies and related products targeted at girls, and imposed similar injunctive relief in the *Girls Life, Inc.* settlements.[35] The defendant had predicated children's participation in the shopping portions of its Web site on the collection of PII from them without parental consent.

SAFE HARBOR

One set of safe harbor rules that has been approved was submitted by the Children's Advertising Review Unit (CARU). These rules apply to advertisers and essentially track the requirements

---

[33] See "FTC Announces Settlements with Web Sites That Collected Children's Personal Data Without Parental Permission" (April 19, 2001), available at http://www.ftc.gov/opa/2001/04/girlslife.htm.

[34] *Id.*

[35] See United States v. Lisa Frank, Inc., Civ. No. 01-1516-A (E.D. Va. Oct. 1, 2001) (consent decree), available at http://www.ftc.gov/opa/2001/10/lisafrank.htm.

of the COPPA rules. The advantage to an advertiser in following these CARU rules to the letter is that, by following them, the advertiser is presumptively in compliance with the COPPA rules— thus eliminating substantial concerns about whether certain efforts to comply actually do satisfy the COPPA rules. To take advantage of the CARU safe harbor program, however, advertisers are subject to CARU's initial review of their Web sites or online services and CARU's ongoing monitoring program. Moreover, when full compliance with the safe harbor rules is not achieved, participating advertisers are subject to the various enforcement mechanisms set up by CARU. For instance, CARU can institute formal cases against noncomplying operators and may refer the matters to the Commission. CARU will also report in press releases and in the monthly Case Reports published by the National Advertising Division the formal cases that it brings against operators for noncompliance. In addition, CARU requires, as a condition of participating in its safe harbor program, that participants abide by CARU's Self-Regulatory Guidelines for Children's Advertising—a set of guidelines and principles addressing, among other things, the content of advertising directed to children.[36]

---

[36] The CARU Safe Harbor Compliance Checklist is available on the FTC Web site at http://www.ftc.gov/privacy/safeharbor/shp.htm.

CHAPTER 5

RELEVANT FEDERAL LEGISLATION: PRIVACY PROVISIONS OF THE GLB AND HIPAA

The privacy provisions of the Gramm-Leach-Bliley Act (the GLB Act) and the Health Insurance Portability and Accountability Act (HIPAA) were, at least in part, intended to address privacy threats posed by digital commerce, where such information as financial and medical information, generally thought to be confidential, is collected and disseminated with unprecedented speed. The GLB Act and HIPAA affect the information-gathering and -use practices of both online and offline entities that deal either in personal financial or personal health information, respectively.

While these laws clearly restrict the collection and use of certain types of information, there are other laws for which application to such practices is less clear, but is nonetheless being extensively used by plaintiffs in their court-based efforts to restrict online information gathering. These laws are the Computer Fraud and Abuse Act (CFAA) and the Electronic Communications Privacy Act (ECPA), the latter of which contains two provisions of interest—the Wiretap Act (which regulates the *interception* of live communications) and the Stored Electronic Communications Privacy Act (which regulates the *accessing* of stored electronic communications). As the chapter on privacy litigation shows,[1] the answer to whether these statutes

---

[1] See Chapter 8.

apply to the online collection and use of personal data is in its preliminary stages and will probably be a source of ongoing uncertainty and litigation.

This chapter describes the basic provisions of the GLB Act and HIPAA, and the duties they impose on certain entities such as Web site operators, financial institutions and/or healthcare entities. It also examines the laws currently being used in court by plaintiffs (the CFAA and the ECPA) because these laws are of particular relevance to online information practices.

The CFAA and the ECPA are prohibitory in nature and, thus, do not impose affirmative duties or have a corresponding set of regulations. They present their own interpretive challenges, however, which courts are still addressing.

THE GRAMM-LEACH-BLILEY ACT

OVERVIEW

Congress enacted the Gramm-Leach-Bliley Act[2] on November 12, 1999 for the purpose of implementing the congressional policy that "each financial institution has an affirmative and continuing obligation to respect the privacy of its customers and to protect the security and confidentiality of those customers' nonpublic personal information."[3] The Act primarily regulates financial institutions,[4] e.g., banks, securities firms and insurance companies. In a significant expansion of its apparent area of operation, however, the GLB Act's provisions also relate to *any party that receives nonpublic personal information from a financial institution.* Among other things, the Act creates certain protections for the "nonpublic personal information" (such as assets, credit history, and, in some cases, names, addresses and telephone numbers) of the consumers of

---

[2] Pub. L. No. 106-102, 113 Stat. 1338 (Nov. 12, 1999)(codified in scattered volumes of the United States Code).

[3] 15 U.S.C. § 6801(a).

[4] The GLB Act is primarily concerned with repealing Glass-Steagall restrictions on permissible affiliations between different types of financial institutions. Title V of the GLB Act sets out the relevant privacy restrictions and is codified at 15 U.S.C. §§ 6801 *et seq.*

financial products and services provided by financial institutions. As with the Children's Online Privacy Protection Act (COPPA),[5] Congress has delegated the responsibility for promulgating regulations, which implement the requirements of the GLB Act, to certain federal agencies, such as the FTC and the Securities and Exchange Commission, and state insurance authorities[6] (the "Agencies"). These regulations have already been promulgated. Financial institutions and parties that receive protected information (i.e., nonpublic, personal information) from financial institutions must have been in compliance with these regulations by July 1, 2001.

The regulations apply to all types of financial institutions in online and traditional settings. They do, however, show an awareness—indeed, a wariness—of online collection practices. For instance, the regulations single out certain types of online activities, such as Internet companies that provide access to a person's online accounts, as being covered by the regulations. Significantly, the regulations also single out information collected by financial institutions through cookies for protection by the regulations.

The key characteristics of the GLB regulations are that they:

- Allow, without restrictions, the sharing of personal information among affiliates;[7]
- Require financial institutions to provide notice to consumers regarding the institutions' privacy policy and practices;
- Limit the ability to share nonpublic personal information with *nonaffiliated third parties* by prohibiting the disclosure of personal information to nonaffiliated third parties unless prior

---

[5] See Chapter 4.

[6] Pursuant to Section 504(a) of the Act, 15 U.S.C. § 6804(a), regulations implementing these provisions are to be promulgated by the Federal Trade Commission, the Securities and Exchange Commission, the Secretary of the Treasury (specifically the Office of the Comptroller of the Currency and the Office of Thrift Supervision), the federal banking agencies (which includes the Federal Reserve System and the Federal Deposit Insurance Corporation), the National Credit Union Administration, and state insurance authorities.

[7] The GLB Act does, however, direct the Secretary of the Treasury to conduct a study of information-sharing practices among financial institutions and their affiliates and to submit a report with its findings and any recommendations for legislative or administrative action. 15 U.S.C. § 6808.

notice and an opportunity to opt out is provided to the individuals whose information is to be disclosed;
* Limit the reuse and redisclosure of personal information by the third parties who receive the information from the financial institutions;
* Limit the disclosure of account number information for marketing purposes.

While the general contours of the GLB regulations are relatively straightforward, the specifics of the regulations are quite complicated and, frankly, are likely not to be fully comprehended or competently followed by a non-lawyer or by someone not trained as a privacy officer. Simply determining whether an entity is a "financial institution" (and thus affected by the regulations) and determining precisely what types of information are covered by the regulations can be painstaking tasks. Thus, unlike COPPA, which can likely be complied with by carefully following the relevant regulations, compliance with the GLB regulations is not likely to be achieved without consultation with a lawyer or other privacy specialist.

As indicated above, the GLB Act required the FTC and numerous other agencies to promulgate regulations to implement the requirements of the Act. In spite of the number of agencies involved, the various regulations that have been issued are in substantial respects identical.[8] Thus, for ease of reference (and because the FTC's regulations have the broadest potential reach), in the discussion that follows we will refer to the FTC regulations and, where appropriate, will note certain differences between the FTC's and other agencies' rules.[9]

SCOPE OF THE GLB REGULATIONS

The threshold questions of (1) to whom the regulations apply and (2) what type of information is covered are in many ways the

---

[8] Examination and comparison of the regulations issued by each state insurance authority is beyond the scope of this book and has not been undertaken.

[9] In addition to the discussion that follows, for further explication of the GLB Act, the FTC has created a guide intended for use by the public. It is available at http://www.ftc.gov/privacy/glbact/glboutline.htm.

most difficult aspects of applying the regulations. As discussed in some specificity below, the GLB Act and regulations broadly apply to any "financial institution"—a term with a highly complex definition that cannot be fully understood without reference to the Bank Holding Company Act (and the related regulations). Making it even more complex, the FTC, in its set of regulations, has defined "financial institution" to be *less* inclusive than the other agencies' definitions. Thus, companies must take care that they are applying the appropriate agency's definition when determining whether the regulations pertain to them or not.

From a practical point of view, however, many companies that technically qualify as "financial institutions" may nonetheless have no obligations under the regulations. This is because the regulations' requirements are triggered by a company's having a particular type of "consumer" or "customer"—specifically, an *individual* who has obtained from the institution financial products or services for personal, family or household purposes. Thus, it is likely that a company engaged in the financial activity of tax preparation for businesses has no obligation under the regulations so long as it does not provide tax preparation services for individuals for personal, family or household purposes. Similarly, a software company that sells tax preparation software would be a financial institution, but if it sells software strictly to other businesses and not to individuals for their own personal, family or household use, such a company would not have to comply with the requirements that apply to financial institutions. Indeed, the FTC has specifically noted that a significant portion of companies that are technically "financial institutions" will "likely not be subject to the disclosure requirements of the rule because not all financial institutions have 'consumers' or establish 'customer relationships'" that trigger the requirements.[10]

By the same token, many companies that are *not* "financial institutions," but have simply received nonpublic personal information from a financial institution, are nonetheless subject to certain aspects of the GLB regulations. A more detailed explanation of the scope of the GLB Act and regulations follows.

---

[10] 65 Fed. Reg. 33,648 n.11 (May 24, 2000).

FINANCIAL INSTITUTIONS

The principal entities to which the regulations apply are "financial institutions," which are institutions engaged—in any "significant way"—in "financial activities."[11] These "financial activities" include traditional financial activities such as lending, exchanging, investing, insuring, issuing or brokering annuities, investment advisory services, underwriting or dealing in securities.[12] "Financial activities," however, *also* include other activities that are simply *associated* with traditional financial activities, such as brokering or servicing loans; leasing or appraising real or personal property; guaranteeing checks, collecting, accessing credit; providing financial or investment advisory activities (for instance, tax planning, tax preparation, and instruction on individual financial management); providing management consulting and counseling activities (including financial career counseling); and selling savings bonds or traveler's checks.

Of particular note to Internet companies is the fact that "financial activities" include the provision of financial data processing and transmission services or facilities (which would include hardware, software, documentation, or operating personnel), financial databases, advice, or "access to these by technological means," e.g., Web sites and online services. This could potentially bring an unexpectedly large class of Internet companies into the fold of "financial institutions." The FTC, however, noted that certain Internet industries are affected by its regulations and that many Internet companies, like other companies that are technically "financial institutions," will not have obligations under the regulations unless they have, as their consumers or customers, individuals who obtain financial products or services for personal, family or household

---

[11] 16 C.F.R. § 313.3(k)(1).

[12] "Financial activities" can be more completely defined by referring to Section 4(k)(4) of the Bank Holding Company Act, 12 U.S.C. § 1843(k), which describes activities that are considered financial in nature, and the Federal Reserve Board's list of "associated" activities, found in 12 C.F.R. §§ 225.28 and 225.86(a). The other agencies have adopted an even broader definition of "financial institution," which includes not only activities that are financial in nature, but also activities that are "incidental" to such financial activities ("incidental activities" being a different category of activities than "associated activities"). See, e.g., 17 C.F.R. § 248.3(n)(1).

needs. In particular, the FTC stated that for Internet companies to determine whether they have obligations under the regulations, the companies "will have to evaluate (1) whether they are engaged in a financial activity, and, (2) if so, whether they have consumers or customers that trigger the disclosure or other requirements of the Act."[13]

The FTC gave a number of illustrations to assist such a determination. For instance, the FTC specifically noted that "an Internet company that compiles, or aggregates, an individual's on-line accounts (such as credit cards, mortgages, and loans) at that company's web site as a service to the individual, who then may access all of its account information through that Internet site," would be within the definition of a financial institution.[14] What the FTC did not add, although it seems self-evident, is that the individual who accesses all the account information through the Web site is also a customer. Therefore, such an Internet company would appear to be subject to the regulation's requirements. Another example offered by the FTC was of "financial software and hardware manufacturers," which, the FTC stated, would fall within the definition of "financial institutions but will have no disclosure obligations if they sell only to businesses." Similarly, a management consultant, while a "financial institution," is not likely to be subject to the regulations' requirements because it is unlikely that "any individual obtains management consulting services for personal, family or household purposes." Similarly, "courier services, data processors, and real estate appraisers who perform services for a financial institution, but do not provide financial products or services to individuals, will not be required to make the disclosures mandated by the regulation because they do not have 'consumers' or 'customers.'"[15]

The FTC has provided other non-Internet-specific examples of entities that are not significantly engaged in financial activities (and, therefore, are not financial institutions). For instance, a retailer that only extends credit through "lay away" or deferred payment

---

[13] 65 Fed. Reg. 33,655 (May 24, 2000).
[14] *Id.*
[15] 65 Fed. Reg. 33,655-33,656 (May 24, 2000).

plans is not a "financial institution." A retailer or merchant is not a "financial institution" merely because it accepts payment in the form of cash, checks or credit cards, or permits individuals to "run a tab."[16]

"OTHER PERSONS" SUBJECT TO THE FTC'S RULES

Unlike the other agencies, whose regulations only apply to certain types of "financial institutions," the FTC regulates "other persons." These "other persons" are "third parties that are not financial institutions, but that receive nonpublic personal information from financial institutions with whom they are not affiliated."[17] The FTC regulates these other persons insofar as they reuse and redisclose the information they received from financial institutions.

TYPE OF INFORMATION PROTECTED BY THE GLB ACT: NONPUBLIC PERSONAL INFORMATION

The Act and the applicable regulations apply to "nonpublic personal information" about consumers who obtain such products or services for personal, family or household purposes.[18] Such personal information is not protected if it is that of individuals obtaining financial products or services for business, commercial or agricultural purposes.

The term "nonpublic personal information" is defined in a highly complex manner, but can reasonably be said potentially to encompass virtually *any* information that a consumer provides a financial institution to obtain financial products or services for personal, family or household use *or* any other information that the financial institution "otherwise obtain[s]" in connection with such a transaction.[19] Moreover, any list, description or grouping of consumers that *includes or is derived from* any of this information is also considered "nonpublic personal information" and, therefore, its disclosure is regulated by the GLB Act.

---

[16] 16 C.F.R. § 313.3(k)(4).
[17] 16 C.F.R. § 313.1(b).
[18] 15 U.S.C. § 6809(9) (definition of consumer); and 16 C.F.R. § 313.1(b).
[19] See 16 C.F.R. § 313.3(n) and (o).

An important point is that the information need not be financial in nature (such as assets or credit history) but can include such information as names, telephone numbers, addresses and the mere fact that a consumer obtained a service or product. Of particular importance to any financial institution with a Web site is the fact that information "collect[ed] through an Internet 'cookie'" is specifically included in the definition of "nonpublic personal information."[20] Accordingly, it would seem that the Web usage history that a financial institution could derive from a cookie would be covered (i.e., nonpublic personal) information. Unfortunately, there are no rules or comments that would serve to clarify some of the possible ramifications of this rule. For instance, whether information collected by an advertiser through its *own* cookie, rather than the cookie of the financial institution, can be nonpublic personal information that is covered by the regulations is as yet undetermined. It is worth noting, however, that the FTC, in the context of COPPA, clarified that advertisers that collected children's personal information on Web sites were subject to COPPA rules themselves.[21] Similarly, whether the GLB regulations' reference to "cookies" applies to other information-gathering devices is also undetermined, although it is highly likely that it does.

"Publicly available information," i.e., information that one has a reasonable basis to believe is lawfully available to the general public, is not covered by the regulations. Examples are information contained in telephone books, government records, newspapers and Web sites accessible to the general public. Thus, mortgage information is "publicly available" if such information is generally contained in public records in the relevant locale. But a person's telephone number, which can easily be unlisted, is publicly available only if it can actually be located in the telephone book or the consumer stated that the telephone number is, in fact, listed.[22] The rules make clear that lists of names of customers of an entity that is not a financial institution, as well as aggregate or blind data that

---

[20] 16 C.F.R. § 313.3(o)(2)(F).
[21] 64 Fed. Reg. 59,892 (Nov. 3, 1999).
[22] See 16 C.F.R. § 313.3(p).

do not contain personal identifying information (such as account numbers, names or addresses), are not included in the definition of "nonpublic personal information."

Finally, it is important to understand that, given the broad meaning of "nonpublic personal information," health-related information can be covered by the GLB regulations. In the event that a financial institution collects such information, it should be aware that the Health Insurance Portability and Accountability Act may come into play to regulate the information's use and disclosure. The FTC has specifically noted that when both HIPAA and the GLB Act apply, the greater protections afforded by HIPAA—such as demanding consent and opt-in requirements, not to mention extensive administrative burdens—will prevail.

JURISDICTION OF THE VARIOUS AGENCIES

Each of the agencies that issues regulations under the GLB Act enforces its own set of regulations. Because the regulations issued by each agency are not identical—and, indeed, differ from time to time in important respects—it is critical for every financial institution (or other persons who received nonpublic personal information from financial institutions) to understand which agency will enforce its regulations against the institution.

The least specialized, probably broadest jurisdiction to enforce the Act, lies with the FTC. All agencies other than the FTC have jurisdiction over specific types of financial institutions. The particular area of each agency's jurisdiction is set forth below.

- Brokers, dealers, investment companies and investment advisors registered with the SEC are subject to the regulations of the SEC.[23]

---

[23] 15 U.S.C. § 6805(a)(3)-(5); 17 C.F.R. § 248.3(w). The regulations of the various agencies make clear that all such brokers, dealers, investment companies and investment advisors are, with respect to the GLB Act, within the sole jurisdiction of the SEC even if such brokers, dealers, investment companies and investment advisors are subsidiaries of financial institutions that fall within the jurisdiction of the Federal Reserve System, Federal Deposit Insurance Corporation, Office of Thrift Supervision, Office of the Comptroller of the Currency, or National Credit Administration.

- State member banks, bank holding companies and certain of their nonbank subsidiaries or affiliates, state uninsured branches and agencies of foreign banks, commercial lending companies owned or controlled by a foreign bank, and Edge and Agreement corporations are subject to regulations of the Federal Reserve.[24]
- Savings associations whose deposits are insured by the Federal Deposit Insurance Corporation and their subsidiaries are subject to the rules of the Office of Thrift Supervision.[25]
- National banks, federal branches and agencies of foreign banks, and subsidiaries of such entities are subject to the rules of the Office of the Comptroller of Currency.[26]
- Federally insured credit unions are subject to the National Credit Union Administration rules.[27]
- Insurance companies are subject to any applicable regulations issued by the relevant state insurance authority.[28]

In contrast to these agencies' specifically delineated areas of jurisdiction, the FTC has jurisdiction over all financial institutions that do not specifically fall within the jurisdiction of any of the agencies described above.[29] A non-exclusive list of financial institutions within the FTC's jurisdiction would include "mortgage lenders, 'pay day' lenders, finance companies, mortgage brokers, account servicers, check cashers, wire transferors, travel agencies operated in connection with financial services, collection agencies, credit counselors and other financial advisors, tax preparation firms, non-federally insured credit unions, and investment advisors that are not required to register with the Securities and Exchange Commission."[30] As indicated above, the GLB Act further extends the reach

---

[24] 15 U.S.C. § 6805(a)(1)(B); 16 C.F.R. § 216.3(q).
[25] 15 U.S.C. § 6805(a)(1)(D); 16 C.F.R. § 573.1(b)(1).
[26] 15 U.S.C. § 6805(a)(1)(A); 16 C.F.R. § 40.1(b)(1).
[27] 15 U.S.C. § 6805(a)(2); 16 C.F.R. § 716.3(t).
[28] 15 U.S.C. § 6805(a)(6).
[29] 15 U.S.C. § 6805(a)(7). Specifically, the statute provides that the FTC has jurisdiction over "any other financial institution or other person that is not subject to the jurisdiction of any agency or authority under paragraphs (1) through (6) of this subsection." 15 U.S.C. § 6805(a)(7).
[30] 16 C.F.R. § 313.1(b).

of the FTC by providing that the FTC has jurisdiction to enforce the Act's limits on reuse and redisclosure of nonpublic personal information against "other persons," i.e., persons or entities that are not financial institutions, but that received nonpublic personal information from a financial institution.[31]

TIME FOR COMPLIANCE

The GLB Act directs that the privacy regulations promulgated by these various agencies take effect twelve months after the date of the enactment of the Act. The various agencies, however, have recognized the difficulties associated with compliance. Thus, while the regulations took effect on November 13, 2000, the *date for compliance* with the regulations occurred on July 1, 2001.

WHEN DISCLOSURE OF NONPUBLIC PERSONAL INFORMATION IS PERMITTED

Here are the guts of the regulations. Financial institutions may not disclose any nonpublic personal information about any consumer to a non-affiliated third party unless all of the following have occurred:

- The consumer has received an initial privacy notice (which, generally speaking, notifies the consumer about the kinds of information that are to be disclosed and to whom);
- The consumer has received an "opt-out notice" that gives the consumer an opportunity to opt out of having his or her information disclosed; and
- The consumer has not opted out.[32]

In addition, financial institutions may not disclose information about a consumer in a manner inconsistent with what is stated in the initial privacy notice unless, prior to this disclosure, the institution sends each consumer a revised privacy and opt-out notice.[33]

---

[31] 15 U.S.C. § 6805(a)(7) and 16 C.F.R. § 313.1(b).
[32] 16 C.F.R. § 313.10.
[33] 16 C.F.R. § 313.8.

Application of these fairly straightforward-sounding requirements is less than straightforward. For instance, any initial or revised privacy notices and any opt-out notices must comply with the many rules relating to who gets such notices, as well as the content, timing and method of delivery of such notices. In addition, there are numerous exceptions to whether and when privacy notices and/or opt-out notices must be sent at all. Moreover, it is important to note that financial institutions may have to comply with certain notice requirements *even if they do not intend—or even wish to reserve their right—to disclose nonpublic personal information*. These and additional factors that complicate the regulations are discussed below.

NOTICE REQUIREMENTS AND RESTRICTIONS ON DISCLOSURE OF NONPUBLIC PERSONAL INFORMATION AND THE "CONSUMER"/ "CUSTOMER" DISTINCTION

Once a company has done the Byzantine analysis of whether it is a financial institution, it must then turn, yet again, to complex regulations that actually deal with the notice and disclosure requirements that are imposed on financial institutions. Generally, the regulations require financial institutions to provide certain individuals with privacy notices that alert the individuals to the types of information collected and/or disclosed and the types of parties to whom that information is to be disclosed. The regulations also require financial institutions to send opt-out notices that provide individuals with an opportunity to choose not to have their nonpublic personal information disclosed.

These regulations are complicated and detailed. There are, for instance, many different types of privacy notices, which are required to be delivered in varying circumstances. The content of the notices will vary as well, depending upon such factors as the type of disclosure intended by the company, and whether the individual is merely a "consumer" or a "customer."

Indeed, the distinction between consumers and customers is the most important touchstone in understanding how the notice requirements operate. Although the meanings of "consumer" and "customer" are delineated in detail by the regulations, it is probably safe to say that the class of "consumers" includes individuals who obtain (or apply to obtain) financial services or products for personal, i.e., non-business, needs. An important point is that a person can be a consumer even if he or she never obtains a product or service. For instance, an individual who applies for credit is a "consumer," even if the credit is not extended. Similarly, an individual who provides nonpublic personal information in order to obtain a determination about whether he or she may qualify for a loan is also a "consumer," regardless of whether the loan is extended.[34]

The class of "customers" is a subset of "consumers" and comprises consumers who have *continuing relationships* with a financial institution through which one or more financial products or services are provided for personal needs. For instance, an individual who has a credit or investment account with a financial institution is a "customer" of that institution. Similarly, an individual who obtains a loan, holds investment products through the institution, or uses an institution to broker a home mortgage is a "customer" of the institution.

Bearing these distinctions in mind, it can be said that if a financial institution has only "consumers" and does not disclose nonpublic personal information (except pursuant to certain transaction/ account servicing-types of exceptions that are explained below), the regulations do not impose any requirements at all. If, however, a financial institution has "customers" or intends to disclose nonpublic personal information of "consumers" to third parties (when such disclosure is not covered by an exception), the institution must comply with the many and varying notice requirements.

CONTENT OF THE PRIVACY NOTICES

There are primarily three types of privacy notices mandated by the regulations: the initial, annual and revised[35] privacy notices. Each of these notices must be "clear and conspicuous" and "accurately reflect [the institution's] privacy policies and practices."[36] In addition, each of these notices must contain the following types of information:

---

[34] 16 C.F.R. § 313.3(e)(1). Notably, an individual is *not* a "consumer" of a company simply because he or she is a participant or beneficiary of an employee benefit plan sponsored by that company. 16 C.F.R. § 313.(e)(2).

[35] 16 C.F.R. §§ 313.4, 313.5, 313.8.

[36] See, e.g., 16 C.F.R. § 313.4.

- The categories of nonpublic personal information collected;
- The categories of nonpublic personal information disclosed;
- The categories of affiliates and non-affiliated third parties to whom the information is disclosed (other than those parties that fall under certain exceptions);
- The categories of nonpublic personal information about *former* customers that are disclosed and the categories of affiliates and non-affiliated third parties that receive such information (other than those parties that fall under certain exceptions);
- The categories of information, if any, disclosed to service providers and joint marketers and a description of any such parties;
- An explanation of the consumer's right to opt out of the disclosure of his or her nonpublic personal information;
- The financial institution's policies and practices with respect to protecting the confidentiality and security of nonpublic personal information;
- If nonpublic personal information is disclosed pursuant to certain exceptions created by the regulations,[37] a statement that the financial institution makes disclosures to other non-affiliated third parties "as permitted by law."

INITIAL NOTICE

Financial institutions must provide an initial notice to all customers *and* to consumers in more limited circumstances. In essence, the initial notice must be sent to all customers at the time that the customer relationship is established *regardless of whether information is to be disclosed.* With respect to customers, the initial notice need only be delivered if the financial institution wishes to disclose personal information to non-affiliated third parties, unless the disclosures are subject to an exception. When a financial institution wishes to disclose a consumer's personal information, the notice must be sent to the consumer *before* the disclosure has taken place. A "short-form" initial notice is permitted for consumers

---

[37] Specifically, exceptions for processing and servicing transactions (16 C.F.R. § 313.14) and other miscellaneous exceptions, such as disclosure with the consent of consumer or to protect against fraud, the security of records or to resolve disputes (16 C.F.R. § 313.15).

who are not customers and must be delivered along with any required opt-out notice.[38]

A "simplified" initial notice (not to be confused with the "short-form" notice for consumers) is permitted to be sent if the financial institution does not disclose—or does not wish to reserve its right to disclose—nonpublic personal information to affiliates and non-affiliated third parties (except pursuant to certain exceptions, such as disclosure for transaction processing and servicing). This notice should simply explain this policy and include other limited information.[39]

ANNUAL NOTICE

Financial institutions must provide an annual notice only to *customers*. No annual notices are required for consumers or for former customers. For annual notices, the regulations specifically permit that this notice can be delivered by posting it on the institution's Web site (in a clear and conspicuous manner), but only for those customers who use the Web site to access financial products and services electronically *and* agree to receive notices at the Web site.[40]

REVISED NOTICES

If the privacy policies and practices of an institution have changed since the time initial notice was delivered, no nonpublic personal information may be disclosed (other than as described in the initial notice) until revised privacy notices—along with opt-out notices—have been sent and the consumer given a reasonable opportunity to respond.[41]

OPT-OUT NOTICES

Prior to disclosing any nonpublic personal information, financial institutions must provide to all consumers and customers opt-out

---

[38] Essentially, the short form must state that the financial institution's privacy notice is available upon request and must explain a reasonable means by which the consumer may obtain a such privacy notice, e.g., a toll-free telephone number that the consumer may call to get a copy of the notice. 16 C.F.R. § 313.6(d).

[39] 16 C.F.R. § 313.6(c)(5).

[40] 16 C.F.R. § 313.9(c)(1).

[41] 16 C.F.R. § 313.8.

notices that clearly and conspicuously explain the right to opt out.[42] The opt-out notice can be sent with the initial notice and must: (1) state that the institution will disclose (or reserves the right to disclose) nonpublic personal information about the consumer to a nonaffiliated third party; (2) state that the consumer has the right to opt out of the disclosure; and (3) set forth a reasonable means by which the consumer may exercise the opt-out right.[43]

In addition, financial institutions must give the consumer "reasonable means" and "reasonable opportunity" to opt out of the disclosure prior to disclosing the information.[44] For instance, institutions should make it easy for a consumer to respond by providing forms with prominent check-off boxes. If a consumer agrees to receive notices electronically, the FTC specifically provides that the institution can send such an opt-out form by electronic mail or set up a process at its Web site.[45]

In addition, financial institutions must give consumers a reasonable amount of time to respond to the notice—though what is "reasonable" varies from situation to situation. For example, an institution need not wait at all if, for instance, the institution intends to disclose nonpublic personal information that it obtains through an electronic transaction and the consumer is provided with a convenient means of opting out of the disclosure as part of the transaction.[46] In other instances, however, such as when the opt-out notice is provided by mail, it is appropriate to allow the consumer thirty days from the date the opt-out notice was mailed to opt out by mailing back a form, by calling a toll-free number, or "by any other reasonable means."[47] When the notice is provided electronically, i.e., in an instance in which the consumer *agrees* to receive the notice electronically, institutions must *still* allow the consumer thirty days to opt out—which seems a little more than "reasonable," given almost instant e-mail time.

---

[42] 16 C.F.R. § 313.10(a)(1)(ii).

[43] 16 C.F.R. § 313.7.

[44] 16 C.F.R. §§ 313.7(a)(1)(iii), 313.10(a)(1)(iii).

[45] 16 C.F.R. § 313.7(a)(2)(ii)(C).

[46] 16 C.F.R. § 313.10(a)(2).

[47] *Id.*

DELIVERY OF NOTICES

Delivery of all notices—privacy and opt-out—must be undertaken in such a way that each consumer and customer reasonably can be expected to receive actual notice *in writing*; oral explanation is not sufficient. With the exception of consumers who conduct transactions electronically, it appears that the only acceptable delivery of notices is individualized delivery. For instance, posting a sign in an office or branch or publishing an advertisement with privacy policies is insufficient.[48] Rather, satisfactory delivery can be accomplished by hand-delivery of a printed copy of the notice or mailing a printed copy to the last known address of the consumer. As indicated above, however, electronic delivery of annual notices on the Web site is permitted for the consumer who conducts transactions electronically and agrees to receive notices on the Web site. In addition, electronic delivery is permitted for other privacy and opt-out notices for consumers who conduct transactions electronically and specifically acknowledge having received the particular notice as a necessary step to obtaining the financial product or service.[49] An important point is that the regulations specify that sending the notice via e-mail is an insufficient method of providing notice if the consumer does not obtain a financial product or service electronically.[50]

PRIMARY EXCEPTIONS TO PRIVACY AND/OR OPT-OUT NOTICE REQUIREMENTS

The regulations provide for specific exceptions to the initial privacy and opt-out notice requirements. In keeping with the spirit of the regulations, these exceptions are fairly complicated and detailed. Broadly speaking, however, the exceptions permit certain types of disclosures of personal information without complying with the initial privacy and opt-out notice provisions. For instance, the exceptions permit disclosure without notice of any sort if the disclosure (1) is necessary to process and service transactions with the consumer, (2) is made with the consumer's permission, (3) is to

---

[48] 16 C.F.R. § 313.9(b).
[49] 16 C.F.R. § 313.9(b)(1)(iii).
[50] 16 C.F.R. § 313.9.

protect the security of records, (4) is made for institutional risk control, or (5) is made to various governmental authorities under other provisions of law.[51]

The regulations also provide for an exception to the *opt-out* (but not notice) requirements for disclosure of personal information to service providers and joint marketers, as long as the consumer received notice that such disclosure would be made *and* the financial institution contracts with the third party to prohibit it from disclosing or using the information except for the purposes for which it was disclosed.[52]

REUSE AND REDISCLOSURE LIMITATIONS

There are limits placed on the reuse and redisclosure of non-public personal information by the third party receiving such information—regardless of whether such third party is a financial institution. If, for instance, a third party received personal information pursuant to one of the exceptions discussed immediately above, then the third party can only disclose and use the information for the purpose for which it was given. For example, if a third party received personal information to process a request by the consumer, the third party can only use and disclose the information for that particular purpose and no other.[53] The third party could also, for example, disclose that information in response to a properly authorized subpoena, but could not disclose the information to a third party for marketing purposes or use the information for its own marketing purposes.[54]

There are also limits on the ability of third parties to use and disclose information even if they received the information outside of one of the account-processing types of exceptions. In essence, if a company receives personal information (which, of course, is virtually any information pertaining to a consumer or customer of a financial institution), that company steps into the shoes of the

---

[51] 16 C.F.R. §§ 313.14, 313.15.
[52] 16 C.F.R. § 313.13.
[53] 16 C.F.R. § 313.11.
[54] 16 C.F.R. § 313.11(a)(iii)(2).

financial institution that made the initial disclosure. In other words, no disclosure is made by the third party unless it could have been made by the financial institution. This requires the company receiving the information to comply with the privacy policy (as it was disclosed to the consumers and customers) of the financial institution and to comply with any opt-out instructions given by the consumer or customer to the financial institution.

As the FTC notes, to be able lawfully to redisclose the information, a third party "must have procedures in place to continually monitor the status of who opts out and to what extent."[55] Thus, and as the FTC explicitly observed, the practical difficulty of complying with another company's privacy and opt-out notices will in most circumstances prevent companies from redisclosing the information.

OTHER RESTRICTIONS

The regulations also prohibit the disclosure to third parties of consumer account numbers, as well as access codes for credit card, deposit or transaction accounts, for marketing purposes. As always, there are exceptions, such as disclosure to an agent or service provider for purposes of marketing the products of the financial institution itself, or to a participant in programs such as private label credit card programs in which the participants are identified to the customer when he or she joins.

A FURTHER WORD ON OPT-OUT VS. OPT-IN RESTRICTIONS

The opt-in/opt-out debate is playing itself out across the United States, as well as abroad, in areas outside of the regulation of customer information usage by financial institutions under the GLB Act. Many states, for instance, have proposed legislation that favors an opt-in regime over GLB's opt-out requirements. For example, the California legislature is currently considering a bill that would require an opt-in mechanism before financial institutions could disseminate personal identifying information.[56]

---

[55] 65 Fed. Reg. 33,668 (May 24, 2000).
[56] See A.B. 1775, 2001-02 Reg. Sess. (Cal.).

The opt-in/opt-out debate has also come to a head in the telecommunications arena. In 1998, the Federal Communications Commission promulgated regulations pursuant to Section 222 of the Telecommunications Act of 1996, which addresses privacy of customer information. The regulations were designed to place restrictions on the use by telecommunications companies of Customer Proprietary Network Information (CPNI). The FCC adopted an opt-in approach, and the regulations required a carrier to obtain prior express approval from a customer before the carrier could use the customer's CPNI. The Telecommunications Act defines CPNI as:

(A) information that relates to the quantity, technical configuration, type, destination, and amount of use of a telecommunications service subscribed to by any customer of a telecommunications carrier, and that is made available to the carrier by the customer solely by virtue of the carrier-customer relationship; and

(B) information contained in the bills pertaining to telephone exchange service or telephone tool service received by a customer of a carrier; except that such term does not include subscriber list information.[57]

U.S. West challenged the FCC's regulation, claiming, among other things, that CPNI is information the communication of which is subject to First Amendment protection as commercial speech, that the requirement of prior consent from customers before carriers can use CPNI is an unconstitutional burden on free speech, and that the FCC's analysis of this First Amendment issue was technically flawed.[58] Many other telecommunications companies filed friend-of-the-court briefs. The Court of Appeals for the Tenth Circuit invalidated the regulations to the extent that they required opt-in consent of customers.[59] The court, in a 2-1 decision, agreed with U.S. West and held that the FCC had "failed to adequately consider the

---

[57] 47 U.S.C. § 222(f)(1)(A)-(B).

[58] U.S. West also argued that the regulations constitute a taking under the Fifth Amendment by asserting that CPNI belongs to the customer and not to the carriers.

[59] U.S. West, Inc. v. Federal Communications Commission, 182 F.2d 1224 (10th Cir. 1999), cert. denied 120 S.Ct. 2215 (June 5, 2000).

constitutional ramifications of the regulations . . . and that the regulations violate the First Amendment."

The FCC is currently engaged in a rulemaking proceeding to reconsider its earlier regulations and to comply with the court's conclusion that it had failed to consider adequately the constitutional ramifications of the earlier regulation.[60] Many interested parties on both sides of the issue have submitted comments on the subject. As of this writing, it is unclear whether the FCC will attempt to mandate an opt-in approach again, after attempting to demonstrate that it has adequately considered the constitutional ramifications of such a rule, or whether the FCC will adopt an alternative to the opt-in regime.

HEALTH INSURANCE PORTABILITY AND ACCOUNTABILITY ACT OF 1996

OVERVIEW

The Health Insurance Portability and Accountability Act of 1996 (HIPPA) required the Department of Health and Human Services (HHS) to promulgate regulations governing the disclosure and use of health information. The regulations are the subject of intense lobbying by physician and insurance groups.

There is little wonder as to why these groups are lobbying to modify the regulations. The version of the regulations as of the middle of 2002 consists of highly complicated and, in some instances, ambiguous rules that protect the disclosure and use of certain "protected health information"—information that includes nearly all health-related information that can identify an individual and that exists in *any* form (e.g., paper, electronic or oral). The overall thrust of the regulations is to create an opt-in framework for the use and disclosure of protected health information. The regulations implement this opt-in framework by requiring individual consent before most types of use or disclosure, including, for

---

[60] In the Matter of Implementation of the Telecommunications Act of 1996, Telecommunications Carriers' Use of Customer Proprietary Network Information and Other Customer Information; Implementation of the Non-Accounting Safeguards of Sections 271 and 272 of the Communications Act of 1934, as Amended, CC Docket Nos. 96-115, 96-149.

instance, routine use by healthcare providers for treatment and payment. It is widely anticipated that compliance with the HIPAA regulations will be difficult and expensive.[61] Indeed, HHS projects that compliance with the privacy regulations will cost approximately $17.6 billion.[62]

The current version of HIPAA regulations applies to certain healthcare-related entities. The entities covered by the regulations (the "covered entities") are (1) health plans, which are any individual or group plans that provide or pay the cost of medical care; (2) healthcare clearinghouses; and (3) healthcare providers that transmit health information in electronic form (given the widespread and ever-growing use of electronic transmission in the medical community for, among many other things, obtaining insurance payments, transmitting digital images, and providing online healthcare, this limitation will likely amount to very little).[63] Obviously, the regulations apply with particular force to Web-based healthcare providers—some of which have come under particular scrutiny by the FTC for, among other things, their information practices.[64] Absent a change in the current version of the regulations, these covered entities (with the exception of small health plans) must comply with them by February 26, 2003.[65]

---

[61] State laws offering more stringent protection (like those covering mental health, HIV infection, and AIDS information) continue to apply. Thus, the HIPAA regulations do not offer the benefit of a uniform standard for treating individuals' health information. 45 C.F.R. § 160.203.

[62] December 20, 2000 HHS Fact Sheet. This cost has been projected to be offset by a projected $29.9 billion savings engendered by HHS's electronic claims regulations that will standardize the transmission of electronic data.

[63] 45 C.F.R. § 160.102.

[64] For instance, operators of a group of online pharmacies, including Worldwidemedicine.com and Focusmedical.com, were charged with touting medical and pharmaceutical facilities they didn't actually have and making privacy and confidentiality assurances they didn't keep. The operators settled the FTC charges and, among other things, were prohibited from "selling, renting, leasing, transferring or disclosing the personal information that was collected from their customers without express authorization from the customer." FTC Press Release, "Online Pharmacies Settle FTC Charges" (July 12, 2000).

[65] 45 C.F.R. § 164.534. Small health plans—health plans with annual receipts of $5 million or less—have an additional year and must comply by February 26, 2004. *Id.* Certain organizations, such as insurance companies, may be a covered entities

While entities can attempt to minimize the effects and burdens of the regulations by minimizing their uses and disclosures of protected health information to those that are absolutely necessary, the burdens of compliance should not be underestimated. For instance, the regulations require that each covered entity designate a privacy officer, who will develop and implement a written and detailed description of all of the entity's privacy policies and procedures that guide the entity through the maze of regulations.[66] The regulations also mandate training of staff who have access to protected health information in how to treat the information. For existing staff, this training must have been provided by no later than the compliance date and must be provided on an ongoing basis to staff hired subsequently.[67] The regulations require that covered entities put in place a grievance process for persons who believe that their personal health information has been improperly disclosed. Moreover, the regulations require covered entities to implement administrative, technical and physical safeguards to protect the privacy of protected health information, for example, (1) shredding documents containing protected health information prior to disposal, (2) requiring that doors to medical records departments (or to file cabinets housing such records) remain locked and limiting which personnel are authorized to have the key or passcode, and (3) instituting verification procedures to establish the identity and authority of persons to whom disclosures of protected health information are made. This latter requirement, for instance, may call for the standard use of devices that have only recently entered the popular vocabulary, such as digital certificates.[68] It is also worth noting that the proposed HIPAA Security Standards will

---

under HIPAA *and* be "financial institutions" subject to the Gramm-Leach-Bliley Act, which regulates disclosure of personal information collected by a financial institution. While protected health information collected by financial institutions is, in theory, covered by the GLB Act, the FTC has clarified that the greater protections provided by HIPAA will apply to such information. Thus, certain organizations will have to comply with both the GLB and HIPAA regulations.

[66] 45 C.F.R. § 164.530.

[67] 45 C.F.R. § 164.530.

[68] 45 C.F.R. §§ 164.530 and 164.514(h). Organizations such as the Association for Testing and Materials and the American Health Information Management Association have developed a body of recommended practices for handling protected health information that covered entities may find useful.

require covered entities to safeguard the privacy and integrity of health information. For electronic information, compliance with both the privacy and security regulations will likely be required.

Finally, the penalties in place for violations of the regulations' standards range from nominal to highly significant. Health plans, providers and clearinghouses that violate any of the many standards set forth in the regulations would be subject to civil liability. Civil monetary penalties are $100 per incident, up to $25,000 per person, per year, per standard. There are also federal criminal penalties for health plans, providers and clearinghouses that knowingly and improperly disclose information or obtain it under false pretenses. Penalties will be higher for actions designed to generate monetary gain. Criminal penalties are up to $50,000 and one year in prison for obtaining or disclosing protected health information; up to $100,000 and five years in prison for obtaining such information under false pretenses; and up to $250,000 and ten years in prison for obtaining or disclosing such information with the intent to sell, transfer or use it for commercial advantage, personal gain or malicious harm.[69] At this stage, however, while individual consumers may lodge complaints with the covered entities and with HHS,[70] individuals do not have the right to bring a claim in court against the covered entities for violations of the regulations. Instead, HHS possesses enforcement power.

Given that compliance with these regulations will probably require the guidance of a lawyer or privacy officer, we do not parse the regulations in detail.[71] Below is a fairly general description of their current contours.

LIMITATIONS ON USE AND DISCLOSURE OF PROTECTED HEALTH INFORMATION

The regulations prohibit covered entities from using or disclosing protected health information except for purposes and under

---

[69] 42 U.S.C. § 1320d-6.

[70] 45 C.F.R. § 160.306.

[71] In addition to the discussion that follows, a guide to HIPAA intended for the public has been posted on the HHS Web site at http://www.hhs.gov/ocr/hipaa/final-master.html.

conditions specified by the regulations. In general, the regulations require healthcare providers to obtain a general patient consent for even routine use and disclosure of health records—such as for treatment and payment or internal data gathering by a provider. The regulations contain highly detailed requirements regarding content and other aspects of the consent.[72]

The regulations, however, do permit the *other non-provider* covered entities, i.e., healthcare plans and healthcare clearinghouses, to use or disclose the information without consent solely for purposes of carrying out treatment, payment or healthcare operations.[73]

With the exception of certain disclosures relating to certain public interests (such as public health),[74] all other uses or disclosures can only take place pursuant to a specific authorization from the individual.[75] For instance, disclosures for most marketing purposes or disclosures to employers to make personnel decisions or to financial institutions require specific authorization. Unlike the more general consent that permits healthcare providers to use and disclose information for routine purposes, an authorization is a specific agreement by the individual that a particular type of disclosure, e.g., disclosure of a health condition for purposes of marketing, is acceptable. As with consents, authorizations must meet the highly detailed standards set forth in the regulations.[76]

---

[72] 45 C.F.R. § 164.506.

[73] 45 C.F.R. §§ 164.502 and 164.506.

[74] 45 C.F.R. §§ 164.502 and 164.512. Other public policy uses and disclosures that do not require prior consent are, for instance, uses and disclosures required by law; uses and disclosures for public health activities; disclosures about victims of abuse, neglect or domestic violence; uses and disclosures for health oversight activities; disclosures for judicial and administrative proceedings; disclosures for law enforcement purposes; uses and disclosures about decedents; uses and disclosures for cadaveric donation of organs, eyes or tissues; uses and disclosures for research purposes; uses and disclosures to avert a serious threat to health or safety; uses and disclosures for specialized government functions; and disclosures to comply with workers' compensation laws. 45 C.F.R. §§ 164.512.

[75] 45 C.F.R. §§ 164.502 and 164.508.

[76] The rule also mandates an individual's verbal "agreement" before using or disclosing protected health information for facility directories and to persons assisting in the individual's care. 45 C.F.R. § 164.510.

The HIPAA regulations not only create a sliding scale of consent requirements, but they also specify in detail other conditions under which the protected information may be disclosed to third parties. For instance, the regulations provide that covered entities may disclose health information to third parties that carry out "a function or activity for the covered entity that involves the use or disclosure of individually identifiable health information." These functions can be as diverse as claims processing, data analysis, billing, quality assurance, benefit management, practice management, data aggregation, and services relating to accounting, legal, management, financial or any consulting needs.[77] The regulations provide, however, that before any disclosure, certain specific contractual agreements, which are designed to ensure that the business associate appropriately safeguards the information, must be in place between a covered entity and these sorts of third parties (termed "business associates" by the regulations).[78]

In addition, whether made pursuant to a consent, authorization, verbal agreement or one of the public policy exceptions built into the regulations, disclosure of protected health information must be made in accordance with the "minimum necessary" rule. As the name implies, this rule requires that, with the exception of medical treatment, entities ensure that only the minimum amount of information necessary to fulfill the purpose of any disclosure is actually disclosed.[79]

In short, the regulations have erected an opt-in framework that will likely deter/prevent most covered entities from using or disclosing protected health information for most purposes other than a routine medical purpose.

MARKETING AND FUND RAISING

The regulations permit the use and disclosure of protected health information *without prior consent, authorization or verbal agreement* for certain, limited types of marketing and fund raising. While in general, protected health information cannot be used or

---

[77] 45 C.F.R. §§ 160.103 and 164.502(e).
[78] 45 C.F.R. § 164.502(e).
[79] 45 C.F.R. § 164.502(b).

disclosed for marketing purposes, i.e., communications intended to encourage individuals to purchase or use a product or service, entities may engage in three types of marketing behavior that involve the use or disclosure of protected information. These three exceptions are geared toward ensuring that individuals can still receive helpful health information that is relevant to their condition and that entities retain a modicum of flexibility in promoting themselves. Entities may use or disclose protected health information for the following types of marketing efforts:

- Face-to-Face Marketing—This permits entities to discuss services or products, including those of a third party, during a face-to-face communication.[80]
- Marketing of Products or Services of Nominal Value—This provision is designed to permit entities to distribute calendars, pens or other nominal merchandise promoting the entity.[81]
- Marketing about Health-Related Products or Services—This provision requires transparency in the marketing by, for instance, requiring the covered entity to identify itself as the marketer and to disclose whether it will receive remuneration for marketing. If individuals are targeted based on their health status, that fact must be disclosed and the product or service should be beneficial to the health of the individual. Individuals may opt out of future marketing.[82]

The regulations also permit the use and disclosure of certain types of protected health information—namely, demographic information and dates on which health care was provided—for fund raising purposes. In addition to limiting the types of information, the regulations, among other things, give individuals a right to opt out of receiving future solicitations.[83]

DE-IDENTIFICATION OF PROTECTED HEALTH INFORMATION

Covered entities may use protected health information to create *de-identified* information (i.e., health information that cannot identify

---

[80] 45 C.F.R. § 164.514(e)(2).
[81] 45 C.F.R. § 164.514(e)(2).
[82] 45 C.F.R. § 164.514(e)(2).
[83] 45 C.F.R. § 164.514(f).

or be linked to an individual).[84] Procedures for de-identifying protected health information are included in the regulations. In
essence, the regulations require the removal of all identifiers of the
individual or his or her relatives, employers or household members.[85] De-identified information created in accordance with the
regulations' procedures is not subject to the requirements of the
privacy rules unless it is re-identified.

NOTICE

With certain exceptions (primarily for group health plans), covered entities must produce and provide to individuals a written
notice containing the entities' respective privacy practices. Under
the regulations, covered entities may not use or disclose protected
health information in a manner inconsistent with the notice of privacy practices. While the notice is not intended to be so detailed
as to include all the entity's policies and procedures, it must conform to the regulations' content requirements. Although the
requirements are quite detailed, the basic elements of the privacy
notice are as follows:[86]

- Header—The regulations mandate specific language for the
  header of the notice: "THIS NOTICE DESCRIBES HOW MEDICAL
  INFORMATION ABOUT YOU MAY BE USED AND DISCLOSED
  AND HOW YOU CAN GET ACCESS TO THIS INFORMATION.
  PLEASE REVIEW CAREFULLY."
- Uses and Disclosures—The notice must, generally speaking,
  describe all uses and disclosures of protected health information that the entity is permitted or required to make and a
  statement that other uses must be with the individual's authorization.
- Individual Rights—The notice must describe individuals'
  rights under HIPAA and how individuals may exercise those
  rights with respect to the covered entity.
- Emphasis: Covered Entity's Duties—The notice must state that
  the entity is required by law to maintain the privacy of

---

[84] 45 C.F.R. § 164.502(d).
[85] 45 C.F.R. § 164.514(b).
[86] 45 C.F.R. § 164.520(b).

protected health information, to provide a notice of its legal duties and privacy practices, and to abide by the terms of the notice currently in effect. Further, if the entity wishes to reserve the right to change its privacy practices and apply the revised practices to protected health information previously created or received, it must make a statement to that effect and describe how it will provide individuals with a revised notice.

- Complaints—The notice must inform individuals about how they can lodge complaints with the covered entity and that they can file a complaint with HHS if they believe their privacy rights have been violated.
- Contact Person—The notice must identify a contact person from whom the individual can obtain additional information about any of the matters identified in the notice.
- Effective Date—The notice must include the date the notice went into effect.
- Optional Elements—The notice may describe privacy practices that are even more limited than those permitted by the regulations, e.g., providers that treat patients with particularly sensitive conditions can distinguish themselves by stating they will only disclose information in very specific circumstances.
- Revisions to the Notice—If a covered entity wishes to change its privacy practices over time—and wishes to have the ability to change its practices with respect to protected health information that has already been collected (that is, when different privacy practices were in effect)—the entity's notice must reserve the right to make such change.

The notice may be delivered electronically by e-mail if the recipient has agreed to receive electronic notice. In addition, an entity that maintains a Web site with information about the entity's services or benefits *must* prominently post the privacy notice on the site.

INDIVIDUAL RIGHTS REGARDING PROTECTED HEALTH INFORMATION

The regulations provide individuals with an array of rights that are designed to give them access to and control over their own protected health information. As the following brief descriptions of the rights indicate, some rights are fairly simple to implement—and indeed are part of current practice—while others may impose on covered entities a more substantial administrative burden.

Right to request restrictions on certain uses and disclosures. An individual may request that a covered entity restrict uses and disclosures made for routine purposes, such as treatment and payment, and disclosures to other individuals, such as relatives and friends, involved in the individual's care. While entities are not required by the regulations to agree to such requests, they are required, if they do agree, to document and abide by any agreed-upon restriction.[87] Individuals, however, may request and health-care providers and health plans must accommodate reasonable requests to receive communications regarding protected health information by particular methods or at particular locations.[88]

Right to inspect and copy protected health information. In general, individuals have a right of access to (i.e., inspect and obtain a copy of) any protected health information that is used to make decisions about them.[89] This information includes, for example, information used to make health care decisions or information used to determine whether an insurance claim will be paid, but would exclude information contained in data systems used solely for quality control or peer review analyses. An entity may deny access in certain enumerated circumstances.[90] Denial, however, triggers an obligation on the part of the covered entity to provide a timely written denial that conforms to various requirements and, where a review of the denial is requested, to designate a licensed healthcare professional to act as a reviewing official to determine whether denial was appropriate.[91]

Right to amend protected health information. Individuals have the right to have a covered entity amend protected health information that is used, in whole or in part, to make decisions about individuals. The covered entity may deny the request, for a number of

---

[87] 45 C.F.R. § 164.522(a).
[88] 45 C.F.R. § 164.522(b).
[89] 45 C.F.R. § 164.524(a)(1).
[90] 45 C.F.R. § 164.524(a)(2).
[91] 45 C.F.R. § 164.524(d).

reasons, including, for instance, that the information is accurate and complete. These grounds for denial are not subject to review by a healthcare professional as they are in the case of denial of access, but do require the covered entity to follow certain procedures that would permit the individual to submit a written statement disagreeing with the entity's decision. The entity, however, is not required to respond, though it may do so with a rebuttal statement that it must provide to the individual and retain in its files. Subsequent disclosures of the protected information by the entity must generally include a copy of or reference to the request to amend and any related material.[92]

Right to an accounting of disclosures of protected health information. Individuals have a right to receive an accounting of disclosures made by a covered entity, including disclosures by or to a business associate of the covered entity, for purposes other than treatment, payment and health care operations. In addition to this primary exception, covered entities are not required to include in the accounting such disclosures as those made to the individual him- or herself, disclosures for facility directories, disclosures to persons involved in the individual's care, or disclosures for national security or intelligence purposes or to correctional institutions or law enforcement officials. The right to an accounting extends to disclosures made in the six-year period prior to the date of the request, but not to disclosures made prior to the covered entity's date of compliance with HIPAA.[93]

ADMINISTRATIVE REQUIREMENTS

The regulations impose a number of administrative requirements on covered entities. Many of these have been touched on in relevant sections above, but for completeness and convenience, a list of these requirements follows. With certain exceptions for group health plans, a covered entity must do the following:[94]

- Designate a privacy official who is responsible for the development and implementation of the policies and procedures of the entity;

---

[92] 45 C.F.R. § 164.526.
[93] 45 C.F.R. § 164.528.
[94] 45 C.F.R. § 164.530.

- Designate a contact person or office to receive complaints for alleged violations of the regulations and to provide further information about the entity's information practices;
- Train all members of its workforce on policies and procedures concerning protected health information;
- Implement appropriate safeguards—administrative, technical and physical—to protect the privacy of protected health information;
- Provide a process for individuals to make complaints concerning the covered entity's policies and procedures;
- Have and apply appropriate sanctions against members of its workforce who fail to comply with the privacy policies and procedures of the covered entity;
- Attempt to mitigate any harmful effect of a use or disclosure of protected health information that was in violation of the covered entity's policies and procedures;
- Not intimidate, threaten, coerce, discriminate against or take other retaliatory actions against individuals for exercising any rights or assisting others to exercise rights under the regulations;
- Not require individuals to waive their right to file a complaint with the Secretary of HHS;
- Implement policies and procedures to ensure that compliance with the regulations is achieved;
- Maintain policies and procedures in written or electronic form;
- Maintain electronic or written copies of all communications required by the regulations; and
- Maintain written or electronic records of any action or activity required by the regulations.

EMPLOYERS THAT SPONSOR GROUP HEALTH PLANS

One of the particular aims of HIPAA and the accompanying regulations was to prevent employers from using protected health information in personnel decisions. While HHS does not have the authority to regulate the actions of employers, it has tried, pursuant to its authority to regulate health plans, to place restrictions on the flow of information from covered entities to non-covered entities—that is, employers. Employers, however, who are sponsors of health plans may need to have access to protected health information in order to administer the plans.

As a result, the regulations permit group health plans to disclose protected health information to plan sponsors if the plan sponsors voluntarily agree to use and to disclose the information only as permitted or required by the regulations and to amend the plan documents of the group health plan to incorporate various required provisions. In essence, the information may be used only for administrative functions performed on behalf of the group health plan and that are specified in plan documents. In addition, the employer must establish firewalls and compliance mechanisms to ensure that the information is used within the limits imposed by the regulations.[95]

COMPUTER FRAUD AND ABUSE ACT

The Computer Fraud and Abuse Act was originally enacted in 1984 as part of the Crime Control Act and was the first statute specifically to address computer crime. In 1990, Congress amended it "to cover all computers used in interstate commerce or communications" and "to prohibit forms of computer abuse which arise in connection with, and have a significant effect upon, interstate or foreign commerce." It seems clear that computers connected to the Internet would be protected by this statute. Whether undisclosed online information-gathering will be considered a form of computer abuse—and if so, under what circumstances—is far from clear.[96]

---

[95] 45 C.F.R. § 164.504(f).

[96] The following are the relevant provisions that could potentially restrict the online collection of information:

> Whoever . . . intentionally accesses a computer without authorization or exceeds authorized access, and thereby obtains . . . information from any protected computer if the conduct involved an interstate or foreign communication . . . shall be punished. 18 U.S.C. § 1030(a)(2)(c).

> Whoever . . . knowingly causes the transmission of a program, information, code, or command, and as a result of such conduct intentionally causes damage without authorization, to a protected computer . . . shall be punished. 18 U.S.C. § 1030(a)(5)(A).

> Whoever . . . intentionally accesses a protected computer without authorization, and as a result of such conduct causes damage . . . shall be punished. 18 U.S.C. § 1030(a)(5)(C).

Generally speaking, the touchstone of the relevant CFAA provisions is that persons are prohibited from accessing a computer *without authorization*. As a result, a fundamental question in virtually any case brought under these provisions will be whether authorization to collect information was given. Certainly, the most obvious way to try to insulate a company from potential liability under the CFAA is to disclose, disclose, disclose. When a company discloses that it gathers information from a user and/or the user's computer, the potential for liability obviously decreases. Indeed, in the cases brought under the CFAA provisions, the linchpin of the CFAA claim is that the privacy policy of the defendant company was misleading or did not disclose that it was collecting information from the users' computers through such methods as cookies, URL captures and GIF tags. While it is arguable—and it is certainly being argued in a number of cases—that this sort of computer "accessing" cannot constitute a violation of the CFAA, regardless of whether full disclosure was made, until the courts directly address this issue, the better course may be to adopt and follow a detailed privacy policy that discloses the methods that are used to collect information and the types of information that are being collected. It would also be wise to require a user to acknowledge that he or she understands and accepts the collection practices of the Web site.

Although the CFAA is a criminal statute, it creates—for purposes of these provisions—a private right of action, which permits private litigants (e.g., consumer groups, or disgruntled Internet users) to bring a civil claim under the statute. Successful private litigants are not entitled to statutory damages, but are entitled to compensatory damages, injunctions and other equitable remedies (such as, theoretically, disgorgement of profits associated with the collection of information in violation of the statute).[97]

THE ELECTRONIC COMMUNICATIONS PRIVACY ACT

The Electronic Communications Privacy Act, an amendment to the federal wiretapping statute, is the primary federal legal protection against the unauthorized interception, accessing, use or disclosure of electronic communications while in transit or in storage.

---

[97] 18 U.S.C. § 1030(g).

Two provisions of the ECPA may apply to online information collection practices—most particularly those that involve the use of cookie-type technology of which users may not be aware. These two provisions, referred to as the Wiretap Act[98] and the Stored Electronic Communications Act,[99] prohibit unauthorized interception of electronic communications and unauthorized access to stored electronic communications. We discuss both of these statutes in greater detail in the chapter on privacy in the workplace, an arena where much of the case law has been developing.[100]

---

[98] The Wiretap Act provides in relevant part as follows:

[A]ny person who intentionally intercepts, endeavors to intercept, or procures any other person to intercept or endeavor to intercept, any wire, oral, or electronic communication . . . shall be punished . . . or subject to suit. 18 U.S.C. § 2511(1)(a).

[A]ny person who intentionally discloses, or endeavors to disclose, to any other person the contents of any wire, oral, or electronic communication, knowing or having reason to know that the information was obtained through the interception of a[n] . . . electronic communication in violation of this subsection . . . shall be punished . . . or subject to suit. 18 U.S.C. § 2511(1)(c).

[A]ny person who intentionally uses, or endeavors to use, the contents of any . . . electronic communication, knowing or having reason to know that the information was obtained through the interception of a[n] . . . electronic communication in violation of this subsection . . . shall be punished . . . or subject to suit. 18 U.S.C. § 2511(1)(c).

It shall not be unlawful under this chapter for a person not acting under color of law to intercept a[n] . . . electronic communication where such person is a party to the communication or where one of the parties to the communication has given prior consent to such interception unless such interception is intercepted for the purpose of committing any criminal or tortious act in violation of the Constitution or laws of the United States or of any State. 18 U.S.C. § 2511(2)(d).

[99] The Stored Electronic Communication Act provides in relevant part as follows:

Whoever intentionally accesses without authorization a facility through which an electronic communication service is provided; or intentionally exceeds an authorization to access that facility and thereby obtains, alters, or prevents authorized access to a communication while it is in electronic storage in such system shall be punished. 18 U.S.C. § 2701(a).

[100] See Chapter 7.

CHAPTER 6

OTHER LEGISLATIVE APPROACHES

FEDERAL AND STATE EFFORTS

Only a few, narrow pieces of legislation specifically designed to limit the collection, use and disclosure of personal information have passed on either a federal or state level. As discussed in some detail in the preceding chapters on federal legislation, these statutes concern specific types of personal information (e.g., medical, financial and children's information) and do not purport to address the overarching issue of whether collection and sale of personal information—regardless of type—should be regulated.

The issue of general protection of personal information is, however, being addressed in the hundreds of bills that have been introduced in Washington, D.C. and the state capitols. The ideas driving the bills and the surrounding debate are familiar: widespread public discomfort over the collection and sale of personal information; concern that this discomfort is a serious impediment to the expansion of e-commerce; and concern that privacy legislation will prove an even greater impediment to the growth and prosperity of e-commerce. Although most of the legislative efforts are general in their application, i.e., do not target Internet companies alone, the focus of legislators on the Internet and the use of personal information by Internet companies cannot be overstated. As one privacy bill[1] neatly summarizes:

---

[1] H.R. 583, § 2, 107th Cong., 1st Sess. (2001).

- Use of the Internet has increased at astounding rates, with approximately 5 million current Internet sites and 64 million regular Internet users each month in the United States alone.
- Financial transactions over the Internet have increased at an amazing rate, with 17 million American households spending $20 billion shopping on the Internet in 2000.
- Use of the Internet as a medium for commercial activities will continue to grow, and it is estimated that by the end of 2000, 56 percent of the companies in the United States were selling their products on the Internet.
- There have been reports of surreptitious collection of consumer data by Internet marketers and questionable distribution of personal information by online companies.
- In 1999, the Federal Trade Commission found that 87 percent of Internet sites provided some form of privacy notice, which represented an increase from 15 percent in 1998.
- The United States is the leading economic and social force in the global information economy, largely because of a favorable regulatory climate and the free flow of information. It is important for the United States to continue that leadership. As nations and governing bodies around the world begin to establish privacy standards, these standards will directly affect the United States.
- The shift from an industry-focused economy to an information-focused economy calls for a reassessment of the most effective way to balance personal privacy and information use, keeping in mind the potential for unintended effects on technology development, innovation, the marketplace and privacy needs.

All of the concerns embodied in these findings are present in legislative debates in both federal and state settings. One concern, however, that is unique to state efforts to protect personal information is what kinds of efforts are constitutionally permissible. Specifically, what kinds of state regulation are permissible under the Commerce Clause of the United States Constitution, which, broadly speaking, does not favor state efforts to control interstate commerce and, in particular, disfavors state efforts to control commercial conduct occurring outside a state's borders. While it seems clear that criminal and fraudulent conduct that occurs over the Internet is, generally speaking, reachable by state action,[2] it is less clear what kinds of state legislation are permissible where the goal is to regulate otherwise legal conduct occurring on the Internet. The primary obstacle to crafting legislation that can survive the restrictions imposed by the Commerce Clause is the well-worn fact that the Internet knows no boundaries—including, of course, state boundaries. This means that most state regulation of Internet conduct would affect not just intra-state conduct, but conduct occurring outside of the state—even conduct occurring outside the United States. Thus, state regulation of the Internet medium would mean an unprecedented expansion of state authority into territories far outside the state itself. Another aspect of this problem is that more than one state can, of course, enact regulations, which raises the specter of inconsistent, and possibly irreconcilable, regulations. These constitutional concerns mirror concerns of the interstate business community—which is to say the entire e-business world. Thus, the Commerce Clause and the business community have the same goal when it comes to state regulation: preventing regulations from burdening the free flow of commerce.

State legislation that fails to take these problems into account will run the risk of being struck down as unconstitutional. Certainly, statutes that *directly* regulate the Internet itself risk being struck down.[3] Even statutes that do not directly target the Internet, but that more indirectly create substantial, unjustifiable burdens on Internet commerce, are at risk of being struck down as well. For instance, an Illinois state law that prohibited the advertising of controlled substances (including FDA-approved pharmaceuticals) by name was struck down as a violation of the Commerce Clause

---

[2] It is well known, for example, that state attorneys general have been successfully using state consumer protection laws to deal with certain types of fraud or misrepresentations over the Internet. This type of law, however, is of general applicability and there is no reason why a prohibited action should go unpunished simply because it was committed over the Internet so long as other jurisdictional requirements are met. Even so, there is still uncertainty as to how far direct criminal regulation of the Internet can go. For instance, one state law that prohibited "communications" depicting nudity that was "harmful to minors" over the Internet was struck down as an unconstitutional burden on interstate commerce. American Librarian Association v. Pataki, 969 F. Supp. 160 (S.D.N.Y. 1997).

[3] See, e.g., *id.*

because of the impossibility of running a national advertising campaign that used the Internet and other national media without violating the statute. In other words, because there was no way to keep Illinois residents from accessing the Web site or to black Illinois out of the national advertising broadcasts, the Illinois law had effects far beyond its boundaries and would, in fact, require a non-Illinois company advertising its product nationwide to tailor all of its advertising to comply with the Illinois law. In addition, the fact that the Illinois statute was inconsistent with other state legislation that permitted the type of advertising prohibited by Illinois was a significant factor in the court's decision to strike the statute down as an unconstitutional burden on interstate commerce.[4]

Certainly *some* state regulation of Internet commerce seems possible—particularly when the legislation protects an important interest and, one hopes, when compliance with the state regulation can be achieved in a reasonable manner. For instance, a Texas statute that, generally speaking, prevented car manufacturers, such as Ford Motor Company, from competing with licensed dealers by selling used cars to Texas consumers over the Internet was upheld.[5] In contrast to the Illinois statute, however, the Texas statute did not require termination of Ford's Web site. Instead, Ford was able to continue promoting its used cars over the Internet so long as it stated that the "offer [was] void where prohibited by law."

---

[4] Knoll Pharmaceutical Co. v. Sherman, 57 F. Supp.2d 615 (N.D. Ill. 1999).
[5] Ford Motor Co. v. Texas Dep't. of Transportation, 106 F. Supp.2d 905 (W.D. Tex. 2000). In that case, Ford was operating an "Internet Showroom" where it offered used cars for sale. Interested consumers could place a hold on a car, which was shipped to participating dealers who would show the car to the prospective buyer. The Texas attorney general filed an administrative complaint against Ford on the ground that it was selling used cars without a dealer's license—a license that was unavailable to Ford by virtue of another Texas statute that prohibited manufacturers from owning an interest in a dealer. Ford challenged the statute in federal court on the ground that, among other things, the state's efforts to enforce Texas law against Internet-based activities unduly burdened interstate commerce. The court rejected the argument, upholding the law on the ground that Ford could both comply with the Texas law and continue to operate its Web site with the simple disclaimer "offer void where prohibited by law." The court was also swayed by the fact that the Texas law prohibiting manufacturers from becoming dealers served the public interest because it tried to equalize the market power between manufacturers and dealers.

The *Ford* case, nonetheless, may not be applicable in the end to answering whether *privacy* legislation can survive constitutional scrutiny. In the *Ford* case, the goods at issue were cars—real space, not cyberspace, goods. Thus, before Ford could consummate the transaction, it had to transport a car to Texas and was in no different position from a non-Internet dealer located in Oklahoma, who, obviously, could not sell a car in Texas without complying with Texas's laws. Moreover, there was no question that Ford *knew* that it was selling cars in Texas. In the context of online gathering of personal information, where the "goods" are digital and the entire transaction takes place on a computer screen, the company gathering the personal information typically would not know the location of an individual and thus would not know if a particular state's law would prohibit or condition the collection or use of the personal information.

Technologies are being developed to permit Web sites to identify the locations of users on the basis of the Internet protocol address of a given user's computer.[6] These technologies are currently more accurate with respect to identifying location at a national level (90 percent-98 percent) than at a state level, where the accuracy rate is only 80 percent-95 percent.[7] Moreover, anonymizers and other similar blocking technologies are additional obstacles to the ability of Web sites to determine the locations of users. Even if these locator-technologies can be brought to the point of enabling Web sites to identify the locations of their users (and thus, which state's law applies)—the relative cost of complying with the laws of fifty different states would seem to be higher for purely digital transactions than for real space transactions. Real space transactions have built-in transaction costs, such as the transport of an object through the mails to the consumer, whereas digital transactions arguably either happen quickly and cheaply or not at all. Thus, even if it is technically possible to identify the location of a user, the cost of then having to tailor the delivery of digital content to comply with fifty potential different sets of regulations might be too great a burden for purposes of the dormant Commerce Clause.

---

[6] Goldsmith and Sykes, "The Internet and the Dormant Commerce Clause," 110 Yale L.J. 785, 810-811 (2001).
[7] *Id.*

Given the complexity involved in crafting privacy bills, it is not surprising that federal and state legislatures are consistently calling for the establishment of privacy commissions (on both the state and federal level) to study how to protect personal information without impairing the growth of e-commerce. Calling for a commission, however, is the mildest of the proposals under consideration. Indeed, a number of bills proposing the establishment of such commissions specifically admonish that the establishment of a commission should *not* prevent other legislative action from being taken to protect the privacy of individuals.[8] Other bills under consideration include more aggressive approaches to protecting privacy and range from voluntary certification programs (similar to TrustE's program), to selectively protecting certain types of personal information (such as that of students), to enhancing already established protections for financial and medical personal information, to imposing broad opt-in schemes that prohibit collecting any personal information without express authorization from consumers. Some bills propose enforcement only by government agency (for instance, the FTC or, for state legislation, a state attorney general), while others propose giving individuals the right to file lawsuits for privacy violations.

It is too early to predict which type of bill will ultimately form the blueprint for regulation—which most believe to be inevitable. It is also too early to tell whether inconsistent state regulations will complicate matters or whether a uniform federal standard will be hammered out. Judging from Congress's approach in the Health Insurance Portability and Accountability Act and the Gramm-Leach-Bliley Act, however, there is the possibility that the result may be somewhere in the middle: a federal rule that sets a minimum standard, but that also permits states to enact consistent regulation further restricting the collection, use and disclosure of personal information.

Certainly, public pressure for some protection appears to be unabated. Legislators, though, are cautious about imposing restrictions that could impede the growth of what has been the most

---

[8] See, e.g., H.R. 583, § 2(13), 107th Cong., 1st Sess. (2001).

promising sector of the U.S. economy—in spite of some heated words coming from certain legislators and consumer groups.

Nevertheless, the large number of privacy bills proposed in both Houses of Congress over the past several years indicates how important privacy issues are to lawmakers and their constituents. The proposed legislation is too voluminous to detail, but those interested in exploring the kinds and scope of the bills may do so on the Library of Congress's legislative information Web site, THOMAS.[9]

STATE-SPONSORED PRIVACY BILLS

Many, if not most, states can be expected to propose some type of privacy legislation. Several states, such as California, Massachusetts, New York, Texas, Virginia and Washington, have taken the same range of approaches as that seen in Washington D.C., i.e., from calling for a study of the issue of personal privacy to broad opt-in schemes that would prohibit all collection of all personal information without express consent of the consumer. These states, along with many others, are enacting additional measures regarding nonpublic personal information collected by financial institutions. These measures are intended to increase the protections offered by the opt-out scheme established by the Gramm-Leach-Bliley Act, which creates a federal, minimum standard for protection of nonpublic personal information collected by financial institutions. In addition, legislators are focused on such issues as enforcement and penalties, e.g., whether individuals will have a private right of action and whether damages should be made available.

Because of the rapidly changing legislative landscape, the only way to keep current on developments is to use electronic bill-tracking services, such as through Lexis, or to visit Web sites that track legislation. There are at present no free Web sites that offer comprehensive tracking of state bills. A number of sites, however, do track federal activity.[10]

---

[9] The THOMAS Internet address is http://thomas.loc.gov/.
[10] Two helpful, well-maintained sites that can be consulted for updates are http://epic.org/privacy/bill_track.html and http://www.cdt.org/legislation.

Chapter 7

Privacy Issues in the Workplace

Privacy issues are being fought out in the workplace, as well as on the Internet. With more and more people using computers and e-mail at work, more and more of us are confronting the prospect of losing a large degree of the anonymity that we used to have at our disposal. E-mail communications have replaced many of the conversations that used to occur around the water cooler. The difference is that the water cooler conversations were not preserved and were not monitored.

- An employee of a New York securities firm claimed to have evidence on his voice-mail of regulatory violations by a senior company official, and threatened to reveal the information if any adverse personnel action were taken against him. He also refused to disclose his voice-mail password and threatened legal action if the company broke into his voice-mail to retrieve the information.
- Several large corporations were subjected to race discrimination lawsuits based on e-mails with racial content sent around the offices by employees using the companies' systems.
- In 1995, a manager at a McDonald's in New York was fired after exchanging impassioned voice-mail messages with another employee with whom he was having an extramarital affair. A co-worker retrieved the steamy romantic messages and played them for the employee's boss and the employee's wife. The employee sued McDonald's and the franchisee under the Electronic Communications Privacy Act, the New York wire-tapping statute, and for various common law torts.

- In 1992, a vice-president at Borland defected to a rival computer software maker, but not before allegedly forwarding trade secrets via MCI Mail. Borland pressed charges against the employee based on the e-mails it retrieved with his password. The employee was indicted, but defended himself by accusing Borland of violating the Electronic Communications Privacy Act's ban on tapping messages sent on commercial e-mail lines.

These are but a few examples of the tensions that exist in the workplace between legitimate business concerns and workers' privacy.

Sexual harassment claims are a good example of how the risk of employer liability has compelled employers to monitor closely employee conduct. Sexual harassment law has shaped the way employers run their businesses in the beginning of the twenty-first century in many respects. When an employee harasses a co-worker, the employer can be liable. As a result, many employers have instituted electronic monitoring programs that "watch" the online conduct of employees or their e-mail communications. One survey concluded that more than 75 percent of major U.S. corporations keep some kind of tab on employees through various surveillance activities; 63 percent of the employers sampled monitor their employees' Internet use and 47 percent store and review employee e-mails.[1]

A host of software programs is available to assist the employer in this effort. For instance, one program takes digital snapshots of everything that appears on a screen of the employee's computer. Another screens each incoming and outgoing e-mail message for evidence of racism and sexism, applying "scores" to the content of each e-mail. E-mails with high scores are automatically forwarded to a supervisor. A whole host of filtering programs or technologies exists for the workplace.

These and similar issues are being played out in the workplace every day. How, if at all, should a business limit employee use of

---

[1] http://www.usatoday.com/careers/news/2001-04-26-monitor.htm.

e-mail or Internet access? How does a company prevent an employee from communicating confidential information instantaneously over the Internet? How does a business ensure that the e-mail system is not abused by employees, for instance, in order to harass or make discriminatory statements about other employees? And, if the business takes precautions to protect itself from liability that might arise as a result of employees using e-mail technology unlawfully (such as to create a discriminatory work environment), does the employee lose all of his or her privacy in communications made by e-mails.

Although reasonable persons can debate what should be the appropriate compromise to draw between employee expectation of privacy in e-mail communications and employer interest in protecting against abuse, the bottom line is that courts to date have come down solidly on the side of employers. Employees have virtually no expectation of privacy in the American workplace, and this applies to Internet browsing and e-mail communications, too.

RELEVANT STATUTES AND LEGAL PRINCIPLES

DO EMPLOYEES HAVE ANY EXPECTATION OF PRIVACY IN THE WORKPLACE?

The question of whether an individual has, under the Fourth Amendment of the U.S. Constitution, an expectation of privacy sufficient to give rise to protection from government invasion has been the subject of many important Supreme Court cases over the years. For instance, in 1967, the Supreme Court held that an individual has a reasonable expectation of privacy in communications at a public telephone booth and that, consequently, the government could not eavesdrop on such conversations absent a search warrant.[2] However, the Supreme Court has qualified what expectations are "reasonable." For example, the Court held that once a person "shares information" with another, she assumes the risk that the other person will not keep the information confidential, and as such she has

---

[2] See Katz v. United States, 389 U.S. 347, 352 (1967).
[3] See Hoffa v. United States, 385 U.S. 293, 302 (1966).

lost her reasonable expectation of privacy.[3] Also, if one voluntarily turns bank records or telephone logs over to a third person, she assumes the risk that the third person will turn the records over to the government.[4]

Courts have held that employees in the workplace have a limited reasonable expectation of privacy. A 1996 case from the Federal District Court for the Eastern District of Pennsylvania is illustrative.[5] In that case, the employee claimed his employer, Pillsbury, wrongfully discharged him because the basis for his discharge was information that Pillsbury had obtained from his stored e-mail communications.[6] Pillsbury had provided its employees with an e-mail system to assist in intra-company communication and had led its employees to believe that their e-mail messages would remain confidential, and that it would not intercept e-mail communications or use intercepted messages against employees as grounds for dismissal.[7] It then accessed the plaintiff's work-related e-mail messages, in which he disparaged a co-worker, and fired him for "sending inappropriate and unprofessional comments on the company's e-mail system."[8]

The court determined that Pillsbury's access of the plaintiff's e-mail was not a tortious invasion of privacy. It held that in order for such an action to be actionable the employer's invasion must be "substantial and highly offensive to the 'ordinary reasonable person.'"[9] In the court's discussion of reasonable expectation of privacy, it stated that the plaintiff did *not* have a reasonable expectation of privacy in his workplace e-mail communications, as one would in physical intrusions such as urinalysis and personal property searches.[10] It then determined that no reasonable person would "find Pillsbury's actions to be a substantial and highly offensive

---

[4] See United States v. Miller, 425 U.S. 435, 442-444 (1976).

[5] Smyth v. Pillsbury Co., 914 F. Supp. 97 (E.D. Pa. 1996).

[6] *Id.* at 100.

[7] *Id.*

[8] *Id.* at 98-99.

[9] *Id.* at 106.

[10] *Id.* at 101.

[11] *Id.* See also, Baum, "E-Mail in the Workplace and the Right of Privacy," 42 Vill. L. Rev. 1011, 1033 (1997).

invasion of an employee's privacy interests."[11] No expectation of privacy was created by Pillsbury's assurances that employee e-mail would remain privileged and confidential. Once the plaintiff sent the message to another person, he had lost any expectation of privacy. The privacy interests of the employees were outweighed by Pillsbury's interest in preventing "inappropriate and unprofessional comments," as well as "illegal activity" on its e-mail system.[12]

This approach by the district court in this case is the general approach taken by courts to date. Employees have no reasonable expectation of privacy in e-mail communications in the workplace. Of course, the lack of privacy applies to *all* e-mail communications from the workplace computer, even those that are nominally personal and not related to business.

THE ELECTRONIC COMMUNICATIONS PRIVACY ACT OF 1986

The Electronic Communications Privacy Act (ECPA) is the most comprehensive piece of federal legislation dealing with the interception of and access to electronic communications such as e-mail and voice mail. But, as the following discussion shows, the courts are still working out what exactly constitutes a violation of Title I of the ECPA.

Congress enacted the ECPA in 1986 to amend Title III of the Omnibus Crime Control and Safe Streets Act of 1968. The 1968 Act provided protection for traditional means of communication, such as the telephone, by placing restrictions on the wiretapping and eavesdropping of these means of communication. The ECPA modernized the 1968 Act to expand the restrictions to all forms of "electronic communication," including specifically e-mail and voice mail transmissions.[13] It exposes violators to civil penalties, and sets out specific exceptions. As we show below, however, employers have been able to circumvent any constraints imposed by the ECPA by obtaining consent of employees. Courts have almost uniformly upheld such consent of employees.

---

[12] Smyth v. Pillsbury Co., 914 F. Supp. 97, 101 (E.D. Pa. 1996).
[13] White, "E-Mail@work.com: Employer Monitoring of Employee E-Mail," 48 Ala. L. Rev. 1079, 1081 (1997).

The ECPA has two principal parts that are relevant to this discussion. Title I prohibits the *interception* of electronic communications.[14] Title II prohibits the unauthorized *access* of stored communications.[15]

Title I of the ECPA defines "interception" as "the aural or other acquisition of the contents of any wire, electronic, or oral communication through the use of any electronic, mechanical, or other device."[16] For such interception to constitute a violation of the statute, the interception must be "intentional."[17] The intentional interception of a voice call, or e-mail communication, arguably, therefore, could be a violation of Title I. But some courts have determined that the window for "intercepting" electronic communications such as e-mail is narrow: the interception must occur *during* transmission.

- The Secret Service comes in and takes stored but unread e-mails from a suspect's computer. Does this constitute a violation of the ECPA—i.e., "interception" of electronic communication?

In one of the leading cases on this issue, *Steve Jackson Games v. United States Secret Service*, the court considered this very question and held that it did not constitute "interception."[18] The court stated that although it is possible for e-mail to be "intercepted" within the meaning of the statute, it must be "in transmission" while it is being accessed in order for the ECPA to apply.[19] This leaves only a few seconds during which the e-mail can be accessed in order to create a cause of action under the Act—after the message has been sent but before it is stored in a temporary electronic area.[20] The court in *Steve Jackson Games* did note that if an employer installed a type of automatic routing software, such that copies of all messages are sent to a supervisor, Title I might apply.

---

[14] 18 U.S.C. §§ 2510 *et seq.*
[15] 18 U.S.C. §§ 2701 *et seq.*
[16] 18 U.S.C. § 2510(4).
[17] 18 U.S.C. § 2511(a).
[18] Steve Jackson Games v. United States Secret Service, 36 F.3d 457, 460 (5th Cir. 1994).
[19] See *id.*
[20] White, "E-Mail@work.com: Employer Monitoring of Employee E-Mail," 48 Ala. L. Rev. 1079, 1082 (1997).

- A co-worker gained access to another employee's voice mail system and discovered that the employee may have committed securities fraud. The co-worker recorded the message, which ultimately started an investigation by the Securities and Exchange Commission and led to indictment of the employee. The indicted employee attempted to suppress the voice mail as evidence, claiming that it was obtained in violation of the ECPA. Did he succeed?

Faced with these facts, a court held that the language of the statute indicated that wire communications, including voice mails, in contrast to electronic communications such as e-mails, could be intercepted within the meaning of the statute even when they were in storage. Thus, the interception of wire communications need not be contemporaneous with the transmission to violate the ECPA.[21] These cases suggest that the scope of protection under the ECPA depends on the technology being used for the communication.

In contrast, in January 2001, the Court of Appeals for the Ninth Circuit decided *Konop v. Hawaiian Airlines*.[22] In this case, Konop, a pilot for Hawaiian Airlines, maintained his own Web site where he posted bulletins critical of the airline, its officers and the union, focusing on labor concessions, which the union and management were negotiating. Access to the Web site required user names and passwords, which Konop gave to fellow employees, but not to Hawaiian Airlines management. A Hawaiian Airlines executive obtained access to the Web site. Konop filed suit claiming, among other things, that Hawaiian Airlines violated the ECPA by improperly accessing his Web site. The Court of Appeals chose to reject the interpretation of the Act advanced by the Court of Appeals for the Fifth Circuit in the *Steve Jackson* case. The court rejected the distinction between electronic communications and wire communications, observing: "We believe that Congress intended the ECPA to eliminate distinctions between protection of private communications based on arbitrary features of the technology used for transmission. . . . It makes no more sense that a private message

---

[21] United States v. Smith, 155 F.3d 1051, 1059 (9th Cir. 1998).
[22] Konop v. Hawaiian Airlines, 236 F.3d 1035 (9th Cir. 2001).

expressed in a digitized voice recording stored in a voice mailbox should be protected from interception, but the same words expressed in an e-mail stored in an electronic post office pending delivery should not."[23] The court concluded saying: "we hold that the Wiretap Act [ECPA] protects electronic communications from interception when stored to the same extent as when in transit."[24]

In another decision, a federal district court in Pennsylvania held that retrieval of an employee's e-mail from storage after the e-mail had been received by the recipient did not violate the Stored Communications Act because, unlike in *Konop*, the retrieval occurred after the recipient had received the communication, and thus not in the course of tranmission.[25]

The point of these examples is that the courts are still working out what exactly constitutes a violation of Title I of the ECPA.

Title II of the ECPA prohibits intentional unauthorized access of a wire or electronic communication while it is in electronic storage.[26] Title II, therefore, more clearly applies to e-mail messages. This section exposes employers to civil damages in the event that they access an employee's stored e-mail or voice mail communications without the employee's permission, or without falling into one of the ECPA's specified exceptions. Stored e-mail includes messages that are unread, and those that have been read and are stored on a computer's hard drive.

There are three exceptions to liability under the ECPA:

The Consent Exception: If one of the parties to the communication consents to the interception.

The Business Extension Exception: If the interception was done by a device provided by the communications provider or subscriber and done in the employer's ordinary course of business.

---

[23] *Id.* at 1046.
[24] *Id.*
[25] Fraser v. Nationwide Mutual Insurance Co., 2001 WL 290656 (E.D. Pa. March 27, 2001).
[26] 18 U.S.C. § 2701(a).

The Provider Exception: If the employer qualifies as a service provider, it may monitor its lines to ensure adequate service.[27]

The Consent Exception is the most interesting and most important of these exceptions for the ordinary business. When an employer notifies its employees that their phone calls will be monitored, the employees will be deemd to have impliedly consented to the policy, and cannot take action under the ECPA. However, an employer's action must not exceed the scope of this notification. For example, an employee sued her employer because the employer had listened to a personal telephone conversation regarding a job interview.[28] The employer had notified employees that it would monitor work-related telephone calls for quality assurance purposes, but the employer's policy stated that the employer would not monitor personal phone calls. The Eleventh Circuit did not extend the employee's consent to personal phone calls and stated that "mere knowledge of monitoring capability cannot be considered implied consent to employer monitoring of all calls."[29] The court noted that consent will be implied only when the policy makes the employees aware that phone calls are continuously monitored or when an employee makes a personal phone call on a phone line reserved for business calls and is aware that the company monitors business calls.[30]

Courts will not infer employee consent in regard to e-mail and voice mail monitoring. Generally, the employee must give actual consent, or the circumstances must illustrate that the employee knew about the monitoring. Employers can increase the likelihood that workers will be deemed to have impliedly consented if the employers place employees on notice of electronic monitoring by adopting a comprehensive electronic communications policy and abiding by the policy's limits.

The Business Extension Exception also deserves some attention. It exempts employers who are furnished with an electronic device

---

[27] See 18 U.S.C. §§ 2510(5)(a)(1), 2511(2)(a)(i), 2511(2)(d), 2701(c)(1), 2701(c)(2).

[28] Watkins v. L. M. Berry & Co., 704 F.2d 577, 581 (11th Cir. 1983).

[29] White, "E-Mail@work.com: Employer Monitoring of Employee E-Mail," 48 Ala. L. Rev. 1079, 1084 (1997).

[30] See *id.*

by a "provider of wire or electronic communication service" for use in the ordinary course of business from liability under the ECPA.[31] Therefore, if an employer uses a device given to it by the phone company, or attached to the phone line, to monitor its employees' business-related telephone calls for quality purposes, it will not be liable for the interception of electronic communications for purposes of the statute.[32] The analysis involves first, whether the use of the device is in the ordinary course of business, and next, whether the actual monitoring is in the ordinary course of business. Courts apply two tests in determining whether the monitoring is in the ordinary course of business or not. A context-based analysis examines the surrounding circumstances of the monitoring,[33] and a content-based analysis examines whether the communication intercepted was business-related or personal.[34]

Without going into too much detail about this exception, the applicability to employers is not free from doubt. Historically, this exception was used to uphold the monitoring of employee phone calls within the ordinary course of the employer's business. Arguably, this may include the providers of an e-mail system. However, there is debate over whether or not an employer would qualify as a "provider" of its own e-mail system, and how the requirement that the intercepting device be a form of telephonic equipment would apply to e-mail.[35]

THE FOURTH AMENDMENT TO THE U.S. CONSTITUTION

In the case of government employees, the Fourth Amendment in theory would apply, since the intrusion in those cases is by the government, as opposed to a private party. But, as mentioned above, before the Fourth Amendment can apply, the individual must have a reasonable and protectible expectation of privacy in the workplace. Most courts have found that an employee's expectation of privacy at work is diminished, especially when the employer has a policy of monitoring employee Internet and e-mail use.

---

[31] 18 U.S.C. § 2511(1)(b).
[32] See Deal v. Spears, 908 F.2d 1153, 1158 (8th Cir. 1992).
[33] See James v. Newspaper Agency Corp., 591 F.2d 579, 582 (10th Cir. 1979).
[34] See Watkins v. L. M. Berry & Co., 704 F.2d 577, 582-584 (11th Cir. 1983).
[35] 18 U.S.C. § 2510(5)(a).

- *No expectation of privacy in Internet use where known policy.*
  A government office monitored its employees' Internet con-
  nections with a "firewall." During a routine check on the system, an employee noticed that the defendant had made many
  visits to sex-related Internet sites. During an investigation of
  the defendant's online activity, the Postal Service found that
  the defendant had accessed several Web pages depicting child
  pornography. At trial for receipt of child pornography, the
  employee had moved to suppress the evidence under the
  Fourth Amendment, arguing that he had an expectation of privacy in his online activity. The Court of Appeals for the Fourth
  Circuit allowed the admission of evidence obtained by the ran-
  dom monitoring of the employee's Internet use at work.[36] The
  court emphasized that the office had a known policy that
  allowed it to audit employee Internet use, and that the government's need to investigate the crime outweighed any privacy interest the defendant had at work.[37]
- *Expectation of privacy in ISP.* In contrast, in a case against an
  Air Force colonel who had used AOL to browse the Internet at
  home, the court did not allow the use of evidence of receipt
  of child pornography obtained by the Air Force by seizing the
  colonel's home computer and searching the files stored in it.[38]
  The court found that the colonel had a reasonable expectation
  of privacy in his home AOL e-mail system, but explicitly limited that protection to e-mails sent person-to-person, not those
  sent to public chat rooms.[39] The rationale behind this distinction lies in the evolution of the reasonable expectation of
  privacy as it has spread from telephone calls to e-mail messages. People talking on cordless telephones do not enjoy a
  reasonable expectation of privacy because their calls can be
  easily intercepted, if only accidentally by their neighbors
  using phones operating on the same frequency.[40] Because

---

[36] See United States v. Simons, 206 F.3d 392, 398 (4th Cir. 2000).
[37] See *id.*
[38] See United States v. Maxwell, 45 M.J. 406, 417-419 (C.A.A.F. 1996).
[39] See *id.*
[40] Sundstrom, "You've Got Mail (and the Government Knows It): Applying the
Fourth Amendment to Workplace E-mail Monitoring," 73 N.Y.U. L. Rev. 2064, 2081 (1998).

messages sent to listservs and chat rooms can be accessed by an infinite number of strangers, the senders similarly have no expectation of privacy in these e-mail messages.[41] Person-to-person e-mails have also been analogized to written mail sent through the postal service, which the government may not access without a warrant, whereas messages sent to chat rooms and listservs are more like postcards, which do not bring with them an expectation of privacy because they can be freely read by anyone who comes in contact with them in the course of their delivery.[42]

STATE SOLUTIONS

States have addressed the privacy rights of employees through state constitutional provisions, common law, and statutory enactments. Constitutional provisions have been added in several states, and generally guarantee the right to privacy, some even applying to private searches. For example, California's privacy statute allows a private (or public) employer to invade an employee's privacy only when the employer has a "compelling interest and the invasion serves a job-related purpose."[43] Common law invasion of privacy claims have been fairly unsuccessful, largely because state courts refuse to recognize an expectation of privacy for employees. These plaintiffs usually must show that the employer "pried or intruded into the plaintiffs' . . . lives in an offensive or objectionable manner and thereby invaded their right to privacy."[44] Such state courts infer consent when the employer has promulgated a policy or had employees sign forms acknowledging the employer's intention to monitor e-mail.[45] Courts have also refused to extend state common law privacy protections to employee e-mail, stating that this extension of employee privacy law should be left to the legislature.[46]

Many states have also enacted statutes that are more restrictive than the ECPA, and protect employees more thoroughly. The

---

[41] See *id.* at 2081-2082.

[42] See *id.* at 2082.

[43] White, "E-Mail@work.com: Employer Monitoring of Employee E-Mail," 48 Ala. L. Rev. 1079, 1094 (1997).

[44] See *id.* at 1095.

[45] See *id.* at 1097.

[46] See *id.*

protection generally mirrors the federal law, but state laws often provide less liberal exceptions for employers.[47] Many states require employers to obtain the consent of all parties to the communication before monitoring can take place, and this may subject out-of-state employers whose employees communicate with a party in a state that has adopted such an exemption to that state's statute.[48] However, other states have afforded employers more protection than the ECPA by allowing the business use exemption to apply to all employers.[49]

EMPLOYER E-MAIL AND INTERNET POLICIES

In order to avoid confusion among employees and litigation over e-mail and Internet usage and searches at work, employers are advised to disseminate policies setting out how such use will be treated. These policies not only provide employees with clear standards and consistency in employment policies, but also may give the employer a means to show that its interest lies in protecting company resources, not in invading the privacy of its employees.[50] Depending on how restrictive an employer desires its policy to be, the following topics should be covered by e-mail and Internet policies:

Key Provisions of an E-mail or Internet Use Policy

- A policy must give employees notice that their electronic communications are not private and expressly provide that the employer reserves the right to access any e-mail messages sent by employees on the employer's system.
- A policy should set out the extent to which the employer will allow employees to use the company e-mail system for personal use, if at all.
- A policy should expressly state that certain types of e-mail content are strictly forbidden, such as sexually explicit and racially offensive messages.

---

[47] See *id.* at 1090.

[48] See *id.* at 1091.

[49] See *id.* (citing Nebraska's employer-friendly statute).

[50] See Baum, "E-Mail in the Workplace and the Right of Privacy," 42 Vill. L. Rev. 1011, 1037 (1997).

- A policy should state that the employer will monitor e-mail and Internet activity and that employees sacrifice any expectation of privacy by using the company e-mail system.
- A policy should provide that an employee will be subject to discipline for retrieving another employee's e-mail, voice mail or electronically stored documents for any reason other than specified legitimate business purposes, such as evaluating the effectiveness of electronic mail; providing assistance in performing departmental duties when employees are otherwise unavailable; finding lost messages; conducting an investigation into suspected criminal acts, breaches of security, or violations of corporate policies; complying with subpoenas or other process; and recovering e-mail, voice mail or electronically stored documents from system failures or other emergencies.
- A policy should also set out the company's retention and backup program.

Such a policy, if disseminated widely to each employee in the workplace, creates a unilateral contract that gives the employer the right to monitor and control its e-mail system. An employee accepts the employer's offer of this contract by agreeing to be employed by that employer. The policy does not create contractual rights for the employee, and as such is not binding on the employer.[51] The Department of Justice recommends that in addition to providing each employee with a written copy of the policy, employers should create a "banner" attached to each user's log-on, stating that monitoring will occur.[52] It is also recommended that employers limit their monitoring of e-mail and Internet usage by employees to what is necessary for legitimate business purposes, paying careful attention to whether their policies continue to conform to any statutory enactments.[53]

Employees do not enjoy an expectation of privacy in their use of employer e-mail, phones or Internet access. Employers may create unilateral contracts allowing them to monitor employee e-mail, and they are protected by exceptions to the ECPA. Employers may be

---

[51] *Id.* at 1036.

[52] White, "E-Mail@work.com: Employer Monitoring of Employee E-Mail," 48 Ala. L. Rev. 1079, 1103-1104 (1997).

[53] See *id.*

exposed to liability more easily under state legislation, but with the implied or express consent of their employees, employers are also protected from these statutes. Even government employers can escape the employee's Fourth Amendment protections by creating well-disseminated policies that allow for employer monitoring of e-mail and Internet usage. Employers can feel comfortable that they will be protected from liability as long as they have policies that explicitly state rules for the workplace and employee behavior.

Chapter 8

Privacy Litigation

An Overview

We are in the midst of a wave of class action Internet privacy litigation. Numerous lawsuits relating to the collection of personal information of Web users have been filed by individual plaintiffs against various Web sites and online advertising companies. Not surprisingly, what may have begun as a grass-roots response to the perceived threats to individual privacy is now being explored and, in many cases, directed by well-known plaintiff class action law firms. As the spokesperson of one of these law firms stated: "There has definitely been a growing focus on this area."[1] To date this wave of privacy litigation has achieved scant success. Nevertheless, one can conclude from the cases filed so far that just as privacy has come to the front page of the newspapers and the top of the legislative agenda, so, too, has it come to the attention of plaintiffs' counsel. More litigation under the new statutes and regulations that have been and are being enacted will undoubtedly follow.

The leading cases to date are: the DoubleClick cookies litigation;[2] lawsuits against Intuit for information gathering by advertisers on

---

[1] "Online ad companies hit with privacy suits," CNET News.com (Nov. 22, 2000), available at http://news.com.com/2100-1023-248999.html?legacy=cnet.

[2] In re DoubleClick, Inc., Privacy Litigation, 154 F. Supp.2d 497 (S.D.N.Y. 2001) (complaint dismissed).

its Quicken.com Web site;[3] cases against Amazon.com challenging data collection and use by its Alexa Internet subsidiary software;[4] and cases against RealNetworks challenging its methods of monitoring usage habits of individuals using its software.[5]

CHARACTERISTICS OF LAWSUITS: TARGET DEFENDANTS AND TYPES OF CLAIMS

Three types of defendants have been sued in the roster of lawsuits targeting information-gathering practices. First are online advertisers, such as DoubleClick, Inc., whose actual and planned consumer profiling practices created tremendous controversy and in no small part triggered the wave of privacy suits. Second are Web sites that utilize third-party advertising companies—hardly a badge of distinction among the many thousands of Web sites that do so. Third are Web sites that offer products—specifically, software—that allegedly have surreptitious information-gathering capabilities.

At first blush, there are a number of significant differences among these three groups of defendants. For instance, while advertisers are ever-present on Web sites, they are, typically speaking, invisibly present. It is probably safe to say that while users are aware of advertisements, they are generally not aware of the "presence" of the third-party advertising companies. Thus, advertisers are unknown to users, but are nonetheless privy to communications between user and Web site. In contrast to advertisers, the Web site defendants are known to users. Indeed, the user has deliberately sought out and communicated with the Web site that is allegedly surreptitiously gathering and/or disclosing his or her personal information. Another difference between the Web sites and advertisers is that because the users are present on the Web site, they have an opportunity to read the Web sites' privacy policies and/or any relevant license agreements relating to the software offered by certain defendants. Certainly, the privacy policies and/or relevant license agreements

---

[3] See In re Intuit Privacy Litigation, No. ED-CV-00-123RT (C.D. Cal. April 10, 2001) (motion to dismiss granted in part, denied in part).

[4] See Supnick v. Amazon.com, No. C00-0221-P, 2000 WL 1603820 (W.D. Wash. April 21, 2000).

[5] See In re RealNetworks, Inc. Privacy Litigation, No. 00C1366, 2000 WL 631341 (N.D. Ill. May 8, 2000).

can potentially disclose any information-gathering practices that are alleged in the many privacy complaints.

Although the nature of the defendants' relationship to users and the defendants' alleged activities are different in significant respects, the claims against these defendants are quite uniform. The great majority of complaints, whether state or federal, allege violations of either the California, New York or Washington state unfair business practices or deceptive acts statute.[6] The extent of monetary recovery under these statutes ranges widely. For instance, the California Business and Professions Code limits private litigants to equitable relief, while other California statutes permit either recovery of damages or substantial statutory damages of up to $2,500 for first-time violators and up to $10,000 for "repeat" offenders.[7] In addition to the specific relief found in each of these California statutes, the California Civil Code has a general provision that permits successful parties in "any action" to recover attorneys' fees when the action has, among other requirements, resulted in "the enforcement of an important right affecting the public interest."[8] This, of course, has potential application when any plaintiff is successful in prosecuting these privacy suits.

The New York and Washington statutes offer less in the way of variety and amount of statutory damages. The New York statute provides for treble damages with a cap of $1,000 for knowing violations, injunctive relief and attorneys' fees.[9] Similarly, the

---

[6] *California:* Calif. Bus. & Prof. Code §§ 17200 and 17500; Calif. Consumers Legal Remedies Act § 1770(a); Invasion of Privacy Act, Calif. Penal Code §§ 631 and 632.

New York: N.Y. Gen. Bus. L., Art. 22A §§ 349(a) and 350.

Washington: Consumer Protection and Deceptive Practices Act, R.C.W. Ch. 19.86.

[7] Specifically, the California Business and Professions Code does not permit recovery of civil penalties by private individuals and limits remedies for such litigants to equitable (indeed, some argue, only injunctive) relief. In contrast, violations of California Consumer Legal Remedies Act Section 1770(a) can warrant the recovery of actual damages, restitution, injunctive relief, punitive damages and attorneys' fees and costs. A violation of the Invasion of Privacy Act, California Penal Code Sections 631 and 632, can result in the imposition of statutory damages of up to $2,500 for first-time violators and up to $10,000 for "repeat" offenders.

[8] Cal. Civil Code § 1021.5.

[9] N.Y. Gen. Bus. L. § 349(h).

Washington state statute provides for recovery of treble damages with a cap of $10,000, injunctive relief and attorneys' fees.[10]

In addition to claims arising under state business practices statutes, each complaint alleges a relatively standard menu of common law claims, such as invasion of privacy,[11] trespass, unjust enrichment, as well as—though less frequently—claims for breach of contract, negligence and fraud. In general, monetary recovery under these claims typically ranges from actual damages to disgorgement of profits and, in some cases, could result in the imposition of punitive damages.

The complaints filed in federal courts also uniformly allege violations of the Wiretap Act and Stored Electronic Communications Act (Titles I and II of the Electronics Communications Privacy Act of 1986). Some, though not all, of the federal complaints also allege violations of the Computer Fraud and Abuse Act, which was enacted as an anti-hacking measure.[12]

From the private litigants' standpoint, it is worth remembering that the Wiretap and Stored Electronic Communications Act provides for the recovery of attorneys' fees by successful plaintiffs. In addition, the damages that are available under these federal statutes are significant. For violations of the Wiretap Act, plaintiffs can recover (1) the greater of (a) the sum of actual damages suffered by the plaintiff *and* any profits made by the violator as a result of the violation or (b) statutory damages of whichever is the greater of $100 a day for each day of violation or $10,000, and (2) punitive damages.[13] For violations of the Wiretap and Stored Electronic Communications Act, plaintiffs can recover the sum of the actual damages suffered by the plaintiff and any profits made by the violator as a result of the violation, "but in no case shall a person entitled to recover receive less than the sum of $1,000."[14] For

---

[10] Wash. Consumer Protection and Deceptive Practices Act, RCW, Ch. 19.86.090.

[11] While in many cases plaintiffs have asserted common law claims of invasion of privacy, in other cases certain California plaintiffs have asserted violations of the statutory version of this claim, Invasion of Privacy Act, Calif. Penal Code §§ 631 and 632.

[12] These statutes are discussed in more detail in Chapters 5 and 7.

[13] 18 U.S.C. 2520 §§ 2520(b) and 2520(c).

[14] 18 U.S.C. § 2707.

violations of the Computer Fraud and Abuse Act, plaintiffs can recover compensatory damages and injunctive or "other equitable" relief.[15]

Obviously, these state and federal statutes, many of which offer the possibility of statutory damages ranging from $1,000 to $10,000 per plaintiff or equitable relief such as disgorgement of profits as well as the possibility of attorneys' fees, are a substantial motivation for the bringing of class action lawsuits. It is likely that in each case concerning statutes that authorize specific statutory damages, a heated issue will be whether the defendant company will be held to have committed a compensable violation for *every class member* or whether the company's practice constitutes simply one compensable violation. Thus, the possible range of liability facing Internet companies for privacy violations is enormous.

OBSTACLES FACING PRIVACY PLAINTIFFS: LACK OF AN APPROPRIATE THEORY OF LIABILITY

As is apparent from the above description of the plaintiffs' claims, the novelty of Internet information-gathering business practices and the lack of any all-purpose Internet privacy legislation have forced the plaintiffs to rely on pre-Internet statutory law and traditional common law theories to frame their claims. Indeed, finding an appropriate theory of liability is one of the chief obstacles facing the privacy plaintiffs.

Probably the overarching question that relates to all of the claims is the question of user consent and whether a user's deliberate communication with a Web site—which communication contains some or all of the collected information—can insulate Web sites and/or third-party advertisers from liability. Another key question—both for purposes of liability and the amount of any recovery—is likely to be whether the plaintiffs can legitimately assert that they have been damaged by the information-collecting practices.

There are also considerable questions surrounding the viability of claims asserted under the various state deceptive business

---

[15] 10 U.S.C. § 1030(g).

practices statutes. While enforcement actions by the FTC and the various state attorneys general indicate that a privacy policy that inaccurately describes information-gathering practices can constitute a "deceptive business practice," it is less clear whether an advertiser, which arguably makes no representations to the users from whom it collects information, can be found to have "deceived" users simply by collecting information.

With respect to the federal statutes, there are basic questions such as whether the ECPA protects users' personal computers at all. In addition, technological questions such as (1) whether advertisers or Web sites collect the information directly from the Web site or directly from the users' computers and (2) whether the collection of information should be characterized as "interception" or the accessing of "stored communications" could determine significant questions of liability under the ECPA and/or the Computer Fraud and Abuse Act.

Whether the claims under the ECPA, Computer Fraud and Abuse Act, and/or the state deceptive business practices statutes are cognizable will have a significant impact on the course of litigation. The majority of these statutes have attorneys' fees provisions, with many providing for minimum statutory damages—both of which create substantial economic incentives for bringing the actions.

A noteworthy decision addressing these issues is the district court decision granting summary judgment for DoubleClick in the consolidated class actions filed in federal court in New York. The court rejected the claims made under Title II of the Electronic Communications Privacy Act,[16] the Wiretap Act,[17] and the Computer Fraud and Abuse Act.[18]

With respect to the ECPA claim, the court concluded that the relevant "users" of the electronic communication at issue were the Web sites that used the DoubleClick technology, as opposed to individuals browsing the Internet, and that the Web sites consented to

---

[16] 18 U.S.C. §§ 2701 et seq.
[17] 18 U.S.C. §§ 2510 et seq.
[18] 18 U.S.C. §§ 1030 et seq.

DoubleClick's interception of their electronic communications. As for cookie communications (specifically, the transmission of cookie identification numbers), the court held that "[t]he cookies' long-term residence on plaintiffs' hard drives places them outside of [the statute's] definition of 'electronic storage' and, hence, Title II's protection."[19] Essentially, the court held that the statute is limited to "temporary" storage—"Title II only protects electronic communications stored 'for a limited time' in the 'middle' of a transmission, i.e., when an electronic communication service temporarily stores a communication while waiting to deliver it."[20]

With respect to the Wiretap Act claim, the court agreed with DoubleClick that the Web sites consented to interception and that DoubleClick did not intercept the information for an unlawful purpose.[21]

Finally, with respect to the Computer Fraud and Abuse Act claim, the court agreed with DoubleClick that, even though DoubleClick technically violated the Act by accessing plaintiffs' computers without authorization, the statute includes a $5,000 damages threshold and that the plaintiffs failed to plead these damages adequately. The court rejected the plaintiffs' contention that damages should be assessed against an aggregation of all of the plaintiffs in order to satisfy the statutory threshold.

LESSONS FROM THE LAWSUITS: WAYS TO AVOID OR MINIMIZE LITIGATION

Because the privacy cases are comparatively young, the primary activity in these lawsuits has been consolidation of the numerous actions against the respective defendants. There are, however, certain consistencies in the complaints that can give guidance on possible ways to avoid litigation altogether. In addition, there have been a few rulings that are instructive both in terms of how companies can try to avoid class action lawsuits and whether there are ways to push the cases out of the courts and into the more desirable—from a defendant's point of view—forum of arbitration.

---

[19] In re DoubleClick, Inc., Privacy Litigation, 154 F. Supp.2d 497, 512 (S.D.N.Y. 2001).

[20] Id. at 513.

[21] Id. at 519.

THE ROLE OF PRIVACY POLICIES AND USER CONSENT

Virtually every complaint against a Web site (as opposed to an online advertising company) alleges that the Web site's privacy policy is inconsistent with the actual information-gathering practices of the Web site. While a privacy policy is hardly a guarantee against litigation, it will without a doubt make a Web site less interesting as a litigation target if its policy accurately describes the relevant information-gathering practices. In addition, it is noteworthy that numerous Web sites have been sued not just for their own information gathering and/or disclosure, but also for the actions of advertising companies, such as DoubleClick, with respect to their collecting information from Web sites users. Thus, it would be wise to include in any privacy policy disclosure of the practices of third-party advertisers that are operating on the Web site. For instance, Intuit, which was sued for the information-gathering practices of *advertisers* on its Web site, Quicken.com, currently uses a privacy policy that states in part:

> Advertising networks that serve ads on this Web site may assign different cookies to you. Those cookies may be used to track your involvement with the advertising on our site. You may choose not to accept these cookies. Intuit does not control those parties. You should review their privacy policies to learn more about what, why and how they collect and use private information. If you have questions about our ad serving networks, please contact us at privacy@intuit.com.

Another feature of many of the complaints is the question of whether users consented to the information gathering. Clearly, a privacy policy can assist in efforts to demonstrate that users did, in fact, consent. When feasible, however, Web sites should also consider implementing click-through agreements, whereby the user must "click" that he or she understands and acknowledges how the information is to be gathered and used. While a click-through agreement will not always be feasible, it may be an option if users are purchasing certain types of products or downloading software or other information. When such agreements are workable, information-gathering disclosures could be made in such agreements.[22]

---

[22] Indeed, as discussed below regarding arbitration clauses, click-through agreements have been used to very positive effect by RealNetworks, which required users of its software to "click through" a license agreement before downloading the software.

TAKING CARE WITH THE FORUM SELECTION CLAUSE: AMAZON.COM PRIVACY LITIGATION

In *Supnick v. Amazon.com,*[23] the court permitted the plaintiffs to bring a class action. Amazon.com's subsidiary, Alexa, distributed software, which was the subject of the litigation. Certain users of the software agreed to various terms set out in a click-through license agreement. One of these terms was a highly specific forum selection clause that required disputes under the license agreement to be brought in "King County, Washington"—which, as the court observed, essentially dictated that all federal lawsuits would ultimately wind up in the Seattle federal courthouse. To the consternation of the court, this concentration of Amazon.com-related litigation posed a serious threat of shutting down the Seattle courthouse with related litigation. As a result, the court rejected Amazon.com's and Alexa's arguments against a class action—which, of course, would permit the disposition of all claims in one, rather than in hundreds, of lawsuits.

Internet companies should take particular note of this result. While a highly specific forum selection clause may be viewed as conferring a home-court advantage on the company, in Amazon.com's case, it appeared to be a significant factor in the court's certification of the class action.

USE OF THE ARBITRATION CLAUSE: REAL NETWORKS PRIVACY LITIGATION

In contrast to the ruling in *Amazon.com,* the ruling in the In re *RealNetworks, Inc. Privacy Litigation*[24] federal case upheld the arbitration clause in RealNetworks' "click-through" user license agreement. The bottom line effect of the decision was to stay all the federal actions pending arbitration and to compel plaintiffs wishing to bring federal claims to do so on an individual, rather than a class action, basis. By forcing individual plaintiffs to go it alone, the

---

[23] Supnick v. Amazon.com, No. C00-0221-P, 2000 WL 1603820 (W.D. Wash. April 21, 2000).

[24] In re RealNetworks, Inc. Privacy Litigation, No. 00C1366, 2000 WL 631341 (N.D. Ill. May 8, 2000).

court's decision exponentially increased the transaction costs of pursuing privacy litigation (based on federal claims) against Real-Networks. Tempering this victory somewhat, however, was the California state court's ruling that RealNetworks' arbitration clause did not cover the state law claims asserted by the plaintiffs.

RealNetworks has substantially lessened its risk of paying considerable amounts in damages under the federal statutes by, at a minimum, making it significantly less efficient and, thus, more expensive to assert a federal claim. RealNetworks avoided a class action lawsuit for federal claims that could potentially render it liable for statutory damages that can range as high as $10,000 for each of the potentially thousands of class members. Instead, each individual federal claimant must hire counsel to pursue RealNetworks for a fairly risky and ultimately fairly modest individual recovery. While the ECPA and Computer Fraud and Abuse Act provide for recovery of attorneys' fees for successful plaintiffs, success is far from certain. Moreover, class-action plaintiff law firms are, no doubt, less interested in pursuing cases in which they can only hope to recover fees rather than a substantial percentage of any court award that could potentially range into the many millions of dollars. Thus, it seems clear that from a practical point of view, companies can learn from RealNetworks' experience and implement, when feasible, an effective arbitration clause in any written or click-through agreements with users.

CERTAIN CONSIDERATIONS FOR EFFECTIVE ARBITRATION CLAUSES

The *RealNetworks'* rulings—particularly the federal ruling—highlight certain factors to be considered in implementing an online arbitration clause. For instance, arbitration clauses must typically be "written" to be enforceable. The RealNetworks ruling shows that the state of the law is unclear as to whether an electronic document (that is neither printed nor stored by the user) can satisfy the writing requirement. Thus, to ensure to the extent possible that an arbitration clause is "written," the *RealNetworks* ruling suggests that companies should make sure that the clauses are easily printable and storable.

In addition, companies should be cognizant of other considerations, such as the font size of the arbitration clause, its placement and its overall prominence in the larger agreement of which the clause is likely to be a part. In making these types of decisions, companies should do so with an eye toward disabling arguments— such as those made in *RealNetworks*—that the arbitration clause is "buried" in a sea of fine print. The clause that passed muster in the *RealNetworks* federal case was in the "attention-getting" last paragraph and was included in a paragraph labeled "Miscellaneous," the font size of which was the same as the font size of the rest of the agreement. Finally, from a substantive point of view, companies should work with counsel to draft an arbitration clause that is broad enough to encompass privacy-related claims, but is not so broad that it risks being invalidated.

CHAPTER 9

THE FEDERAL TRADE COMMISSION: GUARDIAN OF ONLINE PRIVACY

The Federal Trade Commission's Bureau of Consumer Protection has emerged as the dominant federal governmental enforcement agency with respect to the Internet. It has taken the leading role in addressing online consumer fraud and misleading practices. It has also been the lead federal agency addressing online privacy. The FTC's involvement dates back to the inception of the Internet as a marketplace, and clearly dates back to at least April 1995, when the FTC conducted a public workshop on Consumer Protection and the Global Information Infrastructure. The evolution of the FTC's role is instructive because it illustrates the increasing prominence of the matter of Internet privacy and the development of the subjects on which the principal governmental regulatory body is focusing.

What is particularly interesting is the evolution of the FTC's attitude toward regulation of the Internet in general, and online privacy in particular. Prior to 2000, the FTC had taken a relatively cautious position, refusing to advocate federal regulation of the Internet, in part in response to the repeated assertions by the Internet industry that it could effectively regulate itself. After a series of online fraud and consumer protection incidents and the intense attention to online profiling, by the middle of 2000, Chairman Robert Pitofsky (not without dissent from a minority of the Commissioners) agreed to advocate legislation and regulation, at least in selected areas. The FTC has taken an increasingly proactive role in the debate on online profiling, in particular. Its attention ultimately compelled the National Advertising Initiative—a coalition of online advertisers and profiling companies—to adopt a set of rules that largely conformed to the FTC doctrine on acceptable protection of individual information online. The NAI initiative, however, was able to avoid agreeing to an opt-in regime for all personally identifiable information (PII).

This chapter examines the principal investigative and enforcement efforts by the FTC since 1995.

THE FTC'S LEGAL AUTHORITY

The Federal Trade Commission Act[1] grants the FTC the responsibility and power to enforce the FTCA, which prohibits unfair methods of competition and unfair or deceptive acts or practices affecting interstate commerce. The FTCA grants the Commission broad investigative and law enforcement authority over matters affecting interstate commerce, and the Internet falls within the scope of this mandate. The FTCA, however, does not confer on the Commission the power to regulate the Internet generally, or even to regulate online privacy generally, only unfair and deceptive practices. These deceptive practices include false advertising claims made on the Internet, even in cases where other federal agencies are exploring the wrongdoing underlying the advertised claims.[2]

The Commission also has been granted responsibility under many federal statutes, such as the Children's Online Privacy Protection Act and the Gramm-Leach-Bliley Act, specifically to promulgate rules to implement the provisions of the statutes that do have an impact on privacy practices.

BASIC FTC APPROACH TO ONLINE PRIVACY

Although the FTC has moved from what was initially a willingness to permit the online industry to regulate itself to a more proactive approach to federal regulation of Internet privacy, the FTC has consistently defined the elements of a sufficient privacy policy by

---

[1] 15 U.S.C. § 45(a).
[2] See, e.g., FTC v. Ken Roberts Co., No. 00-5266, 2001 U.S. App. LEXIS 27256 (D.C. Cir. Dec. 28, 2001).

reference to the fair information practice principles first espoused in the 1973 HEW Report:

- Notice
- Choice
- Access
- Security
- Enforcement

As set out in Part 2 of *Online Profiling: A Report to Congress* in July 2000, the FTC views these as basic requirements of any privacy program. The FTC has engaged in a number of studies and has issued a number of important reports addressing online privacy over the past several years. It has also commenced investigations of a number of companies that allegedly have violated consumer privacy and has commenced formal enforcement proceedings against several of those companies. Some state attorneys general have also actively participated in the online privacy debate through investigations and enforcement actions. The state enforcement activity complements the federal enforcement work by the FTC. In the absence of more comprehensive federal legislation that preempts state law enforcement, we will continue to see this two-pronged enforcement activity. In some cases, the state attorneys general are *more* activist than their federal counterparts in privacy enforcement matters.

THE JUNE 1996 WORKSHOP AND DECEMBER 1996 REPORT, PUBLIC WORKSHOP ON CONSUMER PRIVACY AND THE GLOBAL INFORMATION INFRASTRUCTURE

The first published study or report by the FTC on Internet Privacy is a December 1996 staff report entitled *Consumer Privacy and the Global Information Infrastructure*. This report summarized the results of a two-day workshop held by the FTC in June 1996. The June 1996 workshop addressed general online privacy concerns, and had specific sessions on "The Use of Medical and Financial Information Online" (Session 4) and "The Collection and use of Information about Children" (Session 6). The FTC staff also conducted a survey of 272 sites for children in connection with this workshop and report.

The FTC June 1996 Workshop addressed many of the key elements of the current debate, including:

- The role of government: regulation versus self-regulation;
- Opt-in versus opt-out regimes;
- Consumer access to information held by marketers and Web companies; and
- Particular sensitivity of financial and medical information, and particular concerns about protection of children.

The workshop also addressed some of the emerging technologies for dealing with privacy concerns. The major technology addressed back in 1996 was the Platform for Internet Content Selection (PICS) developed by the World Wide Web Consortium at MIT to permit blocking of sites on the basis of standardized labeling of sites by content. (Of course, all major browsers and portals provide some blocking mechanism now.) Technology, however, is moving so quickly that the discussions back in 1996 have limited relevance today. Indeed, as noted in its conclusion to the report, the FTC Staff recommended that because "[e]vents continue to unfold with respect to both emerging technologies and self-regulatory initiatives," no specific action be taken at the time and that a follow-up workshop be convened. That follow-up workshop occurred the next year.

THE JUNE 1997 WORKSHOP

In June 1997, the FTC conducted a second workshop on this same subject. Session 1 focused on issues relating to computer databases; Session 2 on consumer online privacy, including issues relating to self-regulation and technological solutions and unsolicited commercial e-mail; and Session 3 on children's online privacy.

INDIVIDUAL REFERENCE SERVICES: A REPORT TO CONGRESS (DECEMBER 1997)

One of the issues hotly debated in 1996-1997 was individual reference services. Individual reference services are "computerized database services that are used to locate, identify, or verify the identity of individuals . . . ."[3] These services are used to provide information about consumers. The information includes public

---

[3] FTC, "Individual Reference Services: A Report to Congress," i (December 1997).

information (such as telephone information) as well as nonpublic information (such as information obtained from credit bureaus). Government and private parties use information from these services for a variety of legitimate purposes, including law enforcement, credit reference and locating relatives or witnesses, for example. In December 1997, the FTC issued a report entitled *Individual Reference Services: A Report to Congress*, which summarized its work on these services. This report analyzed the privacy risks associated with these look-up services and the likelihood that the Individual Reference Services Group (the industry group) would regulate itself.[4]

The FTC commended the IRSG on its proposed self-regulatory efforts, but concluded:

> Despite the laudable efforts of the IRSG Group, important issues related to individual reference services remain. The IRSG principles do not give consumers access to the public information maintained about them and disseminated by the look-up services. Accordingly, consumers will not be able to check for inaccuracies resulting from transcription or other errors occurring in the process of obtaining or compiling the public information by the look-up services. IRSG members have agreed to revisit this issue in eighteen months, and to consider whether to conduct a study quantifying the extent of any such inaccuracies. The Commission strongly urges the IRSG Group to conduct an objective analysis to determine whether the frequency of inaccuracies and the harm associated with them are such that consumer access to public record information or other safeguards are in fact unnecessary.[5]

The *Individual Reference Services Report* thus presented again the fundamental issue of whether industry was going to be able to regulate, and permitted to regulate, itself in this sensitive arena of online privacy. As of December 1997, the Federal Trade Commission remained willing to permit industry to regulate itself, at least pending further study.

---

[4] *Id.*
[5] *Id.* at ii.

PRIVACY ONLINE: A REPORT TO CONGRESS (JUNE 1998)

The workshops and studies conducted in 1995-1997 culminated in the FTC June 1998 report *Privacy Online: A Report to Congress*. In that report, the Commission reaffirmed the standards by which it evaluated practices regarding online privacy:

- Notice/Awareness
- Choice/Consent
- Access/Participation
- Integrity/Security
- Enforcement/Redress

And the Commission applied those standards to information obtained (1) from adult consumers and (2) from children. In response to continued arguments in favor of industry self-regulation, the FTC also examined the online privacy and information practice guidelines and standards of industry groups. Furthermore, in March 1998 the FTC conducted a survey of 1,402 commercial Web sites to determine what information the sites collected and what privacy policies or safeguards they offered.

While 92 percent of the surveyed sites collected some information about individuals, only 14 percent posted any disclosure of their practices, and only 2 percent posted a comprehensive policy. Admittedly, the more developed and busier sites tended to post privacy policies. The numbers for those more developed sites were: 97 percent collected some data, 71 percent provided some disclosure, and 44 percent posted privacy policies.[6]

In its own words, the Commission concluded that:

[The practices of the Web sites surveyed] demonstrate the real need for implementing the basic fair information practices described in the report. The World Wide Web provides a host of opportunities for businesses to gather a vast array of personal information from and about consumers, including children. The online environment and the advent of the computer age also provide unprecedented opportunities for the compilation, analysis,

---

[6] *Id.* at 23-28.

and dissemination of such information. While American businesses have always collected some information from consumers in order to facilitate transactions, the Internet allows for the efficient, inexpensive collection of a vast amount of information. It is the prevalence, ease, and relative low cost of such information collection that distinguished the online environment from more traditional means of commerce and information collection and thus raises consumer concerns.[7]

Recognizing that the "Internet is a rapidly changing marketplace," the FTC reiterated its view that self-regulation remained the preferable mechanism to address privacy concerns. The Commission observed that "[t]o date, however, the Commission has not seen an effective self-regulatory system emerge." The Commission further noted:

As evidenced by the Commission's survey results, and despite the Commission's three-year privacy initiative supporting a self-regulatory response to consumers' privacy concerns, the vast majority of online businesses have yet to adopt even the most fundamental fair information practice (notice/awareness). Moreover, the trade association guidelines submitted to the Commission do not reflect industry acceptance of the basic fair information practice principles. In addition, the guidelines, with limited exception, contain none of the enforcement mechanisms needed for an effective self-regulatory regime. In light of the lack of notice regarding information practices on the World Wide Web and the lack of current industry guidelines adequate to establish an effective self-regulatory regime, the question is what additional incentives are required in order to encourage effective self-regulatory efforts by industry. The Commission currently is considering this question in light of the survey results, monitoring self-regulation efforts since the survey was completed, and assessing the utility and the effectiveness of different courses of action. This summer [1998], the Commission will make recommendations on actions it deems necessary to protect online consumers generally.[8]

---

[7] *Id.* at 40.
[8] *Id.* at 41-42.

Notwithstanding that comment, the Commission deferred any effort to depart from the self-regulatory path, other than in the area of children's privacy. In that area, the Commission made a clear recommendation that Congress enact legislation "placing parents in control of the online collection and use of personal information from their children."[9] These recommendations, of course, led to the enactment of the Children's Online Privacy Protection Act of 1998 (COPPA), pursuant to which the FTC issued regulations that govern operators of Web sites and online services that collect information from children under thirteen years of age.[10]

SELF-REGULATION AND PRIVACY ONLINE: A REPORT TO CONGRESS (JULY 1999)

Given the fast-moving developments in the marketplace, the Commission issued another report in July 1999, following up on its June 1998 report. The July 1999 report, *Self-Regulation and Privacy Online: A Report to Congress*, reflected the Commission's views on the progress, if any, that had been made in self-regulation in the preceding twelve months.[11]

In the July 1999 report, the Commission presented two additional surveys that had been conducted: (1) the Georgetown Internet Privacy Policy Survey (2) and a second survey commissioned by the Online Privacy Alliance, a coalition of companies and trade associations. While the surveys revealed continued improvement in compliance by Internet sites, the Commission noted that "the low percentage of sites in both studies that address all four substantive fair information practice principles demonstrates that further improvement is required to effectively protect consumers' online privacy."[12] The Commission also reported on industry initiatives to improve privacy compliance on the Internet, including the issuance of various guidelines and approval or seal programs.

---

[9] *Id.* at 42.

[10] COPPA and the FTC regulations promulgated thereunder are discussed in greater detail in Chapter 4.

[11] A link to the report can be found at http://www.ftc.gov/os/1999/9907/index. htm#13.

[12] 1999 Report, at 8.

Given the facts mentioned above, the Commission concluded "that legislation to address online privacy was not appropriate at this time,"[13] and set out an agenda as to how it would assess industry progress and evaluate privacy practices over the ensuing year.[14]

FINAL REPORT OF THE FEDERAL TRADE COMMISSION ADVISORY COMMITTEE ON ONLINE ACCESS AND SECURITY (MAY 15, 2000)

In early 2000, the FTC created an Advisory Committee on Online Access and Security to address the increasing public concern over online privacy and to advise on approaches to critical issues regarding fair information practices. The charter of the Advisory Committee, filed on January 5, 2000, stated that the Committee's purpose was "to provide advice and recommendations to the Commission regarding implementation of certain fair information practices by domestic commercial Web sites—specifically, providing online consumers reasonable access to personal information collected from and about them and maintaining adequate security for that information." The Commission, comprised of forty members drawn from industry, academia, law and privacy watchdog organizations, was to meet four times and issue its report by May 15, 2000. (Subcommittees met on other occasions as well.)

From the outset, the Advisory Committee's work was highly contentious. Industry groups were fearful that the Committee's work would serve as additional ammunition for pro-legislation advocates. Privacy advocates suspected industry representatives of participating only to stonewall any challenge to self-regulation. The report went through three significant revisions. At the end of the effort, on May 15, 2000, the Advisory Committee issued a compromise report, *Final Report of the FTC Advisory Committee on Online Access and Security*,[15] that added little to the online privacy debate and did not contain a consensus as to how the various players, including the FTC, should proceed. The report examined alternative views on the

---

[13] *Id.* at 12.
[14] *Id.* at 13-14.
[15] The report is available at http://www.ftc.gov/acoas/papers/finalreport.htm.

problem and solutions, but did not end up setting out any recommendation as to how the sides to the debate might resolve their differences.

SELF-REGULATION WILL NOT SUFFICE

The FTC submitted a prepared statement to the Committee on Commerce, Science and Transportation of the U.S. Senate on May 25, 2000. In that prepared statement, Chairman Pitofsky informed the Committee that the majority of the Commission no longer believed that self-regulation was sufficient:

> Based on the past years of work addressing Internet privacy issues, including examination of prior surveys and workshops with consumers and industry, it is evident that online privacy continues to present an enormous public policy challenge. The Commission applauds the significant efforts of the private sector and commends industry leaders in developing self-regulatory initiatives. The 2000 Survey [the survey conducted by the Commission in February and March 2000 of the busiest U.S. commercial sites], however, demonstrates that industry efforts alone have not been sufficient. Because self-regulatory initiatives to date fall far short of broad-based implementation of effective self-regulatory programs a majority of the Commission has concluded that such efforts alone cannot ensure that the online marketplace as a whole will emulate the standards adopted by industry leaders. While there will continue to be a major role for industry self-regulation in the future, a majority of the Commission recommends that Congress enact legislation that, in conjunction with continuing self-regulatory programs, will ensure adequate protection of consumer privacy online.[16]

ONLINE PROFILING: A FEDERAL TRADE COMMISSION REPORT TO CONGRESS (PART 1, JUNE 2000)

In November 1999, the FTC and the Department of Commerce jointly sponsored a Public Workshop on Online Profiling, focusing

---

[16] Prepared Statement of the Federal Trade Commission on "Privacy Online: Fair Information Practices in the Electronic Marketplace," before the Committee on Commerce, Science, and Transportation, U.S. Senate, Washington, D.C., 4 (May 25, 2000).

on the use of banner ads as a tool to gather information about consumers through the placement of cookies on a consumer's hard drive or "Web bugs," small graphic image files (GIFs), embedded in a Web page that transmit information back to the home server about the computer that downloaded the page containing the GIF.

The FTC defined the problem in Part 1 of the report as follows:

In general, these network advertising companies do not merely supply banner ads; they also gather data about the consumers who view their ads. This is accomplished primarily by the use of "cookies" and "Web bugs" which track the individual's actions on the Web. Among the types of information that can be collected by network advertisers are: information on the Web sites and pages within those sites visited by consumers; the time and duration of the visits; query terms entered into search engines; purchases; "click-through" responses to advertisements; and the Web page a consumer came from before landing on the site monitored by the particular ad network (the referring page). All of this information is gathered even if the consumer never clicks on a single ad.

The information gathered by network advertisers is often, but not always, anonymous, i.e., the profiles are frequently linked to the identification number of the advertising network's cookie on the consumer's computer rather than the name of a specific person. This data is generally referred to as non-personally identifiable information (non-PII). In some circumstances, however, the profiles derived from tracking consumers' activities on the Web are linked or merged with personally identifiable information (PII). This generally occurs in one of two ways when consumers identify themselves to a Web site on which the network advertiser places banner ads. First, the Web site to which personal information is provided may, in turn, provide that information to the network advertiser. Second, depending upon how the personal information is retrieved and processed by the Web site, the personally identifying information may be incorporated into a URL string that is automatically transmitted to the network advertiser through its cookie.

Once collected, consumer data can be analyzed and combined with demographic and "psychographic" data from third-party sources, data on the consumer's offline purchases, or information collected directly from consumers through surveys and registration forms. These enhanced data allow the advertising networks to make a variety of inferences about each consumer's interests and preferences. The result is a detailed profile that attempts to predict the individual consumer's tastes, needs, and purchasing habits and enables the advertising companies' computers to make split-second decisions about how to deliver ads directly targeted to the consumer's specific interests.

The profiles created by the advertising networks can be extremely detailed. A cookie placed by a network advertising company can track a consumer on any Web site served by that company, thereby allowing data collection across disparate and unrelated sites on the Web. Also, because the cookies used by ad networks are generally persistent, their tracking occurs over an extended period of time, resuming each time the individual logs on to the Internet. When this "clickstream" information is combined with third-party data, these profiles can include hundreds of distinct data fields.

Although network advertisers and their profiling activities are nearly ubiquitous, they are most often invisible to consumers. All that consumers see are the Web sites they visit; banner ads appear as seamless, integral parts of the Web pages on which they appear and cookies are placed without any notice to consumers. Unless the Web sites visited by consumers provide notice of the ad network's presence and data collection, consumers may be totally unaware that their activities online are being monitored.[17]

The *Online Profiling Report* contains an excellent discussion of profiling and the privacy issues raised by the collection of personal data online. It does not contain any proposals for addressing those issues. Those recommendations were contained in Part 2 of the report, issued in July. Part 2 of the report came out at the same time as the Network Advertising Initiative issued its principles.

THE NAI PRINCIPLES (JULY 2000)

In an effort to stave off regulation, at the November 1999 Online Profiling Workshop, the leading Internet advertising companies

---

[17] The report can be found at http://www.ftc.gov/privacy/index.html.

formed an industry organization, the Network Advertising Initiative (NAI), to develop privacy recommendations that the members would adopt. Following the Public Workshop, the NAI, the FTC and the Department of Commerce came up with a set of principles that, if implemented, would satisfy the privacy concerns of the regulators. The four NAI principles track the basic 1973 HEW Fair Information Principles—notice, choice, access and security—with the only HEW principle omitted being the one dealing with effective enforcement. The NAI proposal essentially conformed to the fair information principles that the FTC has consistently espoused as basic to any privacy practice:

- *Notice.* The NAI agreed to provide consumers with notice and an opportunity to opt out. If personally identifiable information is to be collected, then "robust" notice (appearing at the time and place of data collection) will be provided. If non-personally identifiable information ("clickstream" data) is to be collected, then notice will be provided in the host Web site's privacy policy.
- *Choice.* The NAI principles adopt an opt-out regime for the most part, although they do adopt a heightened opt-in procedure for certain classes of data.
- *Access.* The NAI principles provide that consumers will be given reasonable access to personally identifiable information. However, the principles do not set out the details of any access program.
- *Security.* The NAI principles provide that network advertisers will make reasonable efforts to protect the profiling data that they collect.

The NAI principles do not set out an enforcement mechanism, either through regulatory oversight or enforcement or through private right of action. In place of an enforcement mechanism, the network advertisers agreed to work with seal and other third-party programs, such as TrustE, to ensure compliance. Privacy advocates believe this to be inadequate.

ONLINE PROFILING: A FEDERAL TRADE COMMISSION REPORT TO CONGRESS (PART 2, JULY 2000)

In the first part of the report, issued on June 13, 2000, the Commission had described the online profiling issues, analyzed industry practices, examined consumer privacy concerns, and had summarized the Commission's efforts to date in addressing those concerns. In the second part, issued on July 27, 2000 and focusing primarily on its approval of the NAI principles, the Commission formally advocated legislation.[18] While commending the NAI "for developing an innovative self-regulatory proposal which addresses the privacy concerns consumers have about online profiling," four of the five FTC Commissioners agreed that federal legislation was necessary to provide effective privacy protection for consumers and to ensure compliance with the NAI principles by non-NAI member companies.[19] As the Commission noted:

> Nonetheless, backstop legislation addressing online profiling is still required to fully ensure that consumers' privacy is protected online. For while NAI's current membership constitutes over 90% of the network advertising industry in terms of revenue and ads served, only legislation can compel the remaining 10% of the industry to comply with fair information practice principles. Self-regulation cannot address recalcitrant and bad actors, new entrants to the market, and drop-outs from the self-regulatory program. In addition, there are unavoidable gaps in the network advertising companies' ability to require host Web sites to post notices about profiling, namely Web sites that do not directly contract with the network advertisers; only legislation can guarantee that notice and choice are always provided in the place and at the time consumers need them.
>
> Accordingly, the Commission recommends legislation that would set forth a basic level of privacy protection for all visitors to consumer-oriented commercial Web sites with respect to profiling. Such legislation would set out the basic standards of practice governing the collection and use of information online for profiling, and provide an implementing agency with the authority to promulgate more detailed standards pursuant to the Administrative Procedure Act, including authority to enforce those standards. In the context of profiling, determining the contours

---

[18] FTC, "Online Profiling: A Report to Congress, Part 2, Recommendations" (July 2000), available at http://www.ftc.gov/privacy/index.html.

[19] (July 27, 2000) FTC Press Release.

of the fair information practice of "choice," in particular, presents special challenges in framing a legislative mandate and in promulgating the required standards, which would require close attention.[20]

Thus, the online profiling area is the second area in which the FTC has advocated federal legislation of online practices, the first being implemented by the Children's Online Privacy Protection Act. We have now seen a clear movement in the five years since the FTC began its work on online privacy, from what had been a willingness to defer to industry self-regulation to a clear recommendation for federal legislation—even in the face of substantial compromise by the NAI—and a willingness to take the lead in promulgating regulations governing the collection and use of personal information online.

THE FTC RETURNS TO INDUSTRY SELF-REGULATION AND INCREASED ENFORCEMENT OF EXISTING LAWS

Since the 2000 reports on online privacy and the passage of COPPA and the Gramm-Leach-Bliley Act in 1998, the FTC seems to be returning to its earlier emphasis on online businesses' self-regulation. In his remarks at the 2001 Privacy Conference in Cleveland, Ohio in October 2001, Chairman Timothy J. Muris announced the Commission's new privacy agenda. Citing the importance of privacy issues to both President George W. Bush and the American people, Chairman Muris outlined an "ambitious, positive, pro-privacy" plan that would begin with the FTC's increasing the amount it spends on privacy-related issues by 50 percent but would not call for the passage of any new Internet privacy legislation.[21]

The first part of the agenda dealing directly with Internet privacy involves cracking down on deceptive spamming practices. The second part deals with the enforcement of privacy policies, including plans (1) to expand and systematize the Commission's review of such policies, (2) to seed lists of consumers with names in order

---

[20] "Online Profiling (Part 2)," N. 18 *supra*, at 10. (Footnotes omitted.)
[21] Remarks by FTC Chairman Timothy J. Muris, "Protecting Consumers' Privacy: 2002 and Beyond," delivered at the Privacy 2001 Conference (Cleveland, Ohio, Oct. 4, 2001), available at http://www.ftc.gov/speeches/muris/privisp1002.htm.

to ensure that businesses honor their restrictions on disclosures to third parties, (3) to work with seal programs and other groups to get referrals of possible privacy violations, (4) to examine claims touting the privacy or security features of products and services, (5) to ensure that U.S. companies adhere to the protections promised under the European Union Safe Harbor Principles, and (6) to improve existing complaint-handling practices.[22]

Third, Chairman Muris emphasized the need for enforcing compliance with COPPA. Fourth, the Commission will conduct workshops with financial regulatory agencies about the readability of the notices required under the Gramm-Leach-Bliley Act. Fifth, it will monitor the progress of the Platform for Privacy Preferences (P3P),[23] an industry-driven initiative that promises to give individuals greater control over the collection of information online by allowing them to specify what level of privacy they wish their Internet browsers to employ while surfing and to screen out sites that do not meet the desired level of privacy. Muris stressed the manageability that P3P offers, claiming it is preferable to the current site-by-site, notice-by-notice regime.[24]

Finally, Muris announced that the FTC would hold back from promulgating new Internet privacy legislation. Although he agreed that federal legislation would help ensure consistency in nationwide information-collection practices, he stressed the difficulty of legislating broad-based privacy protections, the potential difficulties that limiting such protections to the online world could produce (especially in terms of creating two different rules for commercial activity dependent on the medium in which it is conducted), and the need to understand the cost of privacy legislation in the face of slowing Internet growth. Instead, the FTC will concentrate for the time being on enforcing existing privacy legislation while examining the impact of such complicated, far-ranging statutes as the Gramm-Leach-Bliley Act.[25]

---

[22] *Id.*
[23] P3P is discussed in Chapter 13.
[24] *Id.*
[25] *Id.*

FTC ENFORCEMENT ACTIONS

As mentioned above, the FTC does not merely conduct studies and issue reports. It is an enforcement agency. According to the December 1999 FTC report, *The FTC's First Five Years: Protecting Consumers Online (December 1999)*, the FTC had brought over 100 enforcement actions aimed at consumer fraud on the Internet in the period 1994-1999. Although most of the enforcement actions target traditional fraud activities that have migrated onto the Internet (such as pyramid schemes and false healthcare claims), one area of enforcement specifically concerns privacy.

PRIVACY ENFORCEMENT ACTIONS

TOYSMART.COM

Toysmart, an online retailer, went into bankruptcy and during the liquidation sought to sell its database of consumer information along with other assets. The database contained personal and family profiles and such financial information as credit card data. The FTC went to court to stop the sale on the grounds that the sale violated Toysmart's privacy policy, which had stated that Toysmart would "never" disclose that information to third parties.[26] The FTC contended that Toysmart's sale would injure the public by "invading their privacy" in violation of the FTC Act's prohibition on "unfair or deceptive acts or practices in or affecting commerce."[27] The FTC subsequently filed an amended complaint that asserted a second claim for relief under the Children's Online Privacy Protection Act, and the regulations promulgated thereunder.[28] The FTC sought an injunction of any sale of the data by Toysmart. Following the filing of the lawsuit, the FTC and Toysmart reached an agreement on the conditions under which Toysmart could sell the database.[29] Under

---

[26] FTC v. Toysmart.com, 00-CV-11341-RGS (D. Mass. filed July 10, 2000).

[27] Complaint ¶¶ 14, 17.

[28] 16 C.F.R. §§ 312.3-312.5.

[29] FTC Press Release, dated July 21, 2000, available at http://www.ftc.gov/opa/2000/07/toysmart2.htm. See "FTC Approves Toysmart Plan to Sell Its Customer List, With Conditions," *The Wall Street Journal* (July 21, 2000) available at http://interactive.wsj.com/archive/retrieve.cgi?id=SB964205196376235426.djm.

the settlement, Toysmart agreed not to sell the customer database as a stand-alone asset, and agreed to sell it only as part of a package that includes the entire Toysmart Internet site and only to a buyer that was in a related industry and agreed to be bound by Toysmart's privacy policy.

Because Toysmart was in bankruptcy, however, the settlement with the FTC was subject to Bankruptcy Court approval. The Bankruptcy Court rejected the settlement, saying that the settlement could only be considered when an actual buyer presented itself, and until that time it could not determine whether the settlement was in the best interests of the bankrupt estate.[30] In January 2000, Toysmart ended up destroying the database as part of a larger settlement.

A similar issue was presented by the bankruptcy of Living.com, an online furniture retailer. In that case, the Texas Attorney General sued to prevent Living.com from selling its customer data as part of the bankruptcy liquidation. The parties and Bankruptcy Court ultimately worked out a settlement that permitted the sale to third parties as long as customers were given the opportunity to opt out of the sale—presumably requiring their personal information to be removed from the database.[31]

ONLINE PHARMACIES

The FTC charged a group of online pharmacies with making false and deceptive promotional claims. Among other things, the complaint alleged that the sites operated by the defendants misrepresented the security and encryption used to protect consumers' information and that the defendants used the information in a manner contrary to their stated purpose.[32]

---

[30] FTC v. Toysmart.com, Inc., Civ. No. 00-11341-RGS (D. Mass. June 21, 2000). See also, "Judge Rejects Toysmart's Agreement with FTC Because of Lack of Buyer, " *The Wall Street Journal* (Aug. 18, 2000), available at http://interactive.wsj.com/archive/retrieve.cgi?id=SB966545566173284584.djm.

[31] See Richtel, "Technology Briefing: E-Commerce; Limits on Sale of Customer Names," *The New York Times*, at C11 (Sept. 27, 2000). See also, "Dot-Com Liquidations Put Consumer Data in Limbo," *The New York Times*, at C4 (Dec. 4, 2000).

[32] The complaint in FTC v. Rennert can be found at http://www.ftc.gov/os/2000/07/iogcomp.htm.

The defendants entered into a settlement of these and other charges in July 2000. In addition to the settlement of the deceptive claims, the settlement agreement bars defendants from "selling, renting, leasing, transferring or disclosing the personal information that was collected from their customers without express authorization from the customer" and requires defendants to post a privacy policy on their sites conforming with basic fair information practices principles, including disclosure of the information that the sites were collecting through the use of cookies and how that information was used.[33]

REVERSEAUCTION.COM, INC.

The FTC charged ReverseAuction with violating consumers' privacy by taking their personal information from the site of a competitor, eBay, and then sending deceptive spam to the consumers soliciting their business. In addition to agreeing not to engage in these acts in the future, ReverseAuction agreed to delete the personal information of those consumers who did not register with ReverseAuction and to give those who did register notice of the FTC charges and an opportunity to cancel their registration and have their personal information deleted from the ReverseAuction site.[34]

LIBERTY FINANCIAL COMPANIES, INC.

The FTC charged that Liberty Financial falsely represented that it would keep anonymous the personal information it was collecting from children on its Young Investor site. Similar to the remedy in *GeoCities*, discussed below, Liberty Financial agreed to post a privacy policy and obtain parental consent before collecting information from children under thirteen.[35]

---

[33] The FTC press release for this settlement, dated July 12, 2000, can be found at http://www.ftc.gov/opa/2000/07/iog.htm. The settlement can be found at http://www.ftc.gov/os/2000/07/iogstipmort.htm.

[34] The FTC press release for this settlement can be found at http://www.ftc.gov/opa/2000/01/reverse4.htm.

[35] The FTC press release for this settlement can be found at http://www/ftc.gov/opa/1999/9905/younginvestor.htm.

GEOCITIES

This was the first Internet privacy case. The FTC alleged that GeoCities misrepresented the purpose for which it was collecting personal information when it had members register online. GeoCities had represented that the mandatory PII that it was collecting would be used only to provide members with specific advertising or offers that they requested and that the optional information (which included such information as income, marital status and occupation) would not be given to any third party without the member's consent. GeoCities had, in fact, not followed that policy. The FTC complaint also asserted claims with respect to GeoCities' collection of information from children. GeoCities agreed to post a privacy notice and obtain parental consent before collecting information from children under thirteen.[36]

TRANS UNION CORPORATION

Although not strictly an "online" privacy enforcement action, the litigation between the FTC and Trans Union Corporation, one of the leading credit bureaus, is very important.

The FTC and Trans Union Corporation have been engaged in a bitter fight over the credit bureau's rights to use its databases for many years. On April 13, 2001, the Court of Appeals for the D.C. Circuit upheld the order of the FTC prohibiting Trans Union Corporation, which maintains extensive files on almost 200 million adults, from using credit report information about mortgages, automobile loans and lines of credit of individuals without the individuals' consent.[37]

The FTC first challenged Trans Union's practices in 1992. Ultimately, the FTC determined that the lists of names and addresses that Trans Union created and sold were "consumer reports" under the Fair Credit Reporting Act and thus could not be sold for target marketing purposes. Trans Union challenged that determination. The Court of Appeals upheld the determination of the FTC.

---

[36] The FTC press release for this settlement can be found at http://www.ftc.gov/opa/1998/9808/geocities.htm.

[37] Trans Union Corp. v. FTC, No. 00-1141, 2001 U.S. App. LEXIS 6241(D.C. Cir. April 13, 2001).

This ruling affects one of Trans Union's two principal products. Trans Union sells credit reports about individual consumers that it compiles from banks, credit card companies and other lenders. Trans Union receives this credit information from lenders in the form of "tradelines," which typically contain such information as a customer's name, Social Security number, account type, credit limit, account status and payment history. Trans Union receives 1.4 *billion* to 1.6 *billion* records per month, and its credit databases contain information on 190 million adults. The decision of the Court of Appeals does not address or affect this credit report practice.

The decision does affect Trans Union's other principal product— target marketing products. Target marketing products consist of lists of names and addresses of individuals who meet specific criteria, such as possession of an auto loan, credit card or two or more mortgages. Trans Union sells these specialized lists to marketers, who then use them to contact individuals by mail or telephone to offer them services. In connection with its target marketing business, Trans Union maintains a database known as MasterFile, which is a subset of its consumer credit database. MasterFile contains information about every consumer in the credit database that has at least two tradelines with activity during the preceding six months or one tradeline with activity during the previous six months plus a confirmed address. Trans Union can then extract from the MasterFile information about individuals who meet specified criteria of the Trans Union customer, such as, for instance, individuals in a particular geographic area with a minimum credit card limit.

The specific question for the court was whether this sort of report was governed by the Fair Credit Reporting Act of 1970. The FTC determined that this sort of target marketing list was a "consumer report" subject to the Act's limitations.

Trans Union challenged the FTC's determination. The challenge had a lengthy litigation history. The first appeal of the FTC's determination to the D.C. Circuit resulted in a split decision. The court agreed with the FTC that selling consumer reports for target marketing purposes violated the Fair Credit Reporting Act, but set aside the Commission's determination that Trans Union's particular reports violated the Act because the Commission had failed to provide evidence to support the proposition that "the mere existence of a tradeline, as distinguished from payment history organized thereunder," was used or intended to be used for credit-granting decisions, and remanded the matter to the Commission for further proceedings.[38]

Following additional extensive discovery and a lengthy evidentiary hearing before an Administrative Law Judge, the Commission found that the target marketing lists did contain information that credit grantors use as factors in granting credit, and therefore were "consumer lists" governed by the Act. Trans Union appealed to the D.C. Circuit again. This time, faced with a comprehensive evidentiary record, the Court of Appeal affirmed the decision of the Commission that the target marketing lists contain information that is used or is expected to be used for the purpose of serving as a factor in establishing the consumer's eligibility for credit. Among other things, the court rejected Trans Union's challenges to the Fair Credit Reporting Act on grounds of vagueness and under the First Amendment.

AMAZON.COM PRIVACY INVESTIGATION

Note that there is one investigation that did not end up in an enforcement action. In September 2000, Amazon.com altered its privacy policy. Previously, the policy provided that Amazon.com would not share customer data with other companies. The new policy permitted Amazon.com to share customer data with other companies unless a customer expressly opted out and requested that it not. Shortly thereafter, in December, two privacy groups requested that the FTC investigate this change to see if the change constituted an unfair or deceptive trade practice in violation of the FTC Act because it changed a policy that customers had relied on in providing data to Amazon.com in the past. In May 2001, the FTC determined that the revised policy did not materially conflict with representations that Amazon had made in its prior policy and that it likely did not violate the FTC Act because Amazon.com had not sold or traded customer data.

---

[38] Trans Union Corp. v. FTC, 81 F.3d 228, 231-233 (D.C. Cir. 1996).

PRIVACY REGULATION IN THE EUROPEAN UNION AND THE 2000 UNITED STATES-EUROPEAN COMMISSION SAFE HARBOR ACCORD

The Internet market is an international one. There are no technological limits on the exchange of data across international boundaries, and this includes personal information. As Internet businesses and businesses with Internet operations expand their operations globally, they must address differing privacy regulations in different countries. While the name of the game of Internet privacy in the United States has—at least so far—been industry self-regulation, most of the rest of the world has embarked on the road of legislation, in large part modeled after the European Commission 1995 Directive on Data Protection. In addition to the European Union, other countries notable for their advances on the privacy front include the principal trading partners of the U.S.—the United Kingdom and Canada.

How other countries deal with online privacy issues is critically important because the Internet is the paradigmatic global medium. An individual in Thailand can order from Amazon.com just like an individual in Florida—and, soon enough, may also be able to download the desired book just as easily. Personal data can be sent across borders and continents with a push of the "enter" key. Divergent rules governing the use of personal data in different countries will inhibit one of the most significant characteristics of the Internet—the instantaneous movement of any type of digitized information.

Currently, there are fifteen member states in the European Union (the EU): Austria, Belgium, Denmark, Finland, France, Germany,

Greece, Luxembourg, Ireland, Italy, the Netherlands, Portugal, Spain, Sweden and the United Kingdom. Additional countries are likely to join over the next few years.

The need for compatible privacy rules in member states of the EU in order to achieve the goal of barrier-less commerce has driven the EU countries to adopt compatible privacy rules that are stricter than those of the U.S. The regulatory guideposts for privacy matters in Europe are the *OECD Guidelines on the Protection of Privacy and Transborder Flows of Personal Data* (1980), the *Council of Europe Convention on Privacy* (1981), and the *EC Directive on Data Protection* (1995) (effective October 1998). We review those briefly, and then we turn to the Safe Harbor Agreement that the U.S. and European Commission entered into in July 2000.[1]

THE OECD GUIDELINES (1980)

In 1980 the Council of the Organization for Economic Co-operation and Development (OECD) issued recommendations and guidelines governing transborder flow of personal data. The gist of the Council's recommendations was that member countries take into account in their domestic legislation the privacy principles presented in the annexed Guidelines. The Guidelines had eight basic principles:

Collection Limitation Principle
There should be limits to the collection of personal data and any such data should be obtained by lawful and fair means and, where appropriate, with the knowledge or consent of the data subject [i.e., the individual about whom the data are collected].

Data Quality Principle
Personal data should be relevant to the purposes for which they are to be used, and, to the extent necessary for those purposes, should be accurate, complete and kept up-to-date.

Purpose Specification Principle
The purposes for which personal data are collected should be specified not later than at the time of data collection and the subsequent use limited to the fulfillment of those purposes or

---

[1] The European Commission is the executive branch of the EU.

such others as are not incompatible with those purposes and as are specified on each occasion of change of purpose.

Use Limitation Principle

Personal data should not be disclosed, made available, or otherwise used for purposes other than those specified in accordance with Paragraph 9 except: (a) with the consent of the data subject; or (b) by the authority of law.

Security Safeguards Principle

Personal data should be protected by reasonable security safeguards against such risks as loss or unauthorized access, destruction, use, modification or disclosure of data.

Openness Principle

There should be a general policy of openness about developments, practices and policies with respect to personal data. Means of establishing the existence and nature of personal data, and the main purposes of their use, as well as the identity and usual residence of the data controller, should be readily available.

Individual Participation Principle

An individual should have the right:

(a) to obtain from a data controller, or otherwise, confirmation of whether or not the data controller has data relating to him;

(b) to have communicated to him, data relating to him (i) within a reasonable time; (ii) at a charge, if any, that is not excessive; (iii) in a reasonable manner; and (iv) in a form that is readily intelligible to him;

(c) to be given reasons if a request under subparagraphs (a) and (b) is denied, and to be able to challenge such denial; and

(d) to challenge data relating to him and, if the challenge is successful, to have the data erased, rectified, completed or amended.

Accountability Principle

A data controller should be accountable for complying with measures that give effect to the principles stated above.[2]

---

[2] These eight principles are set out in paragraphs 7-14 of the *Guidelines*.

The guidelines were not mandatory, nor did the recommendations provide for any mechanism to enforce compliance with these guidelines. The basic principles track closely the Fair Information Principles of the 1973 HEW Report, although they provide some additional detail and expand on some of the core principles.

COUNCIL OF EUROPE CONVENTION ON PRIVACY (1981)

After the OECD Guidelines, the member states of the Council of Europe next executed a Convention on Privacy, signed on January 28, 1981. The Convention was entered into force on (i.e., had an effective date of) October 1, 1985. The Convention's stated purpose was "to secure in the territory of each Party for every individual . . . respect for his rights and fundamental freedoms, and in particular his right to privacy, with regard to automatic processing of personal data relating to him." (Article 1). Each member state was required by October 1, 1985 "to take the necessary measures in its domestic law to give effect to the basic principles for data protection" set out in the Convention. The Convention set out the following privacy principles, which applied to both public and private entities:

Article 5: Quality of data
a. obtained and processed fairly and lawfully;

b. stored for specified and legitimate purposes and not used in a way incompatible with those purposes;

c. adequate, relevant and not excessive in relation to the purposes for which they are stored;

d. accurate and, where necessary, kept up to date;

e. preserved in a form which permits identification of the data subjects for no longer than is required for the purpose for which those data are stored.

Article 6: Special categories of data
Personal data revealing racial origin, political opinions or religious or other beliefs, as well as personal data concerning health or sexual life, may not be processed automatically unless domestic law provides appropriate safeguards. The same shall apply to personal data relating to criminal convictions.

Article 7: Data security
Appropriate security measures against accidental or unauthorized destruction or accidental loss as well as against unauthorized

access, alteration or dissemination shall be taken for the protection of personal data stored in automated data files.

Article 8: Additional safeguards for the data subject

Any person shall be enabled:

a. to establish the existence of an automated personal data file, its main purposes, as well as the identity and habitual residence or principal place of business of the controller of the file;

b. to obtain, at reasonable levels and without excessive delay or expense, confirmation of whether personal data relating to him are stored in the automated data file as well as communication to him of such data in an intelligible form;

c. to obtain, as the case may be, rectification or erasure of such data if these have been processed contrary to the provisions of domestic law giving effect to the basic principles set out in Articles 5 and 6 of this convention;

d. to have a remedy if a request for confirmation or, as the case may be, communication, rectification or erasure as referred to in paragraphs b and c of this article is not complied with.

Article 9: Exceptions and restrictions

1. No exception to the provisions of Articles 5, 6 and 8 of this convention shall be allowed except within the limits defined in this article.

2. Derogation from the provisions of Articles 5, 6 and 8 of this convention shall be allowed when such derogation is provided for by the law of the Party and constitutes a necessary measure in a democratic society in the interests of:

a. protecting State security, public safety, the monetary interests of the State or the suppression of criminal offences;

b. protecting the data subject or the rights and freedoms of others.

3. Restrictions on the exercise of the rights specified in Article 8, paragraphs b, c and d, may be provided by law with respect to automated personal data files used for statistics or for scientific research purposes when there is obviously no risk of an infringement of the privacy of the data subjects.

Article 10: Sanctions and remedies

Each Party undertakes to establish appropriate sanctions and remedies for violations of provisions of domestic law giving effect to the basic principles for data protection set out in this chapter.

Putting aside some relatively minor differences in the scope of the principles, the main impact of the Convention came from Article 10, which expressly provided that member states would establish sanctions and remedies for violations of the privacy principles.

THE EC DIRECTIVE (DIRECTIVE 95/46/EC)

The next step in the evolution of pan-European privacy standards occurred when the EU adopted 95/46/EC Directive on Data Protection on October 24, 1998. Under Article 32 of the Directive, the member states had three years to put in place the laws or regulations necessary to comply with the Directive.[3]

Overall, the statutory privacy protections of the EC Directive are significantly more stringent and far-reaching than those presently governing American companies. The Directive prescribes, as a general rule, that "data which are capable by their nature of infringing fundamental freedoms or privacy should not be processed unless the data subject gives his explicit consent."[4]

Under the EC Directive, member states are required to provide by legislation or otherwise that any personal data that are processed by automatic means or are otherwise part of a filing system are: (1) processed fairly and lawfully; (2) collected for specified, explicit and legitimate purposes; (3) adequate, relevant and not excessive in relation to the purposes; (4) accurate and kept up-to-date; and (5) kept in a form that only permits identification of the data subject for as long as such identification is necessary.[5]

As stated above, the general rule is that no data can be processed without the express consent of the "data subject." The "explicit consent" rule is not without exceptions, however. If processing is necessary for the performance of a contract to which the data subject is a party; for compliance with a legal obligation;

---

[3] As with any EU directive, the compliance rate is inconsistent among the member states. Consequently, the European Commission announced in January 2000 that it intended to take France, Germany, Ireland, Luxembourg, and the Netherlands to the European Court of Justice in Luxembourg for failure to implement fully the Data Protection Directive.

[4] 95/46/EC Preamble (33).

[5] 95/46/EC Art. 6.

to protect the vital interests of the data subject; or to carry out a task in the public interest, the data can still be processed. In addition, there is a catch-all provision that states that if the processing is necessary for purposes of legitimate interests pursued by the data controller, it is allowed, provided those interests are not over-ridden by the interests of fundamental rights and freedoms of the data subject.[6]

Moreover, the EC Directive contains a special prohibition for processing of data that reveal racial or ethnic origin, political opinions, religious or philosophical beliefs, trade-union membership, and data concerning health or sex life.

United States-European Commission "Safe Harbor" Data Privacy Accord

Article 25 of the EC Directive states that the member states are obliged to provide that transfers of personal data from a member state to a third country (such as, for instance, the United States) may only take place if the third country in question ensures an adequate level of protection, assessed in light of all the circumstances.[7] In essence, Article 25 requires that the level of privacy protection in the third country to which the data are transferred be comparable to EU standards under the Directive, and bars the transfer of PII of EU citizens to countries that do not have "adequate" privacy regulations—i.e., the United States.

Article 25 presented an obstacle to commerce with the U.S., which did not (and still does not) have a level of protection "adequate" by EC standards. Because a transfer of PII occurs each time EU citizens fill out a registration statement on a U.S. site, for example, the EC Directive could, at least in theory, have barred many commercial transactions on the Internet.

Faced with this impediment to transatlantic e-commerce, the U.S. Department of Commerce and the European Commission embarked on lengthy and complicated negotiations to come up with a mechanism to satisfy the Directive's requirement. These

---

[6] 95/46/EC Art. 7.
[7] 95/46/EC Art. 25.

negotiations were called the "Safe Harbor" negotiations because they had the goal of developing a safe harbor that would permit EU companies to transfer PII to U.S. companies that were in compliance with the guidelines that were to be set forth in the Safe Harbor Accord.

After many months of negotiation, on May 31, 2000, the U.S. Department of Commerce and European Commission announced that they had reached a compromise agreement on regulation governing exchange of personal data.[8] Following some wrangling and opposition in the European Union Parliament, the European Parliament, and the U.S. Department of Commerce, the Commission approved the Safe Harbor Accord on July 27, 2000.[9]

The Accord became effective on November 1, 2000. The U.S. Department of Commerce set up a Web site, www.export.gov/safeharbor, to assist companies in taking advantage of the Accord, though companies have been very slow to do so.[10] The reason for the lax attitude of U.S. companies remains unclear. One problem may be lack of knowledge about the protections of the Accord.

On March 27, 2001, the EC approved model contractual clauses for the transfer of personal data to third countries.[11] The U.S. Commerce and Treasury Departments opposed the standard clauses, which would require U.S. firms to operate under the EU privacy standards. Among other things, U.S. companies will be liable in court for actions by their European partners and be bound by any legal settlements that European partner companies enter into. Whether these standard contractual clauses ultimately go into effect remains uncertain, and because they are only one alternative

---

[8] For the letter from the International Trade Association transmitting the Accord to the Department of Commerce, see www.export.gov/safeharbor/larussacovernote 717.htm (visited Feb. 4, 2002).

[9] The text of the Commission decision and related materials, including the safe harbor principles, is located at http://europa.eu.int/comm/internal_market/en/media/dataprot/news/safeharbor.htm.

[10] Id. See "Safe Harbor List," http://web.ita.doc.gov/safeharbor/shlist.nsf/webPages/safe+harbor+list.

[11] The Commission Decision, which includes forms of the standard clauses, can be found at http://europa.eu.int/comm/internal_market/en/media/dataprot/news/clausesdecision.htm.

way to ensure that companies comply with the EC Directive lawfully to transfer personal data to a third country, the dispute may turn
out to be something of a tempest in a teapot.

Key Benefits of the Safe Harbor Accord

The Safe Harbor Accord offers substantial benefits to U.S. companies. These benefits include:

- All fifteen EU member states will be bound by the EC's finding
  of adequacy.
- Companies participating in the safe harbor will be deemed
  adequate, and data flow to these companies will continue.
- Member State requirements for prior approval of data transfers
  either will be waived or approval will be automatically granted.
- Claims brought by an EU citizen will be heard in the U.S.

Basic Structure of the Safe Harbor Accord

From the perspective of U.S. companies, the key to taking advantage of the Accord is following the principles contained in the July
21, 2000 Decision issued by the European Commission. The Department of Commerce issued a set of privacy principles that companies would have to comply with in order to come within the
Accord. The European Commission also stated in its Decision that
compliance with these principles would be sufficient to satisfy the
"adequate level of protection" required by Directive 95/46/EC. The
principles were annexed to the Commission's Decision. Because of
the importance of this annex, we include the full text of the principles below.

Safe Harbor Privacy Principles Issued by the
U.S. Department of Commerce on July 21, 2000

NOTICE: An organization must inform individuals about the purposes for which it collects and uses information about them,
how to contact the organization with any inquiries or complaints, the types of third parties to which it discloses the information, and the choices and means the organization offers individuals for limiting its use and disclosure. This notice must be
provided in clear and conspicuous language when individuals are
first asked to provide personal information to the organization or
as soon thereafter as is practicable, but in any event before the

organization uses such information for a purpose other than that for which it was originally collected or processed by the transferring organization or discloses it for the first time to a third party.

CHOICE: An organization must offer individuals the opportunity to choose (opt out) whether their personal information is (a) to be disclosed to a third party or (b) to be used for a purpose that is incompatible with the purpose(s) for which it was originally collected or subsequently authorized by the individual. Individuals must be provided with clear and conspicuous, readily available, and affordable mechanisms to exercise choice.

For sensitive information (*i.e.*, personal information specifying medical or health conditions, racial or ethnic origin, political opinions, religious or philosophical beliefs, trade union membership or information specifying the sex life of the individual), they must be given affirmative or explicit (opt-in) choice if the information is to be disclosed to a third party or used for a purpose other than those for which it was originally collected or subsequently authorized by the individual through the exercise of opt-in choice. In any case, an organization should treat as sensitive any information received from a third party where the third party treats and identifies it as sensitive.

ONWARD TRANSFER: To disclose information to a third party, organizations must apply the Notice and Choice Principles. Where an organization wishes to transfer information to a third party that is acting as an agent, as described in the endnote, it may do so if it first either ascertains that the third party subscribes to the Principles or is subject to the Directive or another adequacy finding or enters into a written agreement with such third party requiring that the third party provide at least the same level of privacy protection as is required by the relevant Principles. If the organization complies with these requirements, it shall not be held responsible (unless the organization agrees otherwise) when a third party to which it transfers such information processes it in a way contrary to any restrictions or representations, unless the organization knew or should have known the third party would process it in such a contrary way and the organization has not taken reasonable steps to prevent or stop such processing.

SECURITY: Organizations creating, maintaining, using or disseminating personal information must take reasonable precautions to protect it from loss, misuse and unauthorized access, disclosure, alteration and destruction.

DATA INTEGRITY: Consistent with the Principles, personal information must be relevant for the purposes for which it is to be used. An organization may not process personal information in a way that is incompatible with the purposes for which it has been collected or subsequently authorized by the individual. To the extent necessary for those purposes, an organization should take reasonable steps to ensure that data is reliable for its intended use, accurate, complete, and current.

ACCESS: Individuals must have access to personal information about them that an organization holds and be able to correct, amend, or delete that information where it is inaccurate, except where the burden or expense of providing access would be disproportionate to the risks to the individual's privacy in the case in question, or where the rights of persons other than the individual would be violated.

ENFORCEMENT: Effective privacy protection must include mechanisms for assuring compliance with the Principles, recourse for individuals to whom the data relate affected by non-compliance with the Principles, and consequences for the organization when the Principles are not followed. At a minimum, such mechanisms must include (a) readily available and affordable independent recourse mechanisms by which each individual's complaints and disputes are investigated and resolved by reference to the Principles and damages awarded where the applicable law or private sector initiatives so provide; (b) follow-up procedures for verifying that the attestations and assertions businesses make about their privacy practices are true and that privacy practices have been implemented as presented; and (c) obligations to remedy problems arising out of failure to comply with the Principles by organizations announcing their adherence to them and consequences for such organizations. Sanctions must be sufficiently rigorous to ensure compliance by organizations.

As is clear, the Safe Harbor principles track the basic privacy principles that the U.S. has been following since 1973 and that the

FTC has made the core of its enforcement and regulatory efforts: notice, choice, security, access and enforcement, elaborated somewhat by two additional principles—onward transfer and data integrity. Notably, the Safe Harbor Principles rely on an opt-out regime to satisfy the "choice" principle.

The best document for an organization seeking to learn more about the Safe Harbor Agreement to utilize is a set of answers to frequently asked questions issued by the Department of Commerce. These FAQs, along with the other Safe Harbor Accord official documents from both the U.S. and EU, are on the Department of Commerce Web site created for the Safe Harbor Accord.[12]

The topics covered by the FAQs are:

1. Sensitive Data
2. Journalistic Exceptions
3. Secondary Liability
4. Investment Banking and Audits
5. The Role of the Data Protection Agencies
6. Self-Certification
7. Verification
8. Access
9. Human Resources
10. Article 17 Contracts
11. Dispute Resolution and Enforcement
12. Choice—Timing of Opt-out
13. Travel Information
14. Pharmaceutical and Medical Products
15. Public Record and Publicly Available Information

CHECKLIST OF BASIC PRINCIPLES OF SAFE HARBOR ACCORD

Here are some practical pointers for any company seeking to comply with the Safe Harbor Accord. Note that this is not a complete checklist, and you should visit the Department of Commerce Web site for more details and probably consult an attorney familiar with the Safe Harbor Accord.

---

[12] See http://www.export.gov/safeharbor/sh_workbook.html.

1. When you ask an individual to provide personal information, you must inform the individual why you wish to collect the information and how it will be used, including to what third parties you intend to disclose the information.

2. You can only collect personal information that is relevant for the purposes for which it is to be used.

3. You must indicate if and how the individual can limit the use and disclosure of information provided.

4. Generally, you must offer individuals the option to opt out and limit the use of their information.

5. However, if you request particularly sensitive information, you must give individuals an opportunity to opt in. In other words, before you disclose the information to a third party or use it for purposes other than those stated at the time of collection, you must contact the individual and obtain his or her affirmative permission. There are some exceptions to this rule, such as where the processing of information is in the vital interest of the individual or if the processing is necessary to establish legal claims or defenses, or required to provide medical care, or if it relates to data that are manifestly made public by the individual.

6. You must tell those individuals from whom you are obtaining personal information how they can contact your organization with inquiries or complaints.

7. As a general matter, individuals have the right to access personal information about them that you hold and to correct, amend or delete inaccurate information. This right to access is subject to principles of proportionality and reasonableness. The individual's right to access may be weighed against expense and burden, but those factors are not controlling in determining reasonableness. If an access request is broad or vague, you should contact the individual and work out with him or her how access can best be provided. Note that an individual is not required to justify requests for access to his or her own data.

8. You may transfer information to third parties as long as you comply with the principles of notice and choice.

9. You must take reasonable steps to ensure the accuracy and security of the information that you collect.

10. If you have not complied with the choice principle, you may still transfer the information to a third party, but only if you first either (1) ascertain that the third party in question subscribes to the Safe Harbor principles, or (2) enter into a written agreement with the third party that it will subscribe to the principle. If you comply with one of the above alternatives, absent bad faith, you cannot be held liable in the event that the third party transfers or otherwise processes the information obtained in conflict with the principles of notice and choice.

11. You need to demonstrate that you have complied with the Safe Harbor principles. The easiest method of complying is through self-certification. In order to self-certify, you must file a Safe Harbor statement with the Department of Commerce certifying that you will comply with the Safe Harbor principles, including that you will cooperate with the European data protection agencies, will assist those agencies in investigating and resolving complaints under the Safe Harbor, and will comply with advice given by the agencies. The specific information that must be included in the certification is contained in FAQ 7 on the Department of Commerce Web site. Among other things, you must disclose the method of verification that you have adopted (internal or third-party) and the recourse mechanism that you have agreed to follow in the event of complaints.

12. You also must comply with the verification requirement of the Safe Harbor Accord. To do so, you can file a self-assessment verification or can choose verification by an outside organization. A number of organizations offer these third-party privacy verifications.

13. You can comply with the EC Directive without adhering to the Safe Harbor Accord. For instance, the Directive permits the transfer of personal information if the subject has given his or her consent or if the transfer of personal information is made to fulfill a contract involving the data subject (Article 26(1)). The Directive also permits the transfer when the

exporter of the information can demonstrate that adequate safeguards are in place through some other means, such as a contract between the exporter and the importer of the information (Article 26(2)).

14. You need not comply with notice, choice and onward transfer principles if you are dealing with information that is strictly of a public record nature. Public records are records kept by government agencies or other entities that are open to consultation by the public in general. Any time public information is combined with nonpublic information, however, all Safe Harbor principles apply.

15. You need to provide a dispute resolution mechanism. You have some options on this matter, one of which is compliance with a private sector privacy program that includes a satisfactory dispute resolution procedure. Separate and apart from compliance enforcement by private sector bodies, non-compliance is also actionable under Section 5 of the Federal Trade Commission Act, which prohibits misrepresentation and deceptive trade practices.

CHAPTER 11

PRIVACY REGULATION IN OTHER FOREIGN COUNTRIES

In this chapter, we provide a survey of some of the approaches that specific countries outside of the EU have adopted with respect to online privacy. Most important for the United States is likely to be the approaches of its most significant trading partners, Canada and the United Kingdom. In order to make this chapter as comprehensive as possible, however, we include the approaches of a number of other countries as well. As might be expected, the regulatory and statutory environment in more than a few of these countries is in flux, just as it is in the United States. Accordingly, we advise any interested reader to check the current status in each country discussed below.

Certain basic conclusions can be drawn from the study below.

First, the principles set out in the EC Directive[1] (with some modifications) are becoming dominant in most of the countries relevant to U.S. economic activity. In addition to the EU countries, Canada, the United Kingdom and Australia have enacted new privacy legislation, bringing their regulatory regimes into conformity with the EU.

Second, the U.S.'s principal trading partners, and the countries between which there is the most transborder financial investment, have adopted privacy rules that are more stringent than anything in the U.S. What this means as a practical matter is that U.S. companies, even if they have not adopted comparable privacy policies, will

---

[1] The EC Directive is discussed in Chapter 10.

have to do so to the extent that they do business with companies governed by the rules in force in the EU, the United Kingdom and Canada. This includes just about every significant corporation in the United States, and a great number of smaller corporations, too.

Third, the legislative activity by the principal trading partners of the U.S. provides further incentive for similar legislative activity by the U.S. Congress.

CANADA

CANADIAN PERSONAL INFORMATION PROTECTION AND ELECTRONIC DOCUMENTS ACT OF 2000 (EFFECTIVE JANUARY 1, 2001)

Canada has had a Privacy Act comparable to the U.S. Privacy Act since 1983. Just as is the U.S. Act, the Canadian Privacy Act is limited to *governmental* collection of personal information. It does not apply to use of PII by private entities online or offline.

Canada, unlike the U.S., however, has taken concrete steps to address the problems of collection and use of personal data by private organizations. On January 1, 2001, a new law took effect in Canada, the Personal Information Protection and Electronic Documents Act, to regulate comprehensively the way that private organizations can collect, use, keep secure and disclose personal information.[2] Its applicability, initially limited to "federal works, undertakings, and businesses," will be phased in, and by January 1, 2004 anyone doing business in Canada will have to comply with its provisions. Even at the outset, its scope is fairly broad, since federally regulated organizations such as banks and telecommunication and transportation companies are covered. The Act is not limited to online privacy, but applies to personal information gathered offline as well.

In short, Bill C-6, as the legislation is also known, would make it illegal for a company covered by the legislation to collect personal information and use it for purposes other than the stated objective, unless a consumer gives express consent. It gives consumers the right to know what information an organization collects about them and gives them a mechanism to correct errors.

---

[2] The text of the Act can be found at http://www.privcom.gc.ca/legislation/ 02_06_01_e.asp (visited Feb. 7, 2002).

The Canadian Act requires compliance with ten basic privacy principles: (1) providing accountability; (2) identifying purposes; (3) requiring consent; (4) limiting collection; (5) limiting use, disclosure and retention; (6) providing accuracy; (7) supplying safeguards; (8) providing openness; (9) giving individual access; and (10) providing recourse. A short description of these ten principles follows, but the Act contains additional detail and must be consulted by any company doing business in Canada.

1. **Accountability**

   An organization is responsible for personal information under its control and shall designate an individual or individuals who are accountable for the organization's compliance with the following principles.

2. **Identifying Purposes**

   The purposes for which personal information is collected shall be identified by the organization at or before the time the information is collected.

3. **Consent**

   The knowledge and consent of the individual about whom data are to be collected are required for the collection, use or disclosure of personal information, except where inappropriate.

4. **Limiting Collection**

   The collection of personal information shall be limited to that which is necessary for the purposes identified by the organization. Information shall be collected by fair and lawful means.

5. **Limiting Use, Disclosure and Retention**

   Personal information shall not be used or disclosed for purposes other than those for which it was collected, except with the consent of the individual or as required by law. Personal information shall be retained only as long as necessary for the fulfillment of those purposes.

6. **Accuracy**

   Personal information shall be as accurate, complete and up-to-date as is necessary for the purposes for which it is to be used.

7. **Safeguards**
    Personal information shall be protected by security safe-guards appropriate to the sensitivity of the information.

8. **Openness**
    An organization shall make readily available to individuals specific information about its policies and practices relating to the management of personal information.

9. **Individual Access**
    Upon request, an individual shall be informed of the existence, use and disclosure of his or her personal information and shall be given access to that information. An individual shall be able to challenge the accuracy and completeness of the information and have it amended as appropriate.

10. **Challenging Compliance**
    An individual shall be able to address a challenge concerning compliance with the above principles to the designated individual or individuals accountable for the organization's compliance.

Bill C-6 is an important step forward in privacy regulation. What it means as a practical matter is that one of the U.S.'s principal trading partners has moved far ahead of the U.S. in developing a comprehensive approach to protection of personal data, one that is in line with the EU. Bill C-6 will provide added basic economic incentive for the U.S. to take additional steps domestically, since many companies will now have to conform to the Canadian statute and regulation. The Act applies to onward transfer within Canada and abroad. An organization is responsible for information transferred to third parties, and needs consent of the subject before transferring the information to third parties. An organization shall use contractual or other means to provide a comparable level of protection while information is processed by third parties.

In January 2001, the EC Working Party issued a report evaluating the Canadian Act, including some reservations.[3]

---

[3] Available at www.europa.eu.int/comm/internal_market/en/media/dataprot/wpdocs/index.htm.

UNITED KINGDOM

On July 16, 1998, the Data Protection Act of 1998[4] came into force and replaced the U.K.'s previous privacy legislation, the Data Protection Act of 1984. The new law was designed to make U.K. rules compatible with the EC Directive, and had an effective date of March 1, 2000.

AUSTRALIA

In 2000, Australia, like its counterpart Commonwealth countries, Canada and the United Kingdom, enacted legislation to protect consumers' privacy. The Privacy Amendment Act of 2000 imposes requirements on private organizations and regulates comprehensively how private sector organizations can collect, use, keep secure and disclose personal information. The Privacy Amendment provides a mechanism for consumers to review and correct personal information collected about them, and also creates a mechanism for complaints. It applies to all private organizations with a turnover of $3 million (Australian), about $1.6 million U.S. The Privacy Amendment also specifically prohibits transborder transfers of PII unless the transfers are in accordance with the Amendment. The rules apply as of December 21, 2001; small businesses are subject to the rules as of December 21, 2002.[5]

In short, the Australian legislation requires adherence to ten privacy rules, referred to as the National Privacy Principles. A summary of these principles follows:

1. **Collection**
   An organization must not collect personal information unless the information is necessary for one or more of its functions and activities.

2. **Use and Disclosure**
   As a general matter, an organization must not use or disclose personal information about an individual for a purpose other than the primary purpose of collection. (There are some exceptions that follow in the statute itself.)

---

[4] The Act can be found at http://www.hmso.gov.uk/acts/acts1998/19980029.htm.
[5] The law and related information are available at http://www.privacy.gov.au.

3. **Data Quality**

   An organization must take reasonable steps to make sure that the personal information it collects, uses or discloses is accurate, complete and up-to-date.

4. **Data Security**

   An organization must take reasonable steps to protect the personal information that it holds from misuse and loss and from unauthorized access, modification or disclosure, and must take reasonable steps to destroy the information if it is no longer needed for a legitimate purpose.

5. **Openness**

   An organization must set out in a document its policies and must make the document available to anyone who asks for it and must take reasonable steps to let an individual know what sort of information it holds and for what purposes.

6. **Access and Correction**

   An organization must provide the individual with an opportunity to review and correct personal information, but not for certain express exceptions.

7. **Identifiers**

   An organization must not adopt as its own identifier of an individual an identifier of the individual that has been assigned by a governmental agency.

8. **Anonymity**

   Whenever lawful and practical, an individual must have the option of not identifying him- or herself when entering transactions.

9. **Transborder Data Flows**

   An organization may only transfer personal information to someone in a foreign country under specified conditions (comparable to those imposed by the EC Directive).

10. **Sensitive Information**

    An organization must not collect sensitive information (such as health information) except under specified conditions.

In early 2001, the European Commission studied the Privacy Amendment and expressed some concerns about Australia's ability to protect employee data and secondary use of published data.[6]

AUSTRIA

In the Fall of 1999, the Austrian government introduced its new data protection legislation.[7] The statute is quite controversial in that it goes even further than Directive 95/46/EC requires. In particular, under the new Austrian legislation, not only individuals but also corporations and other organizations have a right to privacy.

BRAZIL

There is no privacy policy in Brazil. Federal Senate Bill No. 61, which has been pending in the National Congress since 1996, provides that, "No personal data nor [sic] information shall be disclosed, communicated, or transmitted for purposes different to those that led to structuring such data registry or database, without express authorization of the owner."[8]

CHINA AND HONG KONG

The Chinese Ministry of State Security issued regulations extending the Secrets Act to the Internet.[9] The regulations require individuals and companies to disclose what types of security and encryption systems they are using and to have applied for permission by February 2000.[10] The order sets up a State Encryption Management Commission to enforce the regulations.[11]

Privacy rights in Hong Kong are more extensive than those in China and are clearly outlined in the Personal Data (Privacy)

---

[6] The comments of the EC Working Party can be found at www.europa.eu.int/comm/interna_lmarket/en/media/dataprot/wpdocs/index.htm.

[7] See generally, http://www.parlament.gv.at/ (search available in German only).

[8] See Fed. S. Bill No. 61, 1996, at http://www.privacyexchange.org/legal/ppl/nat/brazilpending.html (visited March 18, 2002) (English translation).

[9] Private Parts Online 2000: The International Privacy Newswire, at http://www.privacyinternational.org/parts/index.html (visited March 18, 2002).

[10] Id.

[11] Id.

Ordinance, which became effective on December 20, 1996. The purpose of the Ordinance is to protect the privacy interests of living individuals in relation to personal data.[12] The Ordinance also contributes to Hong Kong's continued economic well-being by safeguarding the free flow of personal data to Hong Kong from restriction by countries that already have data protection laws.[13]

Specifically, the Ordinance covers any data relating directly or indirectly to a living individual (data subject), from which it is practicable to ascertain the identity of the individual and which are in a form in which access or processing is practicable.[14] It applies to any person (data user) who controls the collection, holding, processing or use of personal data.[15] The Ordinance gives data subjects the right to confirm with data users whether their personal data are held, to obtain a copy of such data, and to have personal data corrected.[16] Any charge for providing personal data to a data subject may not be excessive.[17] Data subjects may also make a complaint to the Privacy Commissioner for Personal Data about a suspected breach of the Ordinance's requirements and claim compensation through civil proceedings for damage they have suffered as a result of a violation of the Ordinance.[18]

FINLAND

After the adoption of the EC Directive, Finland slightly modified its preexisting legislation ensuring Finnish citizens certain rights regarding their personal data, The Personal Data File Act, dating from 1987. Thus, on June 1, 1999, the new Personal Data Act (523/1999) took effect and made Finnish domestic law consistent with the Directive. Finland has a Data Protection Ombudsman who receives complaints and conducts investigations in order to enforce the Act.[19]

---

[12] The Ordinance at a Glance, at http://www.pco.org.hk//english/ordinance/ordglance.html (visited March 18, 2002).
[13] Id.
[14] Id.
[15] Id.
[16] Id.
[17] Id.
[18] Id.
[19] Electronic Privacy Information Center and Privacy International, "Privacy and Human Rights: An International Survey of Privacy Laws and Developments," 70 (1999).

GERMANY

Although Germany is one of the countries that have been criticized by the European Commission for failure to implement fully the Directive, Germany is one of the EU countries that not only had, but enforced, strict privacy legislation even before the Directive came into force. As early as 1994, Citibank was subject to the German privacy laws.[20] Citibank had embarked with the German National Railway on a co-branding agreement that would become the biggest credit card project in German history.[21] But because the project would involve U.S. processing of personal data of millions of German citizens, the German data protection authorities—in responding to a public outcry—threatened to prohibit the agreement unless the privacy of the cardholders could be acceptably ensured.[22] After lengthy negotiations, the two companies reached an agreement setting forth a wide range of privacy protection measures that required Citibank to change significantly its customer information management.[23]

In addition, in 1998, one German court decided that Deutsche Bahn had to erase data relating to its "BahnCard" clients that it had forwarded to Citibank.[24]

The German Federal Data Protection Act of December 20, 1990, last amended December 17, 1997, provides for the protection of individual privacy in the collection, use and handling of the individual's personal data.[25] Personal data is defined as any information concerning the personal or material circumstances of an identified or identifiable individual.[26] Germany is also in the process of

---

[20] Davies, "Europe to US: No Privacy, No Trade," at http://wired.com/wired/6.05/europe.html (visited March 18, 2002).

[21] Id.

[22] Id.

[23] Id.

[24] See reference to judgment at http://www.datenschutz-berlin.de/recht/de/recht_de.htm (visited March 18, 2002).

[25] Federal Data Protection Act, http://www.datenschutz-berlin.de/gesetze/bdsg/bdsgeng.htm (visited March 18, 2002).

[26] Id. at § 3.

amending its data protection law. The federal government adopted a draft bill in June 2000. The amendment takes the Directive into account by expressly referring to the EC Directive in Section 4(b).[27]

GREECE

Greece is one of the member states that are currently in compliance with the EC Directive. (Although every European country has rules on data protection, only Italy, Sweden, Greece and the U.K. fully comply.) In 1997, the law on the Protection of Individuals with Regard to the Processing of Personal Data was approved, thus making Greece's domestic law consistent with the Directive.[28]

INDIA

India's lower house of parliament, the Lok Sabha, passed an Information Technology bill designed to build a framework for electronic commerce. The Senate approved the bill by a voice vote on May 17, 2000.[29] The bill addresses privacy concerns by stipulating punishment with imprisonment for a term which may extend two years or with a fine or both for "any person who . . . has secured access to any electronic record, book, register, correspondence, information, document or other material without the consent of the person concerned [and] discloses such material to any other person."[30] Sections of the bill that required cybercafes to keep detailed records of users and their activities were dropped.[31]

---

[27] Entwurf des Bundesministeriums des Inneren, dated March 16, 2000, http://www.datenschutz-berlin.de/recht/de/recht_de.htm (visited March 18, 2002).

[28] Electronic Privacy Information Center and Privacy International, "Privacy and Human Rights: An International Survey of Privacy Laws and Developments," 78 (1999).

[29] Private Parts Online 2000: The International Privacy Newswire, at http://www. privacy.org/pi/parts/index.html (visited March 18, 2002).

[30] The Information Technology Bill, 1999 § 71, at http://www.mit.gov.in/itbillmain. htm (visited March 18, 2002).

[31] Private Parts Online 2000: The International Privacy Newswire, at http://www. privacy.org/pi/parts/index.html (visited March 18, 2002).

ITALY

Italy fully complies with the EC Directive and there is considerable protection of privacy. As the foreword of the Italian Data Protection Act notes, the Act "regards privacy protection as a part of a larger whole—taking also account of guidelines already included in the European Directive of 1995 . . . ."[32] Under Article I of the Act, personal data are to be processed "while respecting the fundamental rights and freedoms and the dignity of natural persons, with special regard to their right to privacy and personal identity . . . ."[33] Italy views privacy as a "fundamental component . . . the 'electronic citizenship' . . . ."[34]

JAPAN

On March 27, 2001, the Japanese Cabinet approved a privacy protection bill designed to set a legal framework to regulate the acquisition and dissemination of personal information for commercial use. If passed, the legislation would be effective in 2003. The bill adopts the five basic fair information principles, and would bar the transfer of personal information to a third party without the consent of the individual involved.[35] This would bring Japanese data protection practices into general conformity with Europe.

THE NETHERLANDS

Superseding the Act on the Registration of Personal Data, the proposed Act on the Protection of Personal Data (APP) has been submitted to the national legislature as a means of complying with the EC Directive. The Netherlands provides an illustrative example of the intricacies involved in different EU countries implementing the Directive in different ways. It is important to keep in mind that

---

[32] Protection of Individuals and Other Subjects with Regard to the Processing of Personal Data: Act No. 675 of Dec. 31, 1996, at http://www.privacy.it/legge675encoord. html (visited March 18, 2002).

[33] See *id.*, Art 1, § 1.

[34] *Id.*, Foreword.

[35] "Bill on data protection approved by Cabinet," *Japan Times Online* (March 28, 2001).

the Directive prescribes a minimum protection level, but there is nothing to stop individual member states from maintaining a stricter system than the Directive requires. The Netherlands has always had rigorous privacy laws, and the APP takes the legislation even further in that direction. Under the APP, personal data may only be collected for certain specific justified purposes, and in most cases, individual explicit consent is mandated.[36] Thus, the transfer of data between countries *within* the EU itself may turn out to be problematic.

PORTUGAL

In direct response to Directive 95/46/EC, Portugal introduced its Privacy Legislation Act on the Protection of Personal Data in 1998. The Act limits the collection, use and dissemination of personal information in either manual or electronic form.[37]

RUSSIA

Personal privacy in Russia is protected by the Law of the Russian Federation on Information, Informatization and Information Protection, which was passed in January 1995. The law applies to both public and private sectors and outlines individual privacy rights, the lawful use of information, and the lawful use of information technologies. The Russian Duma is attempting to update this law in compliance with the EC Directive. The law prohibits the use of sensitive information and gives both individuals and organizations the right to access, correct and supplement the documented information about them.[38]

SOUTH AFRICA

There is no privacy policy in South Africa specifically relating to technology or the Internet. The Open Democracy Bill, which was

---

[36] Lee, "Globalization: On European Grounds," 23:20 *Legal Times* 40 (May 15, 2000).

[37] Electronic Privacy Information Center and Privacy International, "Privacy and Human Rights: An International Survey of Privacy Laws and Developments," 130 (1999).

[38] *Id.* at 133.

introduced in July 1998, defines the rights of South African citizens to access government information, and also seeks "to provide for the correction of personal information held by governmental or private bodies and to regulate the use and disclosure of that information."[39]

SWEDEN

Sweden was one of the first countries in the European Union to issue new legislation as a consequence of the Directive. The Swedish "Personal Data Statute" is closely modeled after the Directive, and like the Directive applies to automatic and manual processing of personal data, with the exception of processing for purely personal purposes.

The adoption of the Directive did not constitute any significant alterations to what was already the law in Sweden. In fact, in 1995, Sweden's data protection authority took on American Airlines and demanded that the airline delete all health- and medical-related information on its Swedish passengers after each flight, absent the passenger's explicit consent to maintain the information.[40] American Airlines appealed the ruling to Stockholm's District Administrative Court. The court, however, dismissed the airline's claim that it would be impractical to obtain the consent, holding that inconvenience does not constitute a legitimate basis for setting aside privacy rules.[41] The court emphasized that the data were to be considered sensitive, as they related to individual religious beliefs (to customize meal service) and disability (to provide special assistance).[42] The Administrative Court of Appeal agreed that any burden imposed on American Airlines is outweighed by the critical need to protect the integrity and privacy of individual travelers, and affirmed the lower court's decision.[43] The matter is now awaiting decision by Sweden's Supreme Administrative Court.[44]

---

[39] Open Democracy Bill, Republic of South Africa, §§ 56, 59, at http://www.polity.org.za/govdocs/bills/1998 (visited March 18, 2002).

[40] Davies, "Europe to US: No Privacy, No Trade," at http://wired.com/wired/6.05/europe.html (visited March 18, 2002).

[41] Id.

[42] Id.

[43] Id.

[44] Id.

The Directive and the ensuing Swedish legislation have been widely criticized in Sweden as being already outdated. Critics claim that the Directive's very strict rules for processing of personal data, adopted in 1995 before the Internet became as widely used as a public forum of debate as it is today, are in many instances overly harsh for the often harmless purpose for which personal data are processed on the Internet. Instead, say the Swedish critics, the principal objective should be to prevent blatant misuse of personal data. In other words, according to the Swedish critics, there is much to be said for modifying the general rule requiring explicit consent from the data subject before personal data are processed.

Chapter 12

Privacy Policies

Introduction

Every Internet business must consider whether or not to have a privacy policy and, if so, what that policy should be. A few years ago, an online business could legitimately decide not to have a published and formal privacy policy. After all, as hard as it may be to believe, no federal or state statute requires all businesses, or even all online businesses, to publish and adhere to a privacy policy. Furthermore, a business could rationally have concluded that it was better off with no policy since all of the FTC and other enforcement efforts in this area, and most if not all of the civil litigation that has ensued, have resulted from instances when a company *deviated* from its privacy policy, not from failing to have a policy. Indeed, although consumers have consistently ranked privacy among their most significant concerns, a comparatively recent study indicated that only one-third of the companies in the United States have a privacy policy.[1] In short, if a company does not have a privacy policy, the company cannot be accused of departing from it or misleading consumers by failing to adhere to it.

---

[1] See Bartlett, "Only One-Third of US Firms Have Privacy Plans," *Newsbytes* (May 9, 2001) (Consumer Electronics' study of 518 United States companies indicated that only one-third had privacy plans, and that more than 23 percent had not even begun to develop a policy with regard to privacy issues).

Nevertheless, the landscape has changed considerably. First, as discussed in previous chapters, we now have several statutes that require businesses to have privacy policies and set out the disclosure requirements with respect to those policies, specifically the Gramm-Leach-Bliley Act, the Health Insurance Portability and Accountability Act, and the Children's Online Privacy Protection Act. Gramm-Leach-Bliley, in particular, has very broad scope. Thus, businesses covered by these statutes and the regulations promulgated under them no longer have the option of conducting business (offline or online) without a privacy policy.

Second, the policies of our principal trading partners have changed considerably in the past few years. As soon as consent by the subject is required before a data controller can transfer personal information (using EC Directive 95/46/EC parlance), disclosure by the data controller is inevitably required so that the subject can give an informed consent. In most cases, disclosure means having a published privacy policy. Indeed, notice and consent are what are at the core of a privacy policy. The United States-European Commission Safe Harbor Accord provides a way for U.S. companies to comply with the privacy requirements of the EC Directive. However, whether a U.S. company expressly complies with the EC Directive or indirectly complies through the Safe Harbor Agreement, the company must provide a mechanism for notice and consent, among other things. In other words, it must have a published privacy policy. Even a company that does no business with citizens of such "distant" nations as the United Kingdom, for instance, must consider whether it will violate the new privacy law of our neighbor to the north, Canada, with which most major U.S. corporations transact business.

Third, more and more consumers look for, and expect to find, a privacy policy on a Web site. If the numerous surveys mentioned in Chapter 2 are at all accurate, an online commerce site that chooses not to have an express privacy policy does so at considerable business risk.

In short, in theory, U.S. online businesses that do not fall within one of the federal statutes that mandate consent from the data subjects and do not interact with foreign citizens do not therefore need to have a published privacy policy. This "option," however, is increasingly illusive.

How, then, should a company develop a privacy policy? There is "no one size fits all" answer to this question. The place to begin is with a thorough understanding of the basic elements of a privacy policy and what they mean for users.

Next, it is absolutely crucial to understand the nature of the business, the nature of the personal data that the business collects, and how the business uses those data (or wants to them use in the future). The answers to these questions are not always obvious. The privacy policy of a basic e-commerce site is likely to differ considerably from that of, say, DoubleClick. And, unless the company comes within the scope of GLB or HIPAA, for instance, its privacy policy is likely to be very different from that of, for example, American Express Company.

In developing a privacy policy, it is useful to rely on the privacy guidelines developed by various industry groups and privacy organizations. Some organizations also offer "seal" programs, which allow a company to display a seal on its Web site, certifying the company's compliance with certain privacy standards.

Finally, as noted above, there are international considerations that cannot be avoided given the Internet's cross-border reach.

THE FIVE BASIC ELEMENTS OF A PRIVACY POLICY

The Federal Trade Commission (FTC) has identified five basic elements of an online privacy policy.[2] They are (1) notice/awareness, (2) choice/consent, (3) access/participation, (4) integrity/security, and (5) enforcement/redress.

We are therefore illustrating each of the five elements by comparing several different approaches to privacy policies by companies in different industries. For each of the elements, a chart sets forth a comparison of selected portions of the companies' privacy policies as posted on their Web sites.[3]

---

[2] See "Privacy Online: A Report to Congress," at 7-11 (1998), at http://www.ftc.gov/reports/privacy3/index.htm.

[3] Any information from these Web sites is the property of the respective companies.

First, we have selected the privacy policy of a basic e-commerce site, the online catalog site of L.L. Bean. We have selected L.L. Bean not because it is an unsophisticated business, which it clearly is not, but because it is an e-commerce site that theoretically is free from any statutory requirements (in contrast to banks, for instance). We have also included the Amazon.com privacy policy in order to permit a comparison between the approaches of a traditional bricks and mortar company that has migrated online and an Internet e-commerce pioneer.

Second, we have used the privacy policy of a financial services company, Chase Manhattan Bank, to illustrate how a company has chosen to comply with the requirements of the Gramm-Leach-Bliley Act. Third, we have chosen the proposed privacy policy of DoubleClick, which DoubleClick published in early June 2001, asking the public for feedback. Finally, we have selected the privacy policy of peoplesound.com, a foreign music site, to contrast the above approaches with that of a company governed by the EC Directive.

NOTICE/AWARENESS

Notice means providing users with notice of the site's privacy policy. In general, the information provided should be clear, understandable, complete, conspicuously placed and readily accessible from both the site's home page and any other page on which information is collected. Also, users should be informed promptly when the site changes how it gathers or uses information. Some sites notify users of changes by sending e-mail updates to all registered users.[4] E-mail may also be used to communicate with users in the event of a violation of a site's privacy policy. For example, if the site has been "hacked" and confidential user information compromised, events that are often the subject of user concern as well as widespread media coverage,[5] an e-mail distribution may be an excellent means of allaying user concerns regarding the security of their information.

---

[4] See Olsen, "Gaffe at Amazon leaves email addresses exposed," CNET News.com (Sept. 6, 2000) (Amazon e-mails customers regarding revised privacy policy).

[5] See, e.g.: Wolverton, "Ikea exposes customer information on catalog site," CNET News.com (Sept. 6, 2000) (unprotected database file containing customer records was accessible on online catalog); Olsen, id. (software bug in Web page exposes user e-mail addresses).

- **L.L.Bean**

We analyze customer information in aggregate—that is, we collect information about thousands of site visits and analyze it as a whole.

When you visit our site, we do not collect your name, email address or any other personal information unless you provide it to us.

L.L.Bean does not share, sell or trade email addresses, information collected as part of a survey or specific details about you or your household.

- **Amazon.com**

We receive and store any information you enter on our Web site or give us in any other way.

We receive and store certain types of information whenever you interact with us. For example, like many Web sites, we use "cookies," and we obtain certain types of information when your Web browser accesses Amazon.com.

For reasons such as improving personalization of our service . . . we might receive information about you from other sources and add it to our account information.

- **Chase Manhattan Bank**

Chase receives information about you from various sources, including information from: your requests or applications for Chase products or services, such as your income in a loan application, your transactions with us, our family of companies or others, such as your account balance with Chase or mortgage information from Chase or from other consumer reporting agencies (credit bureaus), such as your credit history.

We may disclose information we have about you as permitted by law. . . . We may also share information we have about you, as described above, with firms Chase hires to market Chase products and services or with financial institutions not within the Chase family of companies with whom we have joint marketing agreements to provide you with offers of their financial products and services.

- **DoubleClick**

DoubleClick does not use your name, address, email address, or phone number to deliver Internet ads. DoubleClick does use information about your browser and your prior web surfing to determine which ads to show your browser.

- **peoplesound.com**

In general, we use the personal information and other data that we collect from you and process to fulfil orders, identify personal preferences and match your needs with relevant products and services provided by us or by others. This will, in certain circumstances, involve giving the data we collect to third parties. The consequences of processing of data will include products or services being sent or marketed to you by us and by third parties and not just through our websites.

In our attempt to provide you with the best music and to make peoplesound a truly rich and individual experience, we are now tracking customers as they surf our website in order to provide us with vital information about music tastes which we need to improve the products and services we offer to you.

In addition to using personal data (which identifies you individually), we may also choose to use aggregated statistical information based upon usage of our site which does not identify you individually in any way.

CHOICE/CONSENT

The principle of choice means that users are given the ability to opt out of certain uses of their personal information (for example, sale of e-mail lists to third parties) or opt in to others (distribution of periodic e-mails relating to changes on the site, new services or products, etc.).[6]

Whether a site follows the "opt-in" or "opt-out" model may be the most significant difference among the various privacy policies

---

[6] See Killingworth, "Website Privacy Policies in Principle and Practice," *eCommerce Strategies for Success in the Digital Economy* 663, 687 (PLI Sept. 2000).

currently in use. Under an opt-in policy, user information is not used or disclosed to third parties unless the user specifically consents to its use by the Web site operator. Under an opt-out system, a site will use and/or disclose personal information gathered on the site unless a customer specifically tells the entity not to do so, either by clicking on a button on the site or by sending an e-mail to the operator asking that personal information not be used or disclosed.

The opt-in approach is generally viewed as more protective of user privacy, and tends to engender greater comfort and confidence on the part of users—one study found that 86 percent of users preferred an opt-in policy.[7] Some commentators, however, have asserted that continuously having to opt in can make sites too troublesome to navigate.[8] Others support the opt-in approach, asserting that opt-out policies can be too difficult for users to understand if the information about how to opt out is buried in a complex and confusing privacy policy.[9] Some sites adopt a mix of both approaches, using an opt-out system for the internal collection of demographic and usage pattern information that is used to improve the site, and an opt-in policy for information that will be shared with or sold to third parties.

- **L.L.Bean**

  You can write to the address below to:
  - Eliminate duplicate catalogs
  - Limit the L.L.Bean catalogs you receive
  - Remove your name from our catalog mailing list
  - Remove your name from lists we rent to other direct mail companies
  - Update the name and address information we use when we mail you catalogs. (If you're moving, please indicate when your new address will be in effect.)

  Please include a note of instruction and a catalog mailing label and send your request to: L.L.Bean, Inc.

  Dept. CFM
  Freeport, ME 04033-0001
  USA

---

[7] See Halstead, "Privacy Matters," *Red Herring* 48, 56 (Jan. 16, 2001).
[8] *Id.* at 52.
[9] *Id.*

- **Amazon.com**

If you do not want to receive e-mail or other mail from us, please adjust your Customer Communication Preferences. (If you do not want to receive Conditions of Use and other legal notices from us, such as this Privacy Notice, those notices will still govern your use of Amazon.com, and it is your responsibility to review them for changes.)

- **Chase Manhattan Bank**

You may instruct us not to share information about you, as described in this Privacy Policy.

To opt-out, simply print and complete our Opt-out Form, saving a copy for your records, and follow the directions to call us with your opt-out choices.

- **DoubleClick**

When DoubleClick delivers email for a company, that company must show us that consumers have agreed to receive email messages from that company before we deliver the email messages.

Further, DoubleClick provides the opportunity to opt-out of DoubleClick's unique cookies. If you opt-out, a unique cookie is overwritten with a non-unique DoubleClick cookie that serves as a placeholder, so that no new unique cookie is assigned to your browser.

- **peoplesound.com**

You can opt that we not collect personal data in the first place.
The software that we use to track users cannot be disabled for individuals. In order to ensure we are not collecting data about you, you must either disable the cookie feature on your browser or leave the site by clicking on the back button on your browser until you leave peoplesound. If you require help disabling cookies, please contact our customer service team at customerservice@peoplesound.com. If you choose to continue using the site but never register with us then the information we obtain may only ever be used on an aggregated basis which does not identify you. If you subsequently contact us by e-mail at customerservice@peoplesound.com, we will be happy to confirm

that we are not holding data about you and to delete from our records any data that we may have. If you would like us to remove all information and data collected about you from our records, please send a blank e-mail to privacy@peoplesound.com with the word REMOVAL in the "Subject" field. Please note that if you remove any details you will no longer be able to take advantage of many of the features the site has to offer. By continuing to use this web site, you thereby give your consent to us collecting and processing personal information. If you require any further information upon which to base the giving of consent please contact us at customerservice@peoplesound.com. Should for any reason we elect to change our Policy, we will make those changes available to you here, so that you are always kept informed of how we collect and use the information, and when we would disclose it.

You may require us, at the end of a reasonable notice period, to cease or not to begin using your personal data for the purposes of direct marketing. In order to provide you with the best possible service, peoplesound.com may contact you about products, services and special offers we believe may be of interest to you. If you do not wish to receive information from peoplesound.com about updates to the site, promotional offers, etc. then please send a blank e-mail to privacy@peoplesound.com with the word INTERNAL in the "Subject" field.

On occasion, peoplesound.com may wish to share personal information with other commercial or third parties who may contact you with details of products, services and other special offers that may be of interest to you. Alternatively, if you do not wish to receive information from other companies about offers and services they think might interest you (including by way of direct marketing), please send a blank e-mail to privacy@peoplesound.com with the word EXTERNAL in the "Subject" field.

4.0 You can elect to prevent us from transferring data outside the European Economic Area Your personal information may also be sold, traded or rented to third parties who may be located outside the European Economic Area, including to countries which may not have data protection laws, in order to enable them to send you details that they think will interest you, including by way of direct marketing. By submitting your personal details to us you consent to this transfer. The information that you submit may be transferred outside the European Economic Area for processing by peoplesound.com and its associated companies and to maintain accounts for you at other peoplesound.com sites. By supplying personal data to us, you consent to this transfer. If you do not want your information transferred outside the European Economic Area at any time, please send a blank e-mail to privacy@peoplesound.com with the words EUROPEAN ECONOMIC AREA in the "Subject" field.

ACCESS/PARTICIPATION

Access generally means providing a profile update form that lets users access and update or correct the user profile or other registration information.

- **L.L.Bean**

  You can write to the address below to:
  - Eliminate duplicate catalogs
  - Limit the L.L.Bean catalogs you receive
  - Remove your name from our catalog mailing list
  - Remove your name from lists we rent to other direct mail companies
  - Update the name and address information we use when we mail you catalogs. (If you're moving, please indicate when your new address will be in effect.)

- **Amazon.com**

  Amazon.com gives you access to the following information about you for the limited purpose of viewing and, in certain cases, updating that information. This list will change as our Web site evolves.

  Your Account
  Account Maintenance
  Auction Account
  All About You
  Friends & Favorites

  You can add or update certain information on pages such as those listed in the "What Information Can I Access?" section above. When you update information, we usually keep a copy of the prior version for our records.

- **Chase Manhattan Bank**

  Opting Out

  As a security measure, you may access your account information from the Chase website only if you have registered with Chase for authentication purposes. Information provided to you will be scrambled en route and decoded once it reaches your browser. If you have not registered for authentication purposes and wish to review your account information you may write to the address listed on your account statement, call 1-800-CHASE24 or visit one or our branches.

- **DoubleClick**

  In most cases, when DoubleClick collects personal information online, such as in a sweepstakes or survey, we do so on behalf of another company (as an agent or processor). You can access this information by requesting to see that information from the company to which you provided it. If DoubleClick collects personal information from you for our own purposes (such as to process an employment application on this site), we will provide you with reasonable access to that information.

- **peoplesound.com**

  You can elect to have communicated to you the information we hold which constitutes personal data in respect of you. You can do this by e-mail to customerservice@peoplesound.com or by writing to us at our office at 20 Orange Street, London WC2H 7NN (attn: Customer Services). We are more than willing to correct any errors in the data we hold.

INTEGRITY/SECURITY

Protecting the integrity and security of users' personal information typically means making sure that appropriate security measures, such as secure servers and password protection, are in place to prevent unauthorized access to or use of the confidential information contained on the site.

- **L.L.Bean**

  For privacy purposes, all information relating to our customers is stored on a highly secure server, and all credit card information is stored in an encrypted format.

- **Amazon.com**

We work to protect the security of your information during transmission by using Secure Sockets Layer (SSL) software, which encrypts information you input.

We reveal only the last five digits of your credit card numbers when confirming an order. Of course, we transmit the entire credit card number to the appropriate credit card company during order processing.

It is important for you to protect against unauthorized access to your password and to your computer. Be sure to sign off when finished using a shared computer.

- **Chase Manhattan Bank**

We maintain physical, electronic and procedural safeguards that comply with federal standards to store and secure information about you from unauthorized access, alteration and destruction. Our control policies, for example, authorize access to customer information only by individuals who need access to do their work. From time to time, we enter into agreements with other companies to provide services to us or make products and services available to you. Under these agreements, the companies may receive information about you but they must safeguard this information and they may not use it for any other purpose.

- **DoubleClick**

DoubleClick adheres to reasonable business practices to maintain the security of information collected. In particular, DoubleClick maintains internal practices that help to protect the security and confidentiality of this information by limiting employee access to and use of this information, and by implementing technological and systemic firewalls.

In addition, DoubleClick has implemented generally accepted standards of technology security in order to protect information from loss, misuse, alteration or destruction. Only authorized DoubleClick personnel and agents are provided access to personal information and certain databases containing non-personal information, and these employees have agreed to ensure confidentiality of this information.

- **peoplesound.com**

When you review your account information or order products from us, we offer the use of a secure server. The secure server software encrypts the information that you input before it is transmitted to us. In addition, we have strict security procedures covering the storage and disclosure of your information in order to prevent unauthorized access to comply with the data protection law. This means that sometimes we may ask for proof of identity before we disclose personal information to you.

ENFORCEMENT/REDRESS

Enforcement of the site's own privacy policy/guidelines may mean participation in an industry group that provides mediation/arbitration services for users who believe that a site's privacy policy has been violated or applied in some way that infringes on the users' rights. It may also mean providing a process within the company whereby users can pursue what they believe to be privacy violations. At the very least, the privacy policy should include contact information (e-mail address, mailing address and/or telephone number) for the site's operator so that users who have questions or concerns about the site's privacy policy can bring them to the operator's attention.

- **L.L.Bean**

L.L.Bean is pleased to be a licensee of TRUSTe, an independent organization dedicated to fair information practices on Internet commerce sites. As a licensee, L.L.Bean agrees that TRUSTe will periodically review our privacy practices and this privacy statement for compliance with TRUSTe's standards.

- **Amazon.com**

If you choose to visit Amazon.com, your visit and any dispute over privacy is subject to this Notice and our Conditions of Use, including limitations on damages, arbitration of disputes, and application of the law of the state of Washington. If you have any concern about privacy at Amazon.com, please send us a thorough description to feedback@amazon.com, and we will try to resolve it. Our business changes constantly. This Notice and the Conditions of Use will change also, and use of information that we gather now is subject to the Privacy Notice in effect at the time of use. We may e-mail periodic reminders of our notices and conditions, unless you have instructed us not to, but you should check our Web site frequently to see recent changes.

- **Chase Manhattan Bank**

Consumer Recourse If you believe we have not complied with our stated privacy policies concerning our usage of personally identifiable information that we may collect over the Internet, or that information we have provided to you based upon your Internet activity is inaccurate, you may inform us by utilizing the Contact Us /pages/chase/cc/privacysecurity/contact feature on www.chase.com. Clicking on Contact Us /pages/chase/cc/priva-cysecurity/contact enables you to create an E-mail message to us. We will acknowledge receipt of your message via E-mail within seven business days and endeavor to respond to your concerns within 30 business days.

- **DoubleClick**

To ensure that DoubleClick does what it says and says what it does, there are procedures in place for independent third parties to audit and verify DoubleClick's internal practices. Final audit letters will be posted at this site.

If you have questions about our privacy policy, please contact us and we will address your concerns. Information about us is located at the "privacy team" link on this page, or you can email us at privacy@doubleclick.net.

DoubleClick strives to engage in the best practices of fair trade. Specifically, DoubleClick is a member of the Network Advertising Initiative and abides by the NAI's Self-Regulatory Principles on Online Preference Marketing, which were developed in conjunction with the Federal Trade Commission in July 2000. A copy of these principles is available at http://www.net-workadvertising.org.

Complaints about DoubleClick's practices can be directed to DoubleClick and to www.networkadvertising.org.

Our employees are made aware of and are accountable for compliance with our privacy policies and for any changes to those policies.

DoubleClick is committed to protecting consumer privacy online. Below are some of the organizations of which DoubleClick is a member:

Network Advertising Initiative, www.networkadvertising.org.

Online Privacy Alliance, www.privacyalliance.org.

Internet Advertising Bureau, www.iab.net.

Privacy Leadership Initiative, www.understandingprivacy.org.

Responsible Electronic Communications Alliance, www.responsibleemail.org

Direct Marketing Association, http://www.the-dma.org.

Wireless Advertising Association, www.waaglobal.org.

For more information about protecting your privacy online, please visit these sites. If you have additional questions, please contact us at privacy@doubleclick.net.

- **peoplesound.com**

We welcome your questions and comments about privacy issues and the design of our web site. Should you have such comments or have a complaint about how we are using your personal data, please send an e-mail to customerservice@peoplesound.com.

CREATING A PRIVACY POLICY

Although it is possible in a matter of minutes to cut and paste a privacy policy from others posted on the Internet, the result is likely to be inadequate, and may even create legal exposure by promising more than the site can deliver or misrepresenting how information is collected and used. This is particularly true when the site asks users to click on a button indicating acceptance of the site's terms and conditions, including its privacy policy.[10]

---

[10] Although many sites state that users are presumed to have accepted and agreed to certain terms and conditions by virtue of their use of the site, many privacy policies and legal notices can only be accessed by a link at the very bottom of a Web page, whose label uses a tiny, difficult-to-read font. If it is deemed important to ensure that users have *actually* accepted a privacy policy or any other legal notice, the use of an "accept" or "submit" button on the page following the legal notice offers a much greater likelihood that the policy will actually constitute an enforceable agreement between the user and the site.

A far better approach is to start by analyzing the nature of the site's business (if it has not started operating, the projected operations should be considered), the level of sophistication of the target consumers, the extent to which the site collects information, and the nature and sensitivity of that information—essentially, all of the factors that will have an impact on how much users are likely to care about privacy issues in relation to the site. The questions that should be asked include (1) what type of information, if any, the site collects (personal information or demographic data?), (2) what the site does with user information, if anything (sell it to third parties or use it internally?), (3) who has access to the information (insiders or third parties?), and (4) who the site's users are (are they children or adults, more or less well-educated, more or less affluent?). When information is made available to third parties, it is also important to consider what those entities are likely to do with the information and how much control, if any, the site has over its use.

Answering these questions will typically require the involvement of both the site's technical staff and the business people who provide its content and are knowledgeable about its target users and business partners. When a site is part of a regulated industry, legal counsel should also be part of the process, as the policy may well need to comply with specific regulations.

Having determined what the site does and whom it serves, the next step is determining how best to express to users what the site does with respect to confidential information. A passive, purely informational site that does not collect any information about users, or does so only through cookies, may be able to use a much briefer policy than one that requires users to disclose significant amounts of sensitive information as part of a registration process or conducts e-commerce transactions that require users to enter credit card or other information.

At a minimum, a privacy policy should disclose, in simple, jargon-free language, what the site does and does not do with users' information. If it does not disclose any information to third parties, the policy should say that. If the site collects only demographic information that it uses to enhance its services, that also should be disclosed.

Site operators need to be aware, however, that once a policy has been posted on the site, there *must* be some mechanism in place for ensuring compliance lest a breach of security or a violation of the policy, even if inadvertent, turn into a public relations firestorm. This may mean assigning specific technical, business and/or legal staff to monitor and update the site's privacy practices and respond to consumer inquiries. It may also be desirable to join one of the many "seal" organizations that offer independent monitoring of privacy practices.

CHIEF PRIVACY OFFICER

A growing number of companies have centralized privacy issues, appointing a Chief Privacy Officer, or "CPO," to oversee the implementation of their privacy policies.[11] Although CPOs are relatively new in the United States, where there are estimated to be several hundred such officers, the CPO position is common in Europe, where stricter privacy standards have given rise to thousands of CPOs.[12] The use of CPOs in the United States is growing rapidly, however. Indeed, Privacy & American Business, run by the Center for Social & Legal Research, launched an Association of Corporate Privacy Officers to serve as an independent professional association for corporate CPOs.[13]

Although the CPO's duties will obviously vary depending on the nature of the company's business, they generally include keeping track of pending privacy legislation and new technology, and working with others at the company to ensure that the company's privacy policies and business strategies comply with legal developments as well as take advantage of technical advancements.[14] In

---

[11] See, e.g.: Trombly, "New York Life Names Chief Privacy Officer," Computerworld.com (April 23, 2001) (New York Life names audit and compliance executive as its first CPO); Wilcox, "IBM appoints chief privacy officer," CNET News.com (Nov. 28, 2000) (IBM appoints lawyer and engineer as its first CPO); AT&T, "AT&T Appoints Michael Lamb its Chief Privacy Officer," www.att.com/press (June 20, 2000) (AT&T appoints former chief counsel of AT&T WorldNet Service as its first CPO); Excite@Home, "Excite@Home Appoints Chief Privacy Officer," corp.excite.com (May 2, 2000) (Excite@Home appoints antitrust and intellectual property attorney as its CPO).

[12] See Trombly, N. 11 *supra*.

[13] See Privacy & American Business, "Association of Corporate Privacy Officers Launched," http://www.pandab.org (June 11, 2001).

[14] See: Trombly, "New York Life Names Chief Privacy Officer," Computerworld.com (April 23, 2001); MacMillan, "Chief Privacy Officer: It's a Dirty Job, But . . . ," Newsbytes (March 8, 2001); Mendels, "The Rise of the Chief Privacy Officer," BusinessWeek Online (Dec. 14, 2000).

some instances, this may mean being the one to raise issues about marketing or other strategies that could impact the company's privacy practices.[15] The CPO may also serve as the company's public face with respect to privacy issues, particularly when there has been a breach of security or when the company is seeking to make changes to its privacy policies that are likely to be unpopular with consumers. In order to make such a position effective, however, the CPO has to be sufficiently far up the hierarchy to command real respect from operations executives.[16]

SEAL PROGRAMS

Seal programs are operated by organizations that certify that a particular Web site's privacy policy, including both its guidelines and its implementation of those guidelines, complies with the organization's own privacy standards. The privacy organization effectively provides a "Good Housekeeping"-type seal of approval, signaling to consumers that they can rely on sites displaying the seal to protect confidential information. As concern about privacy on the Internet has escalated, the number of these seal organizations has proliferated. Although each group's basic guidelines typically incorporate the essential elements of a privacy policy identified by the FTC, the specific application varies from group to group, as do the services offered by the groups. While the use of a seal on a site may enhance consumer confidence in the site's privacy practices, it should be noted that at least one study has questioned the importance of seal programs, having found that most consumers do not even understand how such programs work.[17]

BBB*OnLine*

BBB*OnLine* is a subsidiary of the Council of Better Business Bureaus. Its self-described mission is to promote trust and confidence on the Internet, in part through its Privacy Seal Program

---

[15] See Mendels, "The Rise of the Chief Privacy Officer," BusinessWeek Online (Dec. 14, 2000).

[16] *Id.*

[17] See Cranor, Reagle, and Ackerman, *Beyond Concern: Understanding Net Users' Attitudes About Online Privacy*, AT&T Labs Research Technical Reports (April 1999).

(http://www.bbbonline.org/privacy). BBB*OnLine* awards a seal to businesses that post online privacy policies that meet BBB*OnLine*'s "core" principles, including disclosure, choice and security.

In order to ensure that a privacy policy meets its core principles, BBB*OnLine* has formulated a list of requirements for privacy notices. Among other things, the notice must be easy to find and read, explain what types of personal information may be collected on the site, disclose how the information will be used, explain how users can update their data or correct mistakes, and tell users how to contact the entity if they have questions about privacy or data security. BBB*OnLine* audits participating businesses' performance at least once a year and provides a dispute settlement process for consumers.

CPA WEBTRUST

CPA WebTrust (http://www.cpawebtrust.org) is run by the American Institute of Certified Public Accountants. WebTrust is administered by CPAs who certify that a Web site has met the WebTrust standards, and that the site abides by its own disclosed business practices. In order to qualify for certification, companies must tell users what personally identifiable information is being collected, how it will be used, how they can "opt out" of such information gathering, and how they can correct the information that is collected.

ESRB

The Entertainment Software Rating Board (ESRB) has established a privacy program, ESRB Privacy Online, to address consumers' concerns about the collection and use of personal data (http://www.esrb.org/pivacy.asp). ESRB states that its mission, among other things, is to offer a cost-effective means of creating and implementing a privacy policy that will meet consumer concerns without interfering with a company's business goals and objectives, foster consumer security and confidence, promote generally accepted principles of fair information practices, and assure consumer control of personal privacy.

As part of ESRB's Sentinel Program, its staff conducts regular online monitoring of participating companies' sites to ensure that their published privacy practices are being followed and maintained. ESRB also conducts unannounced audits of companies' privacy practices through "spot checks," which involve entering fictitious consumer data on a site and then tracking how that information is collected and used. Consumers who believe that a participating company has committed a privacy violation can report the violation to the Sentinel Consumer Online-Hotline. ESRB also provides a dispute resolution service for privacy disputes.

TRUSTe

TRUSTe (http://www.truste.org) describes its mission as providing consumers with control over their personal information, Web site operators with a standardized, cost-effective means of addressing consumers' privacy concerns, and government regulators with clear evidence that industry can self-regulate privacy issues.

Sites that adhere to TRUSTe's principles of disclosure, choice, access and security, and that agree to comply with ongoing TRUSTe oversight and participate in its dispute resolution process, are permitted to display the TRUSTe seal. The seal may appear directly on the site's privacy statement, or may serve as a link to connect users to the site's privacy statement.

Consumers who have a complaint about a participating company's Web site and have been unable to resolve the issue by contacting the site directly can submit a complaint to TRUSTe. TRUSTe will investigate the complaint and work with the Web site to resolve the issue. If necessary, TRUSTe may implement an on-site compliance review. Among the penalties for noncompliance are revocation of the site's license to display the TRUSTe seal, referral to any appropriate authority (such as the FTC or the appropriate attorney general's office), or breach of contract and trademark infringement claims against the offending site.

OTHER PRIVACY ORGANIZATIONS

In addition to seal-granting organizations, there are a number of other organizations that do not issue seals, but instead establish privacy guidelines by which their members pledge to abide.

DIRECT MARKETING ASSOCIATION

In October 1997, the Direct Marketing Association (DMA) (http://www.the-dma.org) promulgated what it calls the "Privacy

Promise to American Consumers." It required all DMA members to agree, by no later than July 1, 1999, to abide by certain privacy practices, including notice, opt-out and use restrictions. The DMA's Web site also offers a Privacy Policy Generator (http://www.the-dma.org/library/privacy/creating.shtml) that can be used to create a privacy policy for a site. Site operators simply fill out the questionnaire and submit it to the DMA. The DMA then generates a Web page containing a privacy statement based on the responses to the questionnaire.

ONLINE PRIVACY ALLIANCE

Founded in 1998, the Online Privacy Alliance (OPA) (http://www.privacyalliance.org) is a coalition of more than eighty companies and associations across a range of industries, including 3Com, AT&T, Apple Computers, the Business Software Alliance, Disney, DoubleClick, Kodak, Ford, Gateway, IBM, Intel, Microsoft, Nestlé, Proctor & Gamble, Time Warner, Inc., the United States Chamber of Commerce, Verizon Communications, Xerox and Yahoo!. Its members pledge to endorse its mission of, among other things, supporting and promoting effective online privacy policies, self-enforcement mechanisms and activities, and compliance with applicable laws and regulations.

OPA has established guidelines for online privacy policies (http://www.privacyalliance.org/resources/ppguidelines.shtml). According to the guidelines, any organization engaged in online activities or e-commerce should adopt a privacy policy that (1) is easy to find, read and understand, and clearly states what information will be collected and how it will be used, if at all, (2) gives users the opportunity to decide how their information will be used, if at all, (3) provides adequate data security measures, and (4) provides mechanisms for correcting any errors in personal data and protecting against accidental or unauthorized alteration.

WIRELESS ADVERTISING ASSOCIATION

The Wireless Advertising Association (WAA) has established voluntary guidelines for its member organizations regarding the use of users' personal information (http://www.waaglobal.org). The guidelines also cover advertising, marketing and mobile e-commerce through the medium of wireless devices. WAA's guidelines expressly endorse the use of a "confirmed opt in" approach to the collection and use of personal information, and set forth minimum requirements for privacy policies, including informing users regarding what information is being collected, how it will be used, and what security measures are in place, and giving users choice regarding the use of their information. The WAA also condemns the distribution of unsolicited ads unless the user has consented to such messages and the sender is clearly identified.

INTERACTIVE ADVERTISING BUREAU

The Interactive Advertising Bureau (IAB) has promulgated privacy guidelines for use by its members, most of which are required to adopt an online privacy policy (http://www.iab.net). The guidelines establish minimum requirements for members' privacy policies, including informing users about when and how personally identifying information is collected, how it will be used, whether it will be disclosed to third parties, what the member has done to ensure the security of the information, and what enforcement measures are available.

INTERNATIONAL CONSIDERATIONS

Because the Internet is a global medium, online activities are at least potentially subject to widely varying regulations, including widely varying privacy policy requirements. In addition to compliance with United States laws and regulations, it is important for businesses to consider the potential impact of other countries' requirements in this regard. In particular, a company that is already doing business internationally, or that plans to have an e-commerce component on its Web site, should consider whether its privacy policies comply with other countries' requirements, particularly those of the United States's major trading partner, Canada, and the EC Directive. As discussed above,[18] the EC Directive imposes stringent requirements, specially with respect to the consent/opt-out element of privacy practices. This can be seen in the comparisons set forth above—the choice element for peoplesound.com, the

---

[18] See also, Chapter 10.

European company, is significantly more detailed than that of any of the United States-based companies.

One way to make it more likely that one's privacy policy complies with foreign requirements is to use the privacy policy generator developed by the Organization for Economic Cooperation and Development (OECD) (which can be accessed at http://cs3-hq.oecd.org/scripts/pwv3/PWPart1.htm). The OECD is an international organization whose thirty member nations include Canada, France, Germany, Italy, Japan, Korea, Mexico, Spain, the United Kingdom and the United States, among others. Its privacy policy generator was developed in conjunction with industry representatives, consumer groups and privacy commissioners, and has been endorsed by the OECD's members as a means of developing a privacy policy.

Chapter 13

Technology Solutions

In the course of this book, we have considered some of the current online privacy issues and the development of the legal principles governing privacy on the Internet. We have also analyzed some of the likely ways in which government may regulate the collection and use of PII on the Internet. In this chapter, we consider whether technology will render the current debate moot.

Advances in technology have exacerbated privacy concerns by facilitating the collection, organization and transfer of data, but technology may also present the best solution to the current privacy debate. If we assume that privacy advocates base their arguments primarily on the principle that personally identifiable information is a type of personal property belonging to the individual, then the key to solving the privacy dilemma is to provide the individual with an effective means to control dissemination of his or her personal data. If, for instance, an individual can surf anonymously, then he can prevent a site from collecting data about him without his knowledge. If an individual can effectively bar a site from depositing cookies or Web bugs on her hard drive, then she can also limit collection of data without her consent.

Empowerment of this sort requires two things. First, it requires education. Individuals must understand how information is collected about them, and must understand how they can prevent that collection. Second, it requires simple and effective tools that consumers can use without the need for great technical sophistication.

Some of those individuals and organizations that oppose governmental privacy regulation believe that the marketplace can best address privacy matters, at least in general terms. If, as studies suggest, consumers really do care about privacy, then consumers should, in theory, be willing to utilize some of the technological means available to protect against unwanted collection of personal information about them, even if that requires some expense (like purchasing a software tool). The market will set the correct price for privacy protection software programs and other protections—manufacturers will have to price them low enough to induce consumers to purchase them. And the price that a consumer is willing to pay for protection reflects the economic value that he ascribes to his "privacy." That is, a consumer will pay $100 for a software program to permit him to surf anonymously only if the additional degree of privacy protection is worth $100 to him.

All evidence to date, however, suggests that while consumers may care about the collection and distribution of their personal data, they are unwilling to pay for additional protection. Companies have already brought to market a variety of software tools to give consumers additional control over their personal data, but sales of these programs have been remarkably low, particularly given the surveys indicating how strongly consumers care about their privacy.

Indeed, even when the consumer must incur *no* cost, the evidence reveals that few avail themselves of privacy tools currently available. For instance, one study reported that only seven out of 1,000 Internet surfers (0.7 percent) reject cookies.[1] Another study reported that a greater number of surfers block cookies (10 percent),[2] but even that figure is low compared with the high percentage of people concerned about online privacy. How do we square the indications of high consumer concern about online privacy with the low, almost infinitesimal number of surfers who actually take steps to block cookies?

There are several possible answers to this seeming inconsistency between consumers' expressed concerns over privacy and their unwillingness to pay to protect their privacy.

---

[1] "Almost No One Rejects Cookies-Study," *Newsbytes* (April 3, 2001), available at http://www.newsbytes.com/news/01/164047.html. The Web Side Story study is available at http://www.websidestory.com.

First, consumers may lack sufficient information to take steps to protect themselves. We, frankly, believe this is one of the most significant obstacles, but not one that would account for the low number of surfers even taking steps to block cookies.

Second, the cost—both monetary and non-monetary—may be too high, and the market forces have not brought costs into line with consumers' valuation of privacy. Even in the case of blocking cookies, where no monetary cost is involved, there are the non-monetary costs of hassle and inconvenience. Moreover, it is difficult to surf and reject all cookies. Some sites do not permit users to enter without accepting a cookie.

Third, consumers may view privacy as a type of "right" to which they are entitled and for which they are unwilling to pay.

In the next section, we briefly describe some basic technological solutions currently available.

PERSONAL FIREWALLS

It is a relatively simple task now to purchase a personal firewall. The personal firewall can be configured in different ways, but the general purpose of such technology is to prevent other servers from accessing a user's hard drive without his or her consent. Thus, the personal firewall can be configured to reject cookies or to notify a user when a server seeks to place a cookie on the user's hard drive. With such a software program, a user can gain some additional control over unwanted intrusion by third parties. Of course, even before these firewall programs became available, a user could configure his or her browser to reject cookies. Microsoft Internet Explorer 5, for instance, allows a user to disable all cookies by selecting the high level in the security setting under Internet Options. As part of Internet Explorer 6, Microsoft included a function that discloses when a site is attempting to place a cookie on the browser's hard drive.[3]

---

[2] The Pew Internet & American Life Project report can be found at http://www.pewinternet.org/reports/toc.asp?Report=19.

[3] See: "Microsoft to Introduce Privacy Software," www.usatoday.com/life/cyber/tech/review/crh323.htm (visited March 18, 2002); "As Congress Mulls New Privacy Laws, Microsoft Pushes System Tied to Its Browser," *The Wall Street Journal* (March 21, 2001), available at http://interactive.wsj.com/archive/retrieve.cgi?id=SB98513216 538 3902742.djm.

ANONYMOUS BROWSING TECHNOLOGY

Another solution is to browse anonymously. One approach in this model is to give individuals pseudonymous digital identities. Another is to create an entity between the purchaser and seller, which shields not only the browser data, such as IP address or name, but also creates an alternative way to pay for purchases so as to permit purchases without disclosure of credit card numbers over the Internet.[4] If an individual uses a digital signature as is now permitted by statute, however, the very signature will divulge personal information.

P3P

The World Wide Web Consortium, also known as W3C, an industry-dominated standards organization, has endorsed a solution known as P3P, "Platform for Privacy Preferences." P3P is a standard that would permit browsers to recognize the privacy policy of participant Web sites. The individual could then set his browser so that it only would go to sites that met his desired level of privacy protection. For instance, if the individual set his browser so that it only would access sites that agreed not to collect personal information, the standard would be able to recognize those sites that had such a level of privacy protection and not permit access to sites with less rigorous privacy protection. From a technical standpoint, what the P3P standard permits is that a browser search the XML tags tied to elements in a Web site's privacy policy to identify the level of privacy protection.

The success of such a standard depends on acceptance and adoption by a large universe of Web sites, something that has yet to occur, although a number of companies are working on programs that would translate written privacy policies into code that conforms to P3P standards.

P3P has had its share of critics.[5] Some assert that it is another industry attempt to avoid regulation without imposing privacy

---

[4] See http://www.iprivacy.com.

[5] See, e.g., the EPIC report, "Pretty Poor Privacy: An Assessment of P3P and Internet Privacy" (June 2000), available at http://www.epic.org/reports/prettypoorprivacy.html.

principles, since Web sites would not be required to have any particular level of privacy protection. Others assert that it is flawed in that the standard incorporates no mechanism to ensure that a Web site actually complies with the level of privacy protection that it states it follows in its privacy policy. One particular complaint relates to the default settings for the software—those settings that the browser will be adjusted to when shipped. As of the date of this writing, the default setting would essentially require participating sites to adopt an opt-out privacy policy, but would place on the consumer the burden of opting out. It is not clear that this is much better than what the consumer is faced with now, although it obviously simplifies some technical matters for the lay consumer. Another complaint is that the software essentially incorporates an opt-out regime for sites. For those advocates who believe that the standard privacy approach for Web sites should be one that requires consumers to opt in before their personally identifiable information can be collected or disseminated, this is a step in the wrong direction.

Microsoft has inserted P3P technology into the new version of Internet Explorer, version 6.0.[6] Given Internet Explorer's market dominance, the result may well be that P3P becomes the standard.

E-MAIL PROTECTION

VANISHING E-MAIL

A solution now exists that permits one to wipe out e-mail from hard drives and backup storage devices on computers and throughout networks. Indeed, a user can encrypt his or her entire hard drive or erase files, including e-mails, so that they cannot be recovered or undeleted.

ENCRYPTION

The U.S. government has opposed attempts to make encryption technology freely available to the public on law enforcement grounds. It now seems clear, however, that sophisticated encryption

---

[6] See http://www.microsoft.com/windows/ie/evaluation/overview/privacy.asp.

technology is and will be freely available. A host of companies has entered the market offering encryption tools and solutions for the general public.

BLOCKING WEB BUGS

In April 2001, the Privacy Foundation and the University of Denver announced a beta version of a Web Bug Detector software, named Bugnosis, that would provide an easy way to block Web bugs.[7]

EDUCATION AND EXERCISE OF INDIVIDUAL CONTROL

One of the simplest ways to exert control over PII is for the individual to take affirmative steps to limit the distribution of that information. Here are three very easy steps that you can take without the need for any new technology:

- Limit the information that you provide in online registration forms. Never provide optional data and do not use a site that demands more information than you believe you should provide.
- Alternatively, as some privacy advocates suggest, provide fictitious data when sites request personal information.
- Either configure your computer to reject cookies or regularly clean out your cookies file.
- Limit the information contained in your "Temporary Internet Files" folder and in your "History" folder.

THE FUTURE

As these and other privacy products become more prevalent, will governmental regulation be as necessary as some view it today? Already, with a small amount of effort and relatively modest expense, knowledgeable users of the Internet can browse anonymously, purchase without use of actual credit card information, and encrypt and extinguish e-mail communications. But, of course, government regulation is rarely designed to protect the sophisticated. It is precisely the less-informed individual who needs to be protected online as in the offline world. Until effective privacy

---

[7] See http://www.privacyfoundation.org; http://www.bugnosis.org.

protection is bundled with every browser so that with a single, easily understood click of the mouse the individual can go into stealth mode and browse without divulging personal data, the solutions mentioned above will be inadequate to protect most Internet users. Even the P3P technology that is likely to become the standard with the backing of Microsoft is merely a partial solution, at best. Although in theory technology provides a solution, in practice it is unlikely to solve the Internet privacy problem in the near future.

CHAPTER 14

GOVERNMENT MONITORING OF INTERNET USAGE

The privacy issues discussed in the previous chapters are not solely private-sector concerns, but also have increasing relevance in the relationship between governments and citizens. Although a full-fledged examination of the Fourth and Fifth Amendments to the United States Constitution and their interrelation with general Internet privacy concerns is beyond the scope of this book, the United States government's response to the terrorist attacks on New York City and Washington, D.C. in 2001 warrants a brief survey. Specifically, the U.S. has included in its new security agenda measures that involve using the Internet to track suspicious behavior by citizens. The Council of Europe has adopted similar measures in a treaty to which the United States is a signatory.

As criminal activity becomes increasingly international in scope and criminals use the Internet to move money, coordinate plans and communicate with each other, government monitoring of Internet usage is being framed in national security terms. In turn, privacy organizations worry that the government's legitimate interest in security and the meaningful gathering of intelligence will effectively override civil liberties, including the freedom from unreasonable searches and seizures laid out in the Constitution.

Although this book has focused on the use of personal data by private entities, in many ways recent events have brought us full circle to those concerns that started off the privacy movement in the early 1970s—governmental access to and use of data. This chapter will discuss three areas of government monitoring of citizens' Internet usage:

(1) new technologies that aid information collection; (2) new U.S. statutes that facilitate the government's ability to monitor people via the Internet; and (3) international measures that enhance Internet surveillance and information sharing among governments.

INTERNET SURVEILLANCE TECHNOLOGY

Advances in technology that enable users to track components of other people's Internet usage have inevitably made their way into law enforcement officials' arsenal against criminals who use the Internet. Two such technologies employed by the Federal Bureau of Investigation, the Key Logger System (KLS) and the Carnivore communications monitoring application, have raised concern in privacy watchdog circles that law enforcement is using technology either to circumvent or directly to flout existing protections against search and seizure. The debate about technology such as KLS and Carnivore centers on whether the systems allow the government to collect more information than is necessary for it to carry out legitimate law enforcement duties.

KLS AND THE *SCARFO* OPINION

In December 2001, the United States District Court for the District of New Jersey issued an opinion on a pre-trial discovery motion regarding the FBI's use of the Key Logging System to obtain incriminating evidence against a suspect in a gambling and loan-sharking case. In this case, defendants Nicodemo S. Scarfo Jr. and Frank Paolercio had encrypted files on Scarfo's computer using the Pretty Good Privacy (PGP) program. PGP protection requires the user to enter a password into a dialog box to obtain access to the file. The FBI had obtained a warrant to install the KLS on Scarfo's computer to record his keystrokes and thereby obtain the password that would enable them to open the encrypted files.[1] The defendants challenged the legality of the use of the KLS, claiming that it violated the Fourth Amendment and the federal wiretapping statute.[2] Their primary argument was that the KLS gave the

---

[1] See United States v. Scarfo, Crim. No. 00-404 (NHP) (D.N.J. Dec. 26, 2001).
[2] See *id.*

government the ability to collect information beyond the scope of the warrant. When the court ordered the government to file a report explaining how the KLS functioned and demonstrating how it would not violate the wiretapping statute, the government requested that it be allowed to modify the report in accordance with the Classified Information Procedures Act (CIPA)[3] because information on KLS was marked classified and secret.[4] The defendants contended that the government's disclosure of the KLS's operation was inadequate.[5]

The court denied the defendants' motion to suppress the evidence obtained via the KLS. It found that the KLS's ability to "over-collect" data, i.e., record keystrokes that were not related to the sought-for password, did not constitute an unconstitutional general warrant. The initial warrant issued for the FBI to install the KLS stated with sufficient particularity the objects and records to be seized, and any "extra" keystrokes that the KLS recorded were deemed to be "of no consequence." The court likened the extra information obtained to a search through a filing cabinet for documents, each of which must be "cursorily perused to determine whether it is among those to be seized."[6]

The court further found that the information about the KLS's operations released by the government pursuant to CIPA was adequate to describe its overall functioning while still maintaining its classified nature. The information about KLS revealed that it did not function while information was being transmitted via the modem and telephone line attached to Scarfo's computer, and thereby did not violate the wiretap laws. The FBI had deliberately configured the KLS to avoid intercepting communications typed on the keyboard that would be transmitted simultaneously via the computer's communication ports by having it determine whether the communication ports were active or inactive, and by recording the stroke only if the modem was not running.[7]

---

[3] 18 U.S.C. §§ 1 et seq.
[4] See Scarfo, N. 1 supra.
[5] See id.
[6] See id.
[7] See id.

Privacy advocates called the court's decision "unprecedented"[8] and "Orwellian,"[9] especially in light of the expanded powers Congress granted to law enforcement agencies after the World Trade Center attack (discussed below). The technology utilized by the KLS, however, has been publicly available for several years. WinWhatWhere Investigator, a program that provides an audit trail of all computer activity—including date, time, elapsed time, window titles, URLs and keystrokes—was introduced by WinWhatWhere Corp. in 1993 and is downloadable from its Web site.[10] The program appears to be used primarily by individuals, often to monitor the computer usage of a significant other, and is advertised on the site as "ideally suited for the investigative needs of law enforcement, government, business, and private individuals."[11]

THE FBI'S CARNIVORE SYSTEM

An even more controversial data surveillance program, launched by the FBI in 1999 and made public in 2000, is the Carnivore Diagnostic Tool. Carnivore is a type of packet-sniffing software, similar to ones used by Internet service providers for network maintenance, that is installed by the government at the office of a suspect's ISP during criminal investigations.[12] The system can be set to monitor only the "to and from" information in e-mail messages, similar to a traditional telephone pen register or trap-and-trace device. Moreover, it can be programmed to discriminate among different types of online transactions in order to comply with court orders, e.g., to search only for e-mails and not monitor online shopping or banking transactions.[13] Privacy advocates, however, are concerned about the program's wider capabilities; an internal FBI

---

[8] See Port, "FBI's new weapon a lot like a virus," *San Diego Union-Tribune*, at 15 (Dec. 25, 2001).

[9] See Anastasia, "Scarfo case could test cyber-spying tactic," *Philadelphia Inquirer*, at A1 (Dec. 4, 2000).

[10] See http://www.winwhatwhere.com/about.htm (visited Jan. 17, 2002).

[11] See http://www.winwhatwhere.com/ (visited Jan. 17, 2002).

[12] See Schwartz, "Wiretapping System Works On Internet," *The New York Times*, at A19 (Nov. 22, 2000).

[13] See Description of Carnivore Diagnostic Tool, available at http://www.fbi.gov/hq/lab/carnivore/carnivore2.htm.

memorandum acknowledged that Carnivore could reliably capture and archive all traffic passing through an ISP.[14] EPIC, a leading privacy advocacy organization, has claimed that this broad information-gathering capability makes the technology "constitutionally suspect." Privacy advocates' main concern about the system is that it could potentially be used to screen all network traffic passing through an ISP and thereby allow law enforcement officials to "snoop" on all of the ISP's users.[15]

Out of an abundance of caution, the FBI emphasized through the testimony of one of its assistant directors before the Senate Judiciary Committee how Carnivore could operate within the existing constitutional framework.[16] First, Carnivore does not involve "broad-brush" acquisition of the contents of wire or electronic communications or review of communications by FBI personnel beyond those specified by a court order. Second, under Fourth Amendment jurisprudence there is no reasonable expectation of privacy in transactional information conveyed to third parties, including in the form of electronic impulses sent over a telephone wire. Third, Carnivore, like more traditional surveillance methods, is only used after the FBI obtains court approval under the Electronic Communications Privacy Act. Fourth, contrary to initial media reports accompanying the system's release, no human eyes view any of the information passing through the ISP's server; the system is programmed to target only the criminal subject's e-mail and conducts the review purely in machine-readable format. Finally, in the only case that has challenged Carnivore's intended use, the court held for the government, finding that the addressing information acquired through the system was no more intrusive than that acquired through a traditional pen register.[17]

---

[14] See Schwartz, N. 12 *supra.*
[15] See Electronic Privacy Information Center Comments on Carnivore Technical Review (Dec. 1, 2000), available at http://www.epic.org/privacy/carnivore/ review_comments.html (visited Jan. 11, 2002).
[16] See Statement of Donald M. Kerr, Assistant Director, Laboratory Division, Federal Bureau of Investigation, on Carnivore Diagnostic Tool before the United States Senate Committee on the Judiciary (Sept. 6, 2000), available at http://www.fbi.gov/congress/congress00/kerr090600.htm (visited Jan. 11, 2002).
[17] *Id.*

A technical review of Carnivore, conducted at the Department of Justice's request by the Illinois Institute of Technology's Research Institute, found that the system performed exactly as the FBI had revealed.[18] The report did stress, however, the importance of making sure that the human and organizational controls necessary to have the system conform to existing legal search and seizure standards remain in place, and called for similar reviews of any future versions of the system.[19]

THE LEGISLATIVE RESPONSE TO THE EVENTS OF SEPTEMBER 11, 2001: USA PATRIOT ACT

The use of the Internet to combat international and domestic terrorism emerged as a significant issue in law enforcement and privacy watchdog circles following the terrorist attacks on New York, Washington, D.C. and Pennsylvania in September 2001. Recognizing that the Internet has become a fundamental aspect of criminal as well as law-abiding life, in October 2001, Congress passed as part of the USA PATRIOT Act[20] a number of laws expanding law enforcement agencies' authority to monitor electronic communications and otherwise use the Internet to monitor criminal activity.

Section II of the Act, entitled "Enhanced Surveillance Procedures," deals primarily with amendments to federal criminal laws. The new laws authorize the interception of electronic communications to obtain evidence of specified terrorism offenses and computer fraud and abuse.[21] Among some of the salient provisions are the following:

- The federal wiretap statute was amended to include electronic communications as well as wire and oral ones.[22]
- The number of district court judges designated to hear applications for and grant orders approving electronic surveillance was increased from seven to eleven.[23]

---

[18] Schwartz, "Wiretapping System Works On Internet," *The New York Times*, at A19 (Nov. 22, 2000).

[19] See *id.*

[20] Pub. L. No. 107-56.

[21] See *id.* at §§ 201-202.

[22] See *id.* at § 204.

[23] See *id.* at § 208.

- The scope of subpoenas for records of electronic communications was expanded to include the length and types of service utilized for sending and receiving electronic communications, subscriber number or identity information (including temporarily assigned network addresses), and the means and source of payment for electronic communication services.[24]
- Trap-and-trace devices (such as Carnivore) must restrict recoding or decoding so that the contents of an electronic communication are excluded from the information gathered. Such devices must also be allowed to identify the source, but not the contents, of an electronic communication. A court order for use of a pen register or a trap-and-trace device can be served on any person or entity providing electronic communication service in the U.S. whose help may facilitate execution of the order. Law enforcement users of pen registers or trap-and-trace devices on an ISP-provided, packet-switched data network are now required to keep specified records of the communications monitored.[25]
- Interception of the electronic communication of a computer trespasser is legal if (1) the owner or operator of the protected computer authorizes the interception of the computer trespasser's communications on that computer; (2) the investigator is a person acting under color of law; (3) the investigator reasonably believes that the contents of the computer trespasser's communications will be relevant to the investigation; and (4) such interception does not acquire communications other than those transmitted to or from the computer trespasser.[26]
- Nationwide service of search warrants for electronic evidence is now available.[27]
- Providers of electronic communications services shall be reasonably compensated for the expenditures incurred in assisting the government with electronic searches.[28]

---

[24] See *id.* at § 210.
[25] See *id.* at § 216.
[26] See *id.* at § 217.
[27] See *id.* at § 220.
[28] See *id.* at § 222.

The Act provides for a sunset of the provisions of this title on December 31, 2005, for any new investigations arising under it.[29]

Critics of the statute fear that it grants the government overly broad authority to investigate suspected terrorist activity, and that the search powers available under it could be applied to non-terrorist-affiliated criminal activity in the United States.[30] Like the concerns over use of KLS and Carnivore, the primary concern of privacy advocates is that constitutional safeguards, such as the requirement of probable cause for issuance of a warrant by a magistrate judge, remain in place while the new surveillance measures are implemented.

It is too soon to tell how the new surveillance technologies and statutes will fit into existing criminal procedure jurisprudence. For instance, since its introduction two years ago the FBI has used Carnivore only twenty-five times.[31] Moreover, the interaction of the new technology and laws with recent developments in international criminal investigation creates an even greater lack of predictability in how this area will develop.

THE COUNCIL OF EUROPE'S CONVENTION ON CYBERCRIME

On November 23, 2001, the Council of Europe passed a Convention on Cybercrime, which has potentially wide ramifications for operators of computer networks and regular users of the Internet. The Convention's purpose is to foster cooperation among signatory countries and the private sector in investigating online criminal activity.[32] The parties agree to "afford one another mutual assistance to the widest extent possible for the purpose of investigations or proceedings concerning criminal offenses related to computer systems and data, or for the collection of evidence in electronic form of a criminal offense."[33]

---

[29] See id. at § 224.

[30] See, e.g., "Analysis of Provisions of the Proposed Anti-Terrorism Act of 2001 Affecting the Privacy of Communications and Personal Information," Electronic Privacy Information Center (Sept. 24, 2001), available at http://www.epic.org.

[31] See Statement of Assistant Director Kerr, N. 16 supra.

[32] See Convention on Cybercrime, ETS No. 185 (Nov. 23, 2001) available at http://conventions.coe.int/Treaty/en/Treaties/Html/185.htm.

[33] See id. at Chap. III, § 1, Tit. 3., Art. 25.

The Convention's essential purpose is that its members agree to adopt legislation or other necessary measures to criminalize illegal access to computer systems; illegal interception, deletion, damage or alteration of data; the serious hindering of a computer system; and the production, sale, distribution, procurement or import of devices designed to commit any of the foregoing crimes.[34] Furthermore, the Convention requires that each member establish measures to allow its investigative authorities to order or obtain the preservation of computer data, including traffic data, regardless of how many service providers were involved in the communication's transmission.[35] These measures will include empowering the authorities to order service providers offering services in a member's territory to submit subscriber information, including (1) the type of communication service used by the subscriber; (2) the subscriber's identity, mailing address, telephone number and billing/payment information; and (3) any other information relating to the site of communication equipment that was installed for the subscriber on the basis of his or her service agreement.[36] Finally, members agree to allow their investigative authorities to record or compel a service provider to record traffic and content data, in real time.[37]

In addition to the requirements that members update their laws to include different types of computer-related crimes, the Convention mandates that the parties assist each other in carrying out those laws. Under the Convention's mutual assistance provisions, one party may request another to order or obtain the preservation of stored computer or traffic data,[38] or request that the second party search or seize, secure and disclose data stored on a computer within its territory.[39] These provisions were opposed vigorously by high-tech companies and Internet service providers, which argued that they would constantly have to deal with subpoenas for information issued by multiple countries and such cooperation

---

[34] See *id.* at Chap. II, § 1, Tit. 1.
[35] See *id.* at Chap. II, § 2, Tit. 2.
[36] See *id.* at Chap. II, § 2, Tit. 3.
[37] See *id.* at Chap. II, § 2, Tit. 5.
[38] See *id.* at Chap. III, § 3, Tit. 1, Arts. 29-30.
[39] See *id.* at Chap. III, § 3, Tit. 2, Art. 31.

would saddle them with significant financial and technological burdens.[40] United States ISPs were especially concerned, since a majority of Internet communications pass through this country and
thereby potentially leave the entities on whose networks they pass
through subject to being required to assist in an investigation that
has nothing to do with the U.S.

After September 11, 2001, however, many companies and organizations that had actively lobbied against the Convention grew
silent.[41] In the new, security-conscious climate, the Convention was
finalized rapidly and the U.S., along with over two dozen other
countries, signed it.[42] As with the USA PATRIOT Act, the Convention
on Cybercrime's efficacy and ability to balance the interests of
ordinary Internet users remains to be seen.

As criminals use computers more, we can reasonably anticipate
other legislation to empower government to combat such crime.
The scope of such legislation will be the subject of much debate,
and legal cases, in the upcoming years.

---

[40] See Weber, "Treaty on Cybercrime Flew Under the Radar Despite Potential
Risks," *The Wall Street Journal*, at B1 (Dec. 3, 2001).

[41] See *id.*

[42] As of the date of this writing the Senate has not yet ratified the treaty.

POSTSCRIPT

In this book we have attempted to provide an overview of the legal principles and issues surrounding the online privacy debate. Having done so, we make some final observations.

First, technological advances have intensified concerns about personal privacy. While these concerns are not new, we believe that technology at the beginning of the millennium has fundamentally and qualitatively changed the debate. While it is surely correct that data compilers were collecting personal data long before the Internet, the ease of collection, and particularly the potential for collection, is quite different today from what it was in 1971. This profound technological change cannot be denied or disregarded.

Second, we believe that the concerns underscored by technological changes over the past few years will continue for the immediate future. The emergence of the Internet is not the end; it is the beginning. Mobile telephony and the use of mobile phones to browse the Web only create another means of collecting data. Other devices and technologies presenting similar potential for collection of personally identifiable information will follow.

Third, the Fair Data Collection Principles developed a quarter of a century ago have become the principles by which most countries (including the United States through the FTC, at least) evaluate data collection practices. These principles will continue to prevail, and through their incorporation in most of the privacy statutes that have been enacted around the world, including the important European Commission Directive of 1995, have become the dominant construct for discussion of privacy.

Fourth, most of the economic powers in the world have adopted either the EC Directive or laws that conform to it. In addition to the EU nations that have adopted these rules, all of the major Anglophone nations other than the U.S. (the United Kingdom, Canada and Australia) have done so. Even Japan appears to be heading towards adopting consistent rules. The U.S., therefore, stands out as one of the few nations that has not adopted comprehensive privacy laws that embody the Fair Data Collection Principles and conform to the EC Directive.

Fifth, given that most of our major trading partners have adopted comprehensive privacy laws that conform to the EC Directive, the U.S. is falling more and more out of step. Economic pressures and trading practicalities will ultimately compel the U.S. to conform, in our opinion. The issue for the U.S., thus, is not whether, but when and in what format it will conform. To date, the U.S. has resisted a comprehensive federal privacy law. Instead, we have a hodgepodge of subject-specific rules and a variety of enforcement regimes. We doubt that many find this to be a satisfactory state of affairs. While many businesses have resisted a comprehensive federal statute, the huge volume of pending privacy-related bills strongly suggests that Congress will not resist the pressure of public opinion for long, and that additional federal legislation will be forthcoming. We do not believe the prospect of additional federal legislation, in particular a comprehensive federal privacy regime that complies with the emerging international standard, should concern American business particularly. The likely alternative is a mishmash of state legislation and enforcement practices—hardly a desired approach to any rational business.

Sixth, as privacy regulation becomes more developed, we will see more and more enforcement efforts, both private lawsuits and governmental enforcement actions in the U.S. and abroad.

In short, the privacy debate is not over. It is in many respects just beginning. The next few years will witness significant legal and technological advances.

Author Biographies

Andrew Frackman is a litigation partner in the New York Office of O'Melveny & Myers LLP, one of the nation's largest law firms. In the course of his twenty-year career, he has tried many cases in federal and state courts, and has particular expertise in antitrust, securities and technology disputes. He has published and spoken on diverse legal topics, including securities, antitrust, Internet privacy and software patents matters. He is a graduate of Harvard College and Columbia University School of Law.

Rebecca C. Martin was formerly an associate of O'Melveny & Myers LLP, where she specialized in intellectual property with a focus on trademark, copyright and Internet-related disputes. Prior to O'Melveny & Myers, she clerked for the Hon. John C. Lifland of the United States District Court for the District of New Jersey and for the Hon. Theodore McKee for the United States Court of Appeals for the Third Circuit. She graduated cum laude (Order of the Coif) from Rutgers Law School and has published on copyright litigation and Internet privacy. She is currently an Assistant United States Attorney. (The views contained in this book are those of the authors and do not necessarily reflect the position of the Department of Justice.)

Claudia Ray is a counsel in the New York office of O'Melveny & Myers LLP, an international law firm. Ms. Ray specializes in advising foreign and domestic clients in matters involving copyright, trademark, privacy, Internet, and First Amendment issues, including representing them in cases pending in federal and state courts nationwide as well in arbitrations before the International Chamber of Commerce, the American Arbitration Association, and other arbitral institutions. Ms. Ray is a graduate of Macalester College and New York University School of Law.